MW00979872

FILE TRANSFER BETWEEN NETWARE CLIENTS AND UNIX HOSTS

QUICK RECOMMENDATION	PRODUCT OR PRODUCT SOURCE	PAGE
TCP/IP software on the NetWare client	LAN WorkGroup	99
TCP/IP gateways	Novix	107
	Ipswitch	111
	NCM	112
IPX/SPX on UNIX hosts	MCS	109
	RDS PopTerm	114

FILE TRANSFER BETWEEN UNIX HOSTS AND NETWARE CLIENTS

QUICK RECOMMENDATION	PRODUCT OR PRODUCT SOURCE	PAGE
TCP/IP software on the NetWare client	LAN WorkGroup	121
	Ipswitch	125

FILE TRANSFER BETWEEN UNIX HOSTS AND NETWARE SERVERS

QUICK RECOMMENDATION	PRODUCT OR PRODUCT SOURCE	PAGE
FTP services on NetWare servers	Novell's FLeX/IP	119
	NetWare NFS Server	118

NOVELL'S GUIDE TO
Integrating
UNIX AND NetWare
NETWORKS

I NOVELL'S® GUIDE TO
Integrating
UNIX AND NetWare®
N E T W O R K S

J A M E S   E .   G A S K I N

Novell Press, San Jose

Publisher: Peter Jerram
Editor-in-Chief: Dr. R. S. Langer
Series Editor: David Kolodney
Acquisitions Editor: Dianne King
Program Manager: Rosalie Kearsley
Developmental Editor: David Kolodney
Editor: Marilyn Smith
Project Editor: Abby Azrael
Technical Editor: Allan P. Hurst
Editorial Advisor: Kelley Lindberg
Book Designer: Helen Bruno
Production Artist: Charlotte Carter
Technical Illustrator and Screen Graphic Artist: Cuong Le
Desktop Publishing Specialist: Stephanie Hollier
Proofreader/Production Assistant: Lisa Haden
Indexer: Nancy Guenther
Cover Designer: Archer Design
Novell Press Logo Design: Jennifer Gill
Cover Photographer: Tom McCarthy
Screen reproductions produced with Collage Plus
Collage Plus is a trademark of Inner Media Inc.

To Wendy, Alex, and Laura with love forever.

JEG

Acknowledgments

No book like this happens in a vacuum, and there are some people that went above and beyond the call of duty in helping me gather the products and information required. First on the list must be Mike Azzara and Julie Anderson of *Open Systems Today* (formerly *UNIX Today!*). Years before this subject was popular, Mike accidentally contracted a freelance networking columnist with a stronger background in NetWare than in UNIX. As the lone advocate of PC networking, and particularly NetWare, I was given free reign to write articles about topics that interested me and my consulting clients. Those topics were invariably about integrating UNIX and PC networks. Julie, the editor of the Technology section, kept buying the articles and asking for more. Most of the products examined here were first investigated in the pages of *Open Systems Today*.

Jason Levitt of OST helped me understand NetWare from a UNIX person's point of view. His feedback on the organization of the outline and presentation of this book deserves special mention.

The UNIX group at Novell has always given me more time and attention than I probably deserve. Chief among the group are Bob Davis, Jim Jackson, Bob Waterman, and Keith Brown. Willie Donahoo set me off on the right track when I first investigated Portable NetWare. Chris Germann kept me up to date on NetWare 4.0 as it developed, and the lovely Rene Siegel made sure everything promised was delivered.

Equipment for this book was varied and sometimes expensive. Brett Martin of NetFRAME supplied one of the company's excellent file servers. Altos supplied a new ACS4500 system running both UNIX and Altos NetWare for SCO UNIX Systems. Bob Timmons, the local Altos engineer, has been open with support and product whenever needed. The fine group at SUN, including Dave Rosenlund, Mike Moratta, and Luiza de Ruijter, started me on the right track. Their PR person Beth Byer of HiTech somehow found the SPARCstation2 I used in the lab. WordPerfect Corporation and Microsoft both provided software for use and testing.

Outside the computer world, William Scobie showed me years ago that a professional knows the details but an artist owns them.

Many people at Novell Press and SYBEX have worked to make this book a reality, starting with Rose Kearsley at Novell Press. At SYBEX David Kolodney, program manager, and Dianne King, acquisitions editor, got the ball rolling. Editor Marilyn Smith never got flustered as I explained that PING (DOS) and *ping* (UNIX) really must be different. Abby Azrael has the nicest way of making sure an author sticks to the schedule. The rest of the production staff did an excellent job, treating this book as if it were as special to them as it is to me.

CONTENTS AT A Glance

. . . .

TABLE OF *Contents*

. . . .

*I*ntroduction

When faced with a difficult project, the weak hope for divine intervention while the strong look for reference material. This book is for the strong, especially the strong and overworked.

Four years ago, this book was not possible. There were few ways to connect NetWare to UNIX, and few people that wanted to.

Since there are more reasons to connect NetWare to UNIX today, there are more ways to do so. Companies are providing solutions from UNIX down and from NetWare up. Novell has been pushing this market hard, and it has several excellent products for examination. Because Novell has such a strong market leadership position, many third-party companies also have products offering the same features. Some are better than Novell's and some are worse, but they're all different.

This is a hands-on guidebook through the dozens (yes, dozens) of options for connecting NetWare and UNIX. Unfortunately, since this is a new area of networking products, overworked network administrators often know of only one or two options. When choices are limited, it's easy to make a choice but it's apt to be a bad choice. This book provides more choices, more options, and more shortcuts than have ever been available in one place. If a bad choice is made after reading this book, the reasons will be political, not technical.

Motivation for This Book

For several years, I have been doing a series of articles for *Open Systems Today* (previously named *Unix Today!*) on the subject of integrating PC LANs and UNIX systems. As a systems consultant, this topic is of particular interest to me. The number of articles grew, and the people at Novell noticed that no one else was crazy enough to dive into such a topic on such a regular basis.

With Novell's continued interest in UNIX, gradually more and more customers wanted to examine this NetWare to UNIX integration area. That led to the realization that even normal, sane people wish to integrate the leading PC LAN with the leading operating system. You have come to that realization, or you wouldn't be standing in the bookstore reading this now.

THE EXPLOSION OF NETWARE CONNECTIVITY PRODUCTS

An explosion of NetWare connection products, from Novell and from third parties, has hit the market. One of Novell's slogans is "NetWare Everywhere," and it's almost there. And where Novell has not yet penetrated, third-party vendors are blazing trails for them.

UNIX folks may be unaware of exactly the kind of penetration NetWare has today. Even Novell dealers and users are surprised at the coverage. Think there are as many Novell dealers as 7-11's? Yes? Wrong, there are *twice* as many Novell dealers as 7-11's.

This kind of dealer network gets market share by the truckload. Depending on the research firm consulted, NetWare covers from 60 to 75 percent of the PC LAN market. From Corporate America down to the Mom and Pop Shoppe, NetWare connects PCs to shared resources.

As if controlling the PC world wasn't enough, NetWare has infiltrated the UNIX world on three different fronts. First, Portable NetWare (NetWare for UNIX now) runs NetWare file and print services from a UNIX host. Second, Novell's IPX/SPX protocol has been ported to multiple UNIX platforms, eliminating the need to run TCP/IP on NetWare client PCs for UNIX host connection. Third, moves are underway to port Native NetWare directly to traditionally UNIX-only hardware. This includes the announced port to Hewlett Packard's PA-RISC chip, and the coming ports to SPARC, MIPS, and Alpha processors.

THE LACK OF MATERIAL ABOUT NETWARE AND UNIX LANS

With all this activity, there is still a lack of system-administration level material about connecting NetWare and UNIX. These are two environments that are hostile in many ways, but there are multiple overlapping areas to expand.

Beyond the physical, technical, and adminstrative details to explore in this connection process, vast philosophical gaps need to be closed. NetWare and UNIX are cultures that arrived at a somewhat similar point after starting from two distinctly different beginnings. Understanding the past can shed light on the present; examining both NetWare and UNIX from start to status quo will help the connection process. Trust me on this: just wires and configuration files, even done exactly right, will not a successful project make. The cobbled system may work fairly well, but it won't sing until some basic understanding has been reached by both sides of the equation.

THE MOVE TOWARD "OPEN SYSTEMS" CONNECTIVITY OPTIONS

Stepping back from NetWare and UNIX as the primary participants, the entire world of "open systems" must be addressed. "Open" has now officially been entered into the Worthless Buzzword Hall of Fame, since everyone is sure of the definition but no two people agree. Despite these differences, open is now a Good Thing To Be. Notice that every product in the computer world is now open, even if it means only the literature has changed while the product stays the same. The term now carries less credibility than "lite" on a snack food package.

Truth of literature notwithstanding, customers are driving vendors to provide systems that are easier to connect to one another. Once the NetWare and UNIX connection bandwagon gathers steam, there will be even more pressure on the rest of the systems to join the party.

To Corporate America, open often means only the ability for the legacy (older, existing) systems to communicate with the brand new systems. Standards that require replacing legacy systems are doomed to be ignored. Standards that allow legacy systems into the new scheme are welcomed with open arms. Both NetWare and UNIX are the "open-arm" type of standards.

Who Should Read This Book

This is not a user handbook. It's for the lucky people that control and administer either NetWare or UNIX in some capacity. It's also for those managers overseeing technical groups using either platform, today or tomorrow.

BENEFITS FOR MIS MANAGERS

The managers' world, often satirized as a haven for the technically unsophisticated, has never been more difficult. MIS (Management Information Systems) was once primarily a Big Blue (IBM) world, with a single source of products and services. Those days are long gone. Today, that world is crammed with competing technologies and ever-scarcer resources of time, money, and manpower.

Change, even positive change, is stressful. All the buzzwords about "downsizing" and "rightsizing" are fancy wrapping on a painful package of changes. Managers that happily ignored both NetWare and UNIX in the past are suddenly finding both high on their priority list.

The entire thrust of open systems to many people is to make information available across diverse platforms. No longer is it allowable to have data on a UNIX system be unreachable to a NetWare client. This book outlines many ways to make information on one system available to the other.

BENEFITS FOR MIS BUYERS AND PLANNERS

For those in the strategic communications business, the options provided here should be the foundation of network and systems planning for the next several years. If data doesn't pass readily across platforms today, it must traverse that distance soon.

Businesses are reluctant to throw out hardware and software, so any NetWare-to-UNIX option must take legacy (read *leftover*) systems into account. Planners that assume a clean slate in their projections are fooling themselves; the past will always haunt us. Somewhere, work is being done at this very moment on an old IBM PC original model, down to the cassette interface port on the motherboard.

Because of this legacy, options will be covered that allow older systems to play in our new arena of "openness." The older equipment has limitations, especially in the area of memory management for DOS clients, but these machines are not useless. In fact, they have some surprising capabilities left.

BENEFITS FOR NETWARE SYSTEMS ADMINISTRATORS

NetWare systems administrators have conquered the business desktop, including PC, Macintosh, OS/2, and Microsoft Windows clients. Now the race is on to conquer all the other things NetWare can connect. UNIX is one of the biggest and highest growth areas.

NetWare and UNIX are completely different. If NetWare is the area under control in your company, UNIX will be new. The language used by NetWare and UNIX regularly says the same thing using completely different words. Sections of the book are devoted to helping "translate" NetWare experience to UNIX. Those NetWare bigots that believed every other operating system would fall before the Red Horde should know better by now. Whether they know better or not, connections must be made.

The overworked NetWare systems administrator will have on the shelf a valuable guidebook showing the way between NetWare and UNIX.

BENEFITS FOR UNIX SYSTEM ADMINISTRATORS

UNIX people, never known as the most tolerant of computer users, often felt NetWare to be nothing more than a PC with delusions of grandeur. UNIX has not, and will not, sweep every other operating system out the door. In the corporate desktop wars, Novell won hands down over everything else, UNIX included.

UNIX system administrators will need to learn the ways of NetWare more than NetWare administrators will need to learn the ways of UNIX. That's not fair, but think of this as self protection. Most sysadmins believe that UNIX is more involved than NetWare, so the NetWare users will take longer to feel comfortable with UNIX than vice versa. That may be true at the command line, but with assorted menus and front-ends, the NetWare user will never realize which resources are UNIX and which are not.

Some of the options described in this book are disk and CPU intensive but provide strong benefits. Other options are more considerate of system resources, but may not provide everything a company needs. By examining the options available, the world of UNIX can be shared with even the most obtuse DOS user.

BENEFITS FOR RESELLERS AND CONSULTANTS

Resellers and consultants have noticed that customer interest in both UNIX and NetWare have picked up in the last year. If the shingle out front says or implies systems integration, this is the hot topic. Even customers not ready to actually integrate want to be sure that they can in the future. They need a foundation built today that will support those services in the future. This book will provide enough different choices that every customer should be satisfied with at least one of these connection options.

Novell has made UNIX training a top priority with all its resellers. The Unix-Ware product, developed jointly by Novell and Univel (the spinoff from Unix Software Laboratories, the spinoff from AT&T) has been highlighting the need for NetWare resellers to know and understand UNIX. Special certification requirements have been established in order to limit resellers to those that have significant UNIX experience.

UNIX resellers eager to get into the NetWare world also must be certified by Univel to sell UnixWare. If the reseller already supports any major UNIX package, that part of the certification is bypassed. Then the reseller is tested for a certain amount of actual NetWare knowledge.

It's true that there are over 11,000 NetWare dealers, but most are limited to selling only the lower-end products. The Platinum Dealers, the highest ranking group in the Novell reseller pecking order, number about 500. There is plenty of room for NetWare to UNIX integration experts from both sides of the street.

Versions Covered in This Book

One of the things DOS users most enjoy is tweaking their UNIX friends about is "which UNIX is UNIX?" Since hundreds of different UNIX flavors have arrived over the years, it can be a touchy point to defend.

The proper answer is to point out that there are only a handful of major UNIX variants today, and the worst is better than DOS. This is particularly effective if said while leaning on a desktop system running four or five jobs at one time, while sending and receiving mail. Be sure and point out the NFS mount to a machine four floors away. Smile.

One of the things UNIX users most enjoy is tweaking their DOS friends about is "shrink-wrapped applications—who needs them?" The concept of a precompiled and nonmodifiable program sends shivers down true UNIX backbones. What good is a program if you can't adjust it to fit your exact environment?

The proper answer is to point to the thousands upon thousands of DOS and NetWare programs lining shelves of retail stores everywhere. The joy of never seeing a syntax error from a compiler is hard to describe to a UNIX person that lives on Jolt Cola and flourescent lights.

IN THE UNIX CORNER: SUNOS AND SCO UNIX

To test the products covered in this book, two primary machines have been used. The first is a Sun SPARCstation 2, running SunOS version 4.1.3 with 32 MB of RAM, a CD-ROM drive, and a 400 MB hard disk.

The second system is an Altos 4500, a 486 system with an EISA bus, 32 MB of RAM, a cartridge tape drive, and a 400 MB hard disk. The system is running the Altos port of SCO Unix, including the Altos NetWare for SCO Systems. Both systems have internal Ethernet network interface cards, supplied by their respective manufacturers.

The other UNIX flavors most likely to be installed in Corporate America are not overlooked. Attention is paid to SVR4 from USL/Novell, HP/UX from Hewlett Packard, AIX from IBM, Ultrix from DEC, UnixWare from Novell (Univel), and SVR3.2 systems. File and path names follow the most "standard" placement, with explanations for other systems whenever appropriate.

Why these flavors? Market share, corporate penetration, and the fact that these represent multiple other flavors with minor differences.

IN THE NETWARE CORNER: 2.*x*, 3.*x*, AND 4.*x*

NetWare became seriously UNIX friendly with version 3.10, when it included TCP.NLM for the first time. This enabled the server to support TCP/IP and IPX/SPX concurrently. For the first time, the NetWare server could be involved in multivendor UNIX networking.

NetWare Servers

The primary focus here is on NetWare versions 3.11 and 4.0. Earlier versions running a VAP (Value Added Process, an early version of the NLM) are mentioned occasionally. NetWare 3.11 is the most common version for larger companies (large enough to have both UNIX and NetWare in use and in close enough proximity to need to connect the two).

Many of the comments concerning NetWare 3.11 also apply to versions of NetWare for UNIX (Portable NetWare). Of course, having NetWare for UNIX installed indicates a company well down the integration road. Where other options may be valuable in that environment, they are mentioned.

Native NetWare running on non-Intel processors would be part of the NetWare for UNIX program, right? Nope. The idea is to port both the NetWare file and print services and the NetWare Runtime operating system to a new platform. UNIX wouldn't be involved, even though the most common operating system for that particular processor is UNIX.

NetWare Clients

Mainly, NetWare clients are DOS PCs. Although these have the market share, other NetWare clients, such as Macintosh and OS/2-based machines, are discussed as well. Windows is considered DOS for most explanations, but a growing group of programs are Windows specific. Sometimes, these programs require a section to themselves, sometimes just a footnote.

The world of non-DOS clients is growing quickly, and not just the Macintosh and OS/2 users. NeXTstep 3.0, released in the fall of 1992, includes IPX/SPX as a native protocol. Sun's Solaris 2.0 not only includes NetWare protocols, but Sun and NetWare have some joint marketing agreements in place. Whether those survive in the face of the release of UnixWare, slated for those same sales channels, has not yet been decided. Resellers and dealers, being a contrary and self-preserving lot, will no doubt let the market help them decide which version to sell and support.

The IPX/SPX protocols have been available for a fairly nominal license fee from Novell directly for several years. Major companies that want IPX/SPX certainly can afford the license, and many smaller companies are also willing to pay the price, or reverse-engineer the protocol.

Prepare to witness most major operating systems jumping onto the NetWare client bandwagon. By 1994, it will be considered backward to be without NetWare client capability.

How to Use This Book

Where does one piece of spaghetti stop and another one start? Looking down on the plate, how can we tell? That was the question for this book: how to present intertwined information in a linear way.

More important to you, what's the best way to find an answer to a question? You know what you need done, you just aren't sure which is the best way to do it.

The decision was finally made to present the information grouped by services rather than by products, like a dictionary that gives the definitions, then the word. Why this way, when grouping by products works well for so many other books? The dictionary and encyclopedia have been popular formats for hundreds of years, so why mess with the format? Because a UNIX/NetWare integration project is backwards; we have the definition and need to know the word (or rather, the product to use). More and more dictionaries are being arranged this way, so perhaps we're setting a trend.

Most projects have a goal before they have a game plan. Most travelers have a destination in mind before they grab a map; if they don't, it takes much longer to figure out a route. Following that idea, this book is organized by services (goals) with the connection techniques and products (game plan) in that same section. There are always several game plans for every goal, so just start with the one that makes the most sense for the project at hand.

The book begins with the background information you need for this type of integration project. Chapter 1 provides some history, Chapter 2 explains the basics of network connectivity, and Chapter 3 describes how to get your project started (from convincing your bosses to actual planning). NetWare for UNIX (formerly Portable NetWare) is the subject of Chapter 4. The following chapters cover integration services: terminal emulation, basic file transfer, advanced file transfer from UNIX hosts, sharing UNIX file systems, sharing NetWare volumes, printing from NetWare to UNIX and vice versa, and sharing applications. The final chapter provides some insight into the future of NetWare and UNIX.

For those of you who want to read other books about NetWare and UNIX, Appendix A supplies a recommended reading list. It's not all-encompassing, but it does include the books I've used for reference.

Because the book is organized by services, some products are discussed in several chapters. This provides an easy reference for particular needs, but it makes for a messy index. To help clear up some of this confusion, a mini buyer's guide is included as Appendix B. Each product mentioned in the book is listed, along with its manufacturer. Think of this as an executive summary. If we added a few bar charts, even real executives could use it.

The listing of products does not necessarily imply any endorsement or recommendation. Specific details of each product and the applicability to the task at hand are given throughout the book.

Appendix C contains information about where to get NetWare and UNIX information (or upgrades, patches, education, help, and sympathy). These resources provide up-to-date answers to a multitude of questions.

Rather than bore you with the details on installing and configuring the various products within the chapters, I've placed these instructions in a central place: Appendix D. It details the installation procedures, from the convoluted configurations required by some products to the simple "fill in the blanks" of others.

Finally, Appendix E will help you with NetWare and UNIX terminology. It not only includes a "translation table" that equates "NetWarese" to "UNIXspeak," but also includes definitions of the masses of abbreviations used in both the UNIX and NetWare worlds, as well as a regular glossary of common terms.

HOW TO CONTACT THE AUTHOR

To reach me electronically, use one of the following methods:

▸ On the Internet:

jamesg@utoday.com OR
4553186@mci.com

▸ On MCI Mail:

JGaskin OR
455-3186

▸ On CompuServe:

72470,1364

As the networking columnist for *Open Systems Today*, I welcome real-world examples of integration (both good and bad). Perhaps you can show us how you bypassed the pitfalls on the way to Network Nirvana. Perhaps you can tell us first-hand about the pits. Either way, your experiences are valuable. You might even be immortalized in the next NetWare to UNIX book.

Good luck and have fun. Let me borrow a phrase from a network support manager I once worked with, and address it to you ladies and gentlemen of the computer integration world: "Go forth and do great things."

## CHAPTER 1

Puzzling Partners

UNIX is to NetWare as fish are to bicycles. Does that sound right? NetWare is to UNIX as honesty is to congressmen? Oil is to water?

A case could be made for that many years ago, but no more. To many users, NetWare and UNIX are the same thing. Or they do the same things, they just do it completely differently. Or they do things completely differently, but get the same result.

As is often the case in the world of computers, all of the above is true. NetWare and UNIX share some common heritage, and they often are used to accomplish similar goals. In the world of true distributed and intelligent computing (coming Real Soon Now), the operating system will be less important than the job at hand. Until that day, there are plenty of details to worry about, but the big picture is becoming clear.

To make sense of both UNIX and NetWare, it helps to have some feeling for the history and philosophy of both. Working without this understanding is like trying to make a dish you've never tasted before. You can follow all the directions in the recipe, but you still need a reference point when it comes time for the taste test. Your network integration project works in much the same way. If one side of the equation is a total mystery to you, the chance of success is low. As much as it can in a short space, this chapter tries to put the right taste on your palate.

History: Where Did All This Come From?

The computer business is not particularly old in most business terms. Certainly, no one can make a case for any computer business before World War II, and not really much of one before the mid-1950's.

UNIX wasn't around in any form before 1970, so perhaps we can use that as the beginning of the computer business as we know it. NetWare didn't arrive until a decade later. Those that started their computer awareness with PCs will start counting from the early 1980's as well.

A SHORT HISTORY OF NETWARE

NetWare was developed by Novell Data Systems in the late 1970's, up in the hills of Utah. The company built a multiuser microcomputer using the CP/M (Control Program for Microprocessors, the operating system of choice before the PC solidified DOS) and UNIX as the guidelines. It was a typical time-sharing system, with dumb terminals attached by serial cables to a central box containing the CPU (central processing unit), disk, memory, and printer attachments.

This was not a particularly original idea, and the graveyards are full of similar companies started about the same time. The difference between the living and dead is their approach to the hot new item: the IBM PC. Novell embraced it, believing a system that used the intelligence of the end node would always be better than one using dumb terminals (at least this is the story told around campfires).

Another stroke of genius was the search for a "file" server, not a disk server. In the early 1980's, Novell's competitors offered a way to split a large hard disk (maybe 50 or 60 whole megabytes!) into 5 or 10 megabyte (MB) partitions; one for each user and perhaps a common partition. Although this helped contain the capital budget for hardware, it did not allow any better communications between people, applications, or computers than the current rage, SneakerNet.

After the people at Novell moved to include the PC as a file server in their plans, they made another good decision. Rather than offering the Network Operating System (NOS) as a way to sell hardware, as did 3Com and Corvus, they concentrated on promoting the NOS itself. To help differentiate NetWare from its competitors, Novell aggressively supported every network interface card (NIC) that could be found. Novell also made deals with every hardware vendor it could, helping to port NetWare to their hardware. This gave Novell a win-win situation whenever two different hardware vendors were bidding on the same business. No matter which of them won, Novell won as well.

Taking the early lead with NetWare/86 (for the Intel 8088/8086 processors), Novell also started the concept of a remote file system for PC networking. Not just a file repository any more, the file server actually began to control and secure files. Security became stronger, and the file-access controls allowed UNIX software vendors to port their applications to NetWare. This allowed true multi-user programs to help push the sales of NetWare into typically UNIX installations, particularly accounting systems and databases.

By 1986, network hardware independence was a given for NetWare; the file server could support multiple types of interface cards at the same time. Even more amazing, packets could be bridged between network segments without the user being involved.

The push for more NetWare-aware applications was paying off as well. Over 2000 multiuser applications existed for the Novell Operating System.

With the advent of the PC AT, Novell focused most of its operating system development attention on the Intel family of processors. There had been an earlier PC file server, but the AT was such a hot machine that it outstripped the current workhorse: the Motorola 68000 powered S-Net server, an S-100 bus system using 9-pin RS422 connectors (9-pin connectors that look exactly like CGA or Token Ring connectors). With the gradual waning of the S-Net server, the PC server era began. With the new support of the AT and Intel 80286 processor, NetWare officially became Advanced NetWare/286.

In 1988, NetWare for VMS made it's appearance. Macintosh computers could now be supported by NetWare version 2.15, filling the Mac server hole left by Apple.

1989 saw the release of NetWare/386 version 3.0. The rewriting done for NetWare 386 made Portable NetWare (now called NetWare for UNIX) possible. Modularity of the NOS was well underway, continuing a trend Novell started back when it decided to support more than one network interface card.

June of 1989 saw a prophetic (for the world of NetWare and UNIX integration) pairing when Novell merged with Excelan. This gave Novell a solid grip on the world of TCP/IP, OSI, and UNIX. The hardware business Excelan brought has been sold, but the engineers gained through the merger boosted Novell toward becoming a UNIX power.

NetWare 4.0 continues with improved NOS modularity, and it addresses one of the most often-mentioned weak points of NetWare: the lack of a domain-naming service. UNIX people are the envy of the PC world with their large network name control. Novell has taken dead aim at Network Information Service (the new name of Sun's Yellow Pages naming service). Novell's NetWare Directory Services (NDS) is a global, distributed, replicated database, with no single point of failure (the loss of any one server doesn't cripple the network). Little details—integrated image management, on-the-fly file compression, and flexible security auditing—again put NetWare at the head of the LAN class.

A SHORT HISTORY OF UNIX

As with NetWare, the development of UNIX started with a few people with some clear goals. Unlike NetWare, for the first decade or so, UNIX was not a commercial product, but was being used and enhanced by a wealth of programmers, designers, and users.

Ken Thompson is generally given the credit for writing UNIX in 1969. Dennis Ritchie (you C programmers should know that name) heads the list of other important contributors. At Bell Labs, Thompson and others were part of the team of companies writing MULTICS (for MULTiplexed Information and Computing System) for a General Electric (GE) 645 mainframe computer. Bell Labs finally dropped out, but Thompson *et al* continued for a very important reason: they had written a game called Space Travel.

Since MULTICS was no longer available, Thompson and Ritchie rewrote the program on an available Digital Equipment Corporation (DEC) PDP-7. Continuing on, they wrote the earliest UNIX for that same box, and they called it UNICS. The name was a play on the name MULTICS, since it originally tried to do only one thing at a time for one user, unlike the multiuser and complex MULTICS. Just think, the history of computing has been forever changed by bad punsters.

Bell Labs got interested officially when UNIX was ported to a larger DEC PDP-11/20 and some text-processing capabilities were added. By 1972, the second edition of the *UNIX Programmer's Manual* mentioned that more (than the ten currently running it) computers were expected to run UNIX soon. In 1973, the kernel was rewritten in C by Thompson and Ritchie, and the step up to a higher-level language from Assembler made things much more portable. The spread of UNIX was underway.

Commercial Versions

AT&T didn't offer a commercial version of UNIX until 1982. By the mid-70's however, Bell Labs started offering UNIX to universities for a minimal fee. Generations of students are credited with both improving the various flavors of UNIX and carrying those flavors with them into the commercial world. One school, the University of California at Berkeley, made enough changes and improvements to start the popular Berkeley Software Distribution (BSD) strain.

Today, BSD and AT&T's System V versions are dominant. The XENIX version, sold by Microsoft in the early 1980's, put UNIX on desktop computers. Santa Cruz Operation (SCO) ported XENIX to the Intel 80386 processor in 1987. All the UNIX versions offer similar features, but the companies involved are still trying to maintain some differentiation for their products.

DOS and some NetWare users make much of the multiple UNIX flavors, trying to cast doubts on the viability of a technology with so many strains. But note that this is the natural development of a technology that isn't controlled by a single entity. Also note that the versions of UNIX show more common points than do NetWare versus LAN Manager versus Banyan VINES. Going from one UNIX to another is less confusing than going from one NOS to another; common heritage does offer some advantages.

Internet Development

Luckily for the NetWare world, UNIX people solved most of the tough problems of networking before the IBM PC ever saw the light of day. By 1981, when the PC was introduced late in the year, networking was old hat to our friends who were building what has become the Internet. Here's some Internet history (from *Internet System Handbook*, Daniel C. Lynch and Marshall T. Rose, editors, Addison Wesley):

▶ **1969:** Researchers and private-sector representatives met for the first time in Snowbird, Utah to start design of what was to become the Internet. The group became known as the Network Working Group.

▸ **1971**: The first electronic mail was sent between two Bolt Beranek and Newman (BBN) programmers. In October, the Network Working Group had a meeting at MIT where logins to remote systems were successful.

▸ **1972**: The first public demonstration of the network was held at the International Conference on Computers and Communications (ICCC) in Washington, DC.

▸ **1973–74**: TCP/IP (UNIX's networking protocol) was designed.

▸ **1983**: TCP/IP was the only protocol allowed on the Internet.

Those involved with UNIX networking in general and the Internet in particular may take a bow. NetWare and DOS users owe your UNIX friends a pat on the back some time soon. Perhaps lunch would be a nice gesture as well. The next time you despair of connecting that Macintosh to that file server, think of trying to connect an SDS Sigma 7, SDS 940, IBM 360/75, and DEC PDP-10 in 1971.

NetWare and UNIX Operating Systems: Technical Differences

These are the main technical differences between UNIX and NetWare:

UNIX	NETWARE
Preemptive	Non-preemptive
Shaped by a large community of researchers and committees	Developed by Novell
Available on a wide range of processors, including Intel	Currently available on Intel processors

UNIX	**NETWARE**
Several multiprocessor versions	No native multiprocessor versions
Virtual memory (RAM and disk considered valid workspace)	Real memory
Daemons	VAPs (Value-Added Processes) and NLMs (NetWare Loadable Modules)
Distributed file systems (NFS, AFS, RFS)	No distributed file systems
TCP/IP transport protocol	IPX/SPX transport protocol

NETWARE (FOR UNIX PEOPLE)

Much of the scorn heaped by UNIX people toward NetWare has traditionally been misdirected scorn toward DOS. One of NetWare's big selling points has been the fact that the network can appear as a sort of "MegaDOS" that allows multiple users to share disks and printers. It can do other things, of course, but this MegaDOS pitch has great appeal to users of DOS and Windows.

To be fair, other network operating systems played the same game, some perhaps even better than Novell. Microsoft's MS NET and later PC Net and later EtherShare (from 3Com) and PC Network (from IBM) can claim even more DOS compliance than can NetWare. Novell added some features that don't have DOS analogies, such as multiple search paths and a public directory (similar to the long SET and PATH statements in the UNIX environment). These and other features help conceal the fact that NetWare is trying to be a shared computer system built on single-user, non-shareable DOS.

Try to differentiate between DOS and NetWare. It's difficult at first, but important to the task at hand. Remember that NetWare has somewhat of a UNIX background. Also remember that NetWare can turn ordinary DOS PCs into something almost (but not quite) as useful and multitasking as UNIX. The word is *almost*, not more or equally.

The two biggest advantages a dealer will use to sway a customer toward NetWare is cost and PC friendliness. The cost of setting up PCs as Network File System (NFS) clients to a central UNIX NFS server adds up quickly. With an Intel-based PC as a UNIX server (configured exactly as it would be as a NetWare server), the cost of the UNIX operating system, including the NFS server portion, is comparable to the cost of the NetWare server software. Hardware cost is exactly the same, since you can use the same hardware for both systems. The difference is the client software. Client NFS for PCs runs $300 to $500 per machine; NetWare PC client software is included in the cost of the operating system.

Secondly, NetWare is a friendly extension to DOS. If users can accept the idea of disk drives acting like local drives but located on a server, they can handle NetWare. Although that does sound suspiciously like NFS, doesn't it?

The PC's Equal Virtual Sessions

Now that NetWare and DOS are separated in our thinking, let's take the next step. NetWare is a multitasking, multithreaded operating system capable of managing the server hardware, file system, printers, and communications. Sounds much like UNIX, right? The trick is that NetWare has traditionally not done any "processing" at the host, er, server.

The PC at the end of the wire must do all the processing for applications. If you pretend that the PC is only a virtual device, such as an application area in the common memory and CPU pool of a UNIX system, this makes sense.

Squinting your eyes just right, you can almost believe that NetWare is really a UNIX system with each user's memory and application space separated by different PCs rather than by the operating system.

NLMs and VAPs as Daemons

Daemons are moving from UNIX to NetWare in the forms of NetWare Loadable Modules (NLMs) and Value-Added Processes (VAPs). The VAP is the early version that ran in NetWare 286 version 2.*x*, albeit poorly. Dealing with the 80286 processor's real and protected modes made these programs difficult to develop and more difficult to keep working. The NLM is the same process, but done only for NetWare 386 version 3.x and above. The advantages of the Intel 80386 microprocessor have made the NLM a stable platform for true applications.

NLMs have almost turned NetWare into a general-purpose operating system similar to UNIX. NLMs can control printing, watch for mail, manage backups, monitor server load, communicate with outside systems, and even run Oracle and Sybase SQL databases. This is a clear indication of UNIX envy. If they could get a cron NLM working, life would be marvelous.

UNIX (FOR NETWARE PEOPLE)

If NetWare can be considered a MegaDOS, can UNIX be considered a Mega-NetWare? Not really. Although the results may appear similar to the user, the process is markedly different.

First of all, UNIX is a multitasking, multithreaded operating system. It was built from the ground up as a multiuser (in fact, multiprogrammer) operating system. It is more complex than NetWare because it does more things.

Desktop Processing versus Host Processing

The biggest difference between NetWare and UNIX is where the programs are processed. With NetWare, all application processing is done at the client PC or Macintosh. With UNIX, all application processing is done at the host. This saves considerable time, especially in certain applications. If a database needs to be churned, files aren't transferred across the network between the server and the application program; both are at the UNIX host.

Since all programs and data are in the same memory pool, which is accessible to all programs, sharing becomes possible. Running the applications in memory pools in separate PCs makes sharing impossible. Database records that are locked in NetWare stay locked until lots of network traffic is finished, but in UNIX there is much less delay.

The flip side of this is that every keystroke on every terminal requires the host to respond. In the old days, this meant that basic word processing dragged the system down. That is not so true anymore, but the shift toward client-server computing means that host processing is used when necessary, and the clients pull some of their own weight.

Preemptive versus Non-Preemptive Scheduling

UNIX utilizes *preemptive scheduling*, a fancy name for priorities. Certain system functions can interrupt other functions. This allows scheduled jobs to begin and system functions to perform necessary procedures, regardless of what else the system is doing.

NetWare does not have this, which is one of the reasons your UNIX friends look down on NLMs. This is why NetWare does not include a cron (time-keeping and delayed-job scheduling) function. It's possible but much more difficult. And this is why NetWare will never be a real-time system, as some UNIX flavors are. Real-time systems must guarantee that certain functions will happen at exact time intervals, and NetWare can't guarantee that.

Everything Is a File

You'll hear your UNIX friends talk about "files" in strange ways. In UNIX, everything can be considered a file. The keyboard and monitor as files? That's right. That's what *stdin* and *stdout* refer to: your keyboard (STanDard IN) and monitor (STanDard OUT), respectively.

The three types of files are called ordinary files, directories, and special files. Ordinary files and directories are much the same as those in DOS, although we would be more historically correct to say that files and directories in DOS are much like those in UNIX. These can be ASCII (text) files or binary, just as in DOS.

Directories can include files and subdirectories. The nesting of subdirectories within directories was quite an innovation in its day. If you remember, IBM and Microsoft ignored that idea in DOS 1.0 and did not permit subdirectories. When hard disks became available, so did subdirectories (in DOS 2.0).

Now for the weird part: UNIX considers a physical device as a "special" file. Any part of the hardware system and all peripherals can be treated as a file. What DOS considers devices, UNIX considers special files. Any target of output and source of input will be referred to as a file. It's a strange concept, but if you can get it, you'll see the enormous flexibility it offers. Any file or device (in the DOS sense) can be directed to any other file or device. Output from anything can become input to anything.

UNIX is case-sensitive, unlike DOS and NetWare. If you try to execute the file Calendar by typing *calendar*, it won't work. The file ABC is not the same as *abc* or *Abc* or *ABc*. This can cause some trouble when you start trying to link UNIX and NetWare files, so start thinking literally now.

Even more literally, UNIX has never had the lousy naming convention DOS is still stuck with: the 12345678.123 (eight.three) file name limitation. The file Income.December.93 is a legal UNIX file name, but it will be a different file than income.December.93 (capitalization, remember?).

Daemons as NLMs

To quote *Peter Norton's Guide to UNIX* (Peter Norton and Harlan Hahn, Bantam): "The most exotic inhabitants of the UNIX universe are the daemons. A daemon is a process that executes in the background in order to be available at all times." Perhaps this is exotic to DOS-only people, but NetWare folks are used to NLMs.

From *Understanding UNIX* (Stan Kelly-Bootle, SYBEX): "The spelling indicates that such processes are amiable spirits rather than evil demons. Daemons run ceaselessly in the background, performing various essential tasks." This again sounds much like NLMs.

Don't carry this too far, because there is a difference between a daemon and a background process in UNIX. Background processes are programs running actively in the background. They are usually applications or utilities. Any application running on the NetWare server itself must be an NLM. A load-monitoring program for NetWare must be an NLM, but in UNIX it will just be an application running in the background.

Since NetWare doesn't have these background processes available, it must use NLMs. UNIX uses only a few daemons at one time, and the rest are background processes. Any user can spawn background processes and go about his or her business. NetWare users can't start NLMs unless they have console privileges.

THE NETWARE AND UNIX KERNELS

Both NetWare and UNIX have core programs that run all the other programs. In NetWare, it's the SERVER.EXE program, and in UNIX it's the *kernel* (often named UNIX or VMUNIX and located in the root directory).

Experienced NetWare administrators are more familiar with kernels than the UNIX people might imagine. The earlier NetWare versions required painful configuration of every detail before a new NET$OS.EXE program was created. The process of making and linking the new NET$OS.EXE program was really relinking a kernel called by another name.

Today, both NetWare and UNIX try to make the kernels separate from the hardware and software additions that are part of every installation. But both perform the same function: control everything that goes on everywhere. Figures 1.1 and 1.2 illustrate the structures of the NetWare and UNIX systems, respectively.

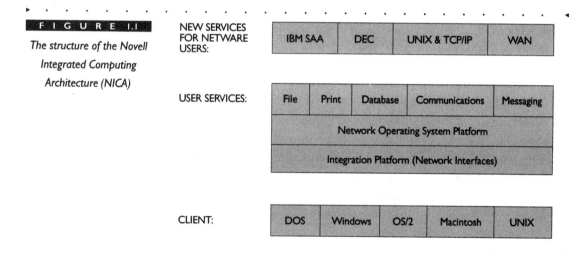

FIGURE 1.1

The structure of the Novell Integrated Computing Architecture (NICA)

NEW SERVICES FOR NETWARE USERS:

IBM SAA	DEC	UNIX & TCP/IP	WAN

USER SERVICES:

File	Print	Database	Communications	Messaging
Network Operating System Platform				
Integration Platform (Network Interfaces)				

CLIENT:

DOS	Windows	OS/2	Macintosh	UNIX

NETWORKING SERVICES

While NetWare *is* networking to PC LAN people everywhere, UNIX was networking long before. In fact, the whole DOS excitement over "client-server" computing is laughable to UNIX people raised on distributed file systems and the

FIGURE 1.2

The structure of the UNIX

system

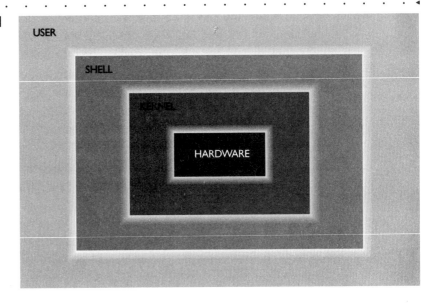

Internet. Allow your UNIX friends a smirk or two when they see some DOS hyperbole concerning the "new world" of distributed computing.

NetWare networking is different from UNIX networking, of course. NetWare has always been a client-to-server network scheme, while UNIX is primarily peer-to-peer. To confuse us now, NetWare has NetWare Lite peer-to-peer networking for DOS clients. For further confusion, many UNIX networks have a server providing file services for a group of workstations in exactly the same manner NetWare provides services for its clients. Just another example of how any system can be improved by incorporating good ideas from other systems.

The differences between NetWare and UNIX networking are in the weakness of the DOS client in PC LAN systems, and the relative structure of UNIX networking. In the world of NetWare client-server networking, the DOS (and Macintosh and OS/2) clients are much weaker than their UNIX counterparts.

This throws much of the weight on the NetWare server. That server has performed well and is getting better, but the feeling has never been one of sharing among equals; it's the weaker client needing the services of the strong server.

The structure of the UNIX world has come through collaborative efforts. The Internet, with its Request for Comment (RFC) procedure building consensus among competitors, is a model of success. The resulting protocols have provided means to connect diverse equipment in a reliable fashion, without allowing one vendor to block the process as so often happens in the DOS world.

One of the main requirements for UNIX networking is support of NFS. Originally developed by Sun in the mid-1980's and release into the public domain, NFS is one of the cornerstones of UNIX-distributed computing. It's so ingrained in the sytem that UNIX programs normally can't tell if they're accessing files on the local system or across the network with NFS.

In the UNIX world, each machine is both a client and a server within the network. In fact, a stand-alone machine functions as both a client and a server. This is a difficult concept for DOS users to accept.

In the real world, sharing UNIX services among machines takes the mutual consent of both partners. The print server system, for instance, must give the client permission to use the printing service. Permissions need to be granted and configurations must be made on both ends of the transaction. In NetWare, only the server needs to grant permissions. UNIX cynics among us will take that as an indication of DOS users' level of computer knowledge. However, it's more a restriction of DOS.

NetWare and UNIX: Philosophical Differences

The philosophical differences between NetWare and UNIX are somewhat difficult to discuss, because NetWare is developing a philosophy while UNIX is losing its philosophy.

Some of the UNIX philosophy (and mystique) has been the almost militantly anti-user bias of the operating system. Real UNIX people, it is said, don't buy programs, they write them. If you need a text editor, borrow code from someone and improve it. Or write it from scratch. Those not familiar with the UNIX way of old may wonder why someone would use an editor like *vi* to write an editor just as unfriendly and cryptic as *vi* itself.

Remember that UNIX was developed as a platform for programmers, not regular people. What is easy and logical to programmers, especially the types involved with the birth and development of UNIX, is not easy or logical to the rest of the world.

On the other side are the DOS and NetWare users and administrators who can barely handle a login script within NetWare. Off-the-shelf programs are the norm; the idea of writing a program would never occur to these people. The most the typical DOS user will do is fill out the forms for a flat-file database.

Will these groups ever have anything in common? More than you might think.

The success of UNIX is what will spoil it to the hard-core technical programmer. More programs will come shrink-wrapped like a DOS program, and more and more users that care nothing about the elegance of a good sort algorithm will get on the system. Infidels will ruin what was once a lovely operating system; sadness will reign.

Of course, the technical programmers won't be complaining because they will have more work than ever before (at higher dollar rates than they ever thought possible). The more users, the more programs need to be written, and the more systems need to be administered. UNIX will ooze into the mainstream, to the benefit of all concerned.

Many DOS users swear they never program but build spreadsheets the size of football fields. They administer hundreds of users on a NetWare network that covers floors and buildings and campuses. They must deal with the graphical user interface (GUI), in such forms as Microsoft Windows, IBM's Presentation Manager and Workplace Shell, and Windows NT. Those GUIs take as much care and coddling as a network of X terminals. In fact, they may require more attention, considering the millions of variables created by several hundred individuals modifying dozens of configuration files for one large NetWare network.

The idea of a "neat hack" is coming to NetWare, as users and administrators enjoy tricks for controlling Windows, writing login scripts, managing print queues, and dozens of other daily administrative tasks. The power of a large UNIX system working under control of dozens of users massaging a single database, or even one spread across several states, will purge longings for the old days.

Yes, success will ruin both groups. What a terrible shame it won't happen sooner.

## CHAPTER 2

Basics of Network Connectivity

Your boss comes to you and says, "We have NetWare and we have UNIX: make them work together."

Unfortunately, connecting NetWare to UNIX involves more than adding some NetWare server names to the */etc/hosts* table on your UNIX systems. The issues involved range from the kind of connector that goes on the cable to the file formats used on different systems. Each piece in every system has a corresponding, but different, piece on the other system.

Interconnection Models: Layers in the Network Cake

No computer networking book is legal unless it has the OSI Reference Model of Open System Interconnection somewhere inside. So, to be legal, here it is, along with the corresponding NetWare and TCP/IP layers (from "TCP/IP and TN3270," a White Paper by DCA):

OSI REFERENCE MODEL	NOVELL NETWARE LAYERS	TCP/IP LAYERS
7-Application	NetWare Services ¦ Applications	Application ¦ Mail ¦ File ¦ Transfer ¦ Virtual Terminal ¦ Net Management
6-Presentation	NetWare Core Protocols	Same as above
5-Session	Same as above	Same as above
4-Transport	SPX ¦ TCP	TCP ¦ UDP
3-Network	IPX ¦ IP	IP ¦ ICMP

OSI REFERENCE MODEL	NOVELL NETWARE LAYERS	TCP/IP LAYERS
2-Datalink	IPX ¦ IP(half of 2)	Datalink
1-Physical	Device drivers and hardware (half of 2)	Ethernet ¦ Token Ring ¦ X.25 ¦ FDDI

Now that you've seen it, what is it that you've seen? This is the high-level (non-technical) view of the various slices of our network cake, showing which slice uses which slice as a foundation. If everything goes according to plan in development of new products and services, each slice of this cake will work within the whole properly if it works with the layers just above and just below itself. Each layer is separate and independent of all the layers other than its immediate neighbors. At least that's the idea.

NETWARE AND UNIX PROTOCOLS

Starting from the beginning, someone might ask, "what is a protocol?" According to Douglas Comer in his book *Internetworking with TCP/IP* (Prentice Hall), a protocol is a "formal description of message formats and the rules two or more machines must follow to exchange those messages." This is as good and simple a description as there is.

TCP/IP is generally discussed as a suite of protocols with a single label for ease of identification. Multiple protocols, such as the File Transfer Protocol (FTP) and Internet Control Message Protocol (ICMP), make up this suite.

Here are the primary Novell protocols (from "Inside NetWare for UNIX v3.11," a Novell research report):

▸ IPX (Internet Packet eXchange): Provides datagram (connectionless) transport.

▸ SPX (Sequenced Packet eXchange): Provides connection-based transport.

▸ RIP (Routing Information Protocol): Maintains the router table.

▸ SAP (Service Advertising Protocol): Advertises services.

▸ NCP (NetWare Core Protocol): For manipulating NetWare files.

▸ PBP (Packet Burst Protocol): Performs high-performance reads and writes.

GROUPING OF NETWORKING LAYERS

The seven layers are often grouped as three layers for practical reasons. The lowest layer, the physical, describes in detail the electrical and mechanical specifications for network device connections. Knowing the allowable microvolt variance of connectors is little solace when your spreadsheet won't print across the network.

The layers are often grouped as follows:

▸ Network (or Communications Subnet): The lower three layers, Physical, Datalink, and Network, go in this group. It includes the Media Access Control (MAC) and Logical Link Control (LLC) protocols, which describe Token Ring, Token Bus, and Ethernet. LLC handles low-level error checking, which is primarily limited to verifying packet integrity between network nodes.

▸ Transport: This group is the "mayonnaise" between the physical layers and the applications running on the network. This is where TCP and UDP (User Datagram Protocol, sometimes erroneously labeled Unreliable Datagram Protocol) reside, as does SPX in Novell's IPX/SPX. These protocols help guarantee delivery of packets from one node to another. Two nodes communicating on this level must agree to communicate (establish a session) before data flows back and forth.

▸ Applications: NetWare Core Protocols run in this group. This set of protocols supports NetWare service applications (such as those for file and print access), as well as computer applications (such as spreadsheets). For UNIX, most of the TCP/IP suite of protocols run here, with TCP as the foundation; NFS, Telnet, FTP, and Simple Network Management Protocol (SNMP) belong in the TCP/IP family.

Physical Layer Choices

The early days of NetWare were marked by a profusion of different types of network interface cards. As noted in Chapter 1, Novell took an unusual approach to this proliferation: it supported every card it could find. The early 3Com and Corvus networks ran only on their own interface cards. NetWare ran on all these, as well as on Western Digital's and SMC's and Datapoints and Proteons and on and on.

I once counted (in 1985) about 35 different versions of NetWare available for 35 different interface cards. Now there are more than 200, but they can be neatly categorized as Ethernet, Token Ring, and Other. Other is getting a smaller piece of that pie chart every year.

TOKEN RING AND ETHERNET

If you are mostly UNIX, you are also mostly Ethernet. Many people believe (and have heard from vendors of both UNIX and Ethernet) that *open systems* means UNIX over Ethernet, but that's not exactly true.

If your site is mostly IBM, you are probably mostly Token Ring. IBM introduced Token Ring for the PC in 1984, and it has had great success. By making it easy to connect Token Ring networks to 3270 cluster controllers, mainframes, AS/400s, and the like, IBM has made Token Ring the sales and technical equal to Ethernet.

IBM has now begun to support Ethernet in a major way, as the UNIX vendors have started to support Token Ring. IBM's RS/6000 shipped from the factory with an Ethernet adapter, a first for Big Blue. Sun, DEC, Hewlett-Packard (HP), and other manufacturers now have Token Ring boards available for virtually their entire product lines.

But Token Ring and Ethernet are not interchangeable, not by any means. In fact, technically and philosophically, the two systems are as different as they could be.

Token Ring is a *deterministic* network access control method. This means that each node has a certain slot of time when it can access the network to transmit a packet of information. An electrical signal goes from one station to the next. If nothing is appended to that signal, the network is available. No matter when a node has information, it must wait for an empty token to come by.

Ethernet is a *nondeterministic* network access control method. The network is available at all times for every node. When a node has information ready to transmit, it listens to be sure no one else is using the network, and then sends a packet. The technical jargon is CSMA/CD, for Carrier Sense Multiple Access/Collision Detect. This just means a node listens to the net (carrier sense), any node can get on at any time (multiple access), and if a collision occurs it will be detected.

Collisions occur when two nodes send information at the same time and both electrical signals get garbled. When a collision is detected, both stations wait a random number of microseconds before retransmitting. Users never know if a packet is being retransmitted; it happens randomly, and the retransmission scheme is so good that noticeable delays are avoided.

Token Ring sends signals from one node to the Nearest Active Upstream Neighbor (NAUN). Each node must be connected to a central hub called a Multi-Station Access Unit (MSAU, often shortened to MAU). Each MSAU has an input and output port (Ring In and Ring Out) for connection to other MSAUs. The electrical wire path is circular, with the signal going to each active node in sequence before returning to the original station, hence the name Token Ring.

Ethernet nodes are strung together into an electrical bus, where each node connects to all other nodes. Visualize coax, with the wire running from one node to the next to the next and so on. The new 10Base-T specification details how to run Ethernet over unshielded-twisted-pair (UTP) wiring, like the wiring telephones use. This is still a bus topology, even though every node must be connected to a central hub (like Token Ring and the MSAU). Inside the hub, the electrical signals still act as if they were on good old-fashioned coax.

Here is a quick rundown of some of the major differences between Ethernet and Token Ring:

ETHERNET	**TOKEN RING**
Speed of 10 Mbps (Megabits per second)	Speed of 4 or 16 Mbps
Bus topology	Ring topology
Coax, UTP, fiber media	STP, UTP, fiber media

Token Ring advocates feel they represent civilization while Ethernet is chaos. Ethernet fans feel they have democracy while the Token Ring group has dictatorship. People get really bent out of shape if you criticize their particular choice of physical network connections.

Those of us in the integration business are above this, of course. We realize that both are good systems, and rarely is one considerably better than the other. While we may have our favorites (Ethernet), we know and appreciate both.

ARCNET

An early (1977) network developed by Datapoint is named Arcnet (for Attached Resource Computing network). It uses a token-passing scheme over a bus topology, somewhat of a combination of Token Ring and Ethernet. Slower (2.5 Mbps) and with smaller packet sizes than Token Ring (512 bits versus 4098 bytes), it typically runs over thin coax cable. The cable is the same type used by IBM for 3270 mainframe terminals.

Unfortunately for Arcnet fans, in the past, Datapoint controlled Arcnet completely. Unlike Token Ring and Ethernet, there was never certification by the IEEE (Institute of Electrical and Electronics Engineers) Standards Committee for Arcnet as there was for Token Ring and Ethernet. The move to standardization is underway now, but it will likely be too little too late. There has never been an Arcnet presence in the UNIX world to speak of, and what strength Arcnet had in the NetWare market has dwindled drastically over the last two years.

However, all is not lost for Arcnet-based NetWare users who need UNIX access. Some UNIX systems support Arcnet boards, although the major players are not among them. The interconnection systems that use IPX/SPX all the way from the NetWare client to the UNIX host will support Arcnet with some planning. If the Arcnet-based machines are connected to a NetWare server or router, the traffic can be switched over to Ethernet or Token Ring within that server.

SERIAL CONNECTIONS

Serial cables were the connection of choice for many years in the UNIX world. Most terminals hooked to UNIX hosts use serial connections, although many are migrating to Ethernet for speed. Wide-area networks (WANs) use serial connections between hosts and modems.

Serial connections work well in an older model UNIX host that does all the processing for the dumb terminals. Serial speeds of 9600 bps (bits per second) provide an acceptable response, since only keystrokes and single characters cross the line between the terminal and host. But now that terminals are becoming smarter and more graphics are involved, serial speeds are too slow.

One area where UNIX users have a real advantage over NetWare users is in remote access. To a dumb terminal, the difference between connecting over a modem or over a serial cable is minimal. Since all the processing happens at the host, the delay to send screen characters to a remote terminal is minimal. This allows UNIX systems to connect over a WAN more easily than PCs can connect remotely to their LAN.

The L in LAN stands for *local*, and local is exactly what is needed. Since the processing happens at the client while the NetWare server acts as a shared hard disk, considerably more than single characters are going over the client-to-server link. The high-speed LAN makes this system possible.

LAN-to-LAN links over a WAN will use serial links, but otherwise, serial means little to NetWare. The more balanced client-server methods in UNIX give it an advantage in performance when serial links are involved.

Transport Choices: TCP/IP and SPX/IPX

The main choices for network transports are IPX/SPX for NetWare and TCP/IP for UNIX. Yes, IPX/SPX is being implemented in various UNIX systems. And yes, TCP/IP is becoming ever more important to Novell for NetWare to UNIX communications and even NetWare client-to-server links. But the trick is still to get TCP/IP on NetWare clients on some occasions, and IPX/SPX onto UNIX at other times. PCs don't use TCP/IP out of the box, and the limited memory available under various forms of DOS force some strange machinations.

IPX/SPX is not a "standard" protocol as is TCP/IP, and it has a history of poor performance over WAN links. Novell is addressing these concerns with Burst Mode Protocol, bringing the TCP/IP idea of acknowledging multiple packets with one packet to the world of NetWare. Look for smart UNIX vendors to include IPX/SPX support, but many of the UNIX traditionalists will continue to moan about violating the purity of TCP/IP.

Application Services

Once the network plumbing is connected, what will come from our digital faucets?

Making UNIX systems run DOS programs doesn't help things particularly. But helping NetWare clients access UNIX host systems to run character-based (non-graphic) applications will aid many companies. Since we're working toward a mixed NetWare and UNIX environment, it's fine to let the NetWare clients run their own DOS, Macintosh (System), or OS/2 applications. It would just be nice to share the resulting information between platforms.

And share it we will. With the growing list of applications that offer both DOS and UNIX versions of their product, easy file access between platforms will help greatly. WordPerfect is the leader among word processors to have versions of its product running on DOS, Windows, UNIX, OS/2, and Macintosh platforms. They keep the same file format, so a SunOS user can use a WordPerfect file from a Macintosh left on a NetWare server. Once our network plumbing is in place, of course.

Applications from both sides of the fence are crossing over today. Oracle was the first database to run as an NLM on the NetWare server. This is in keeping with Oracle's wide coverage in the UNIX world. Because of the initial steps Novell made in supporting TCP/IP, starting with NetWare 386 version 3.1, an Oracle database on a NetWare server can communicate with an Oracle client on any UNIX platform.

As much fun as it is to play with these computers, some spoilsports are going to expect real work to be done. For that, applications need a foundation that can support NetWare-to-UNIX interconnections. That foundation is being built today, and it will get stronger with every new player in this cross-platform market.

Open Systems Services

The development of standards in the UNIX world is creating a set of "open" applications. All systems are expected to support these standards, and the world of NetWare is way behind.

THE X WINDOW SYSTEM

One of the hottest areas today is X, or more technically, the X Window System. Those DOS users that believe Microsoft Windows is the ultimate GUI are in for a treat. Originally developed at MIT, X is a powerful, network-transparent windowing system for bit-mapped displays. X is not part of the operating system; it's just another application running on the operating system. This makes it portable and flexible.

NetWare is getting into the world of X, albeit slowly. Starting with the early NetWare for NFS product, remote X consoles were supported for management. Novell knew a mixed environment would likely mean a UNIX management station running X, so the NFS NLM supported the XConsole program.

Before we get carried away, you should know that XConsole is just an ASCII-character program running in a remote X window. Fully windowed X management support is still in the future. But it's noteworthy that Novell's developers felt the need to support X at some level; they could just as easily let it slide.

NETWORK FILE SYSTEM SUPPORT

The same NetWare for NFS product line addressed one of the other main requirements for UNIX networking: support of NFS. Better and better support of NFS is important for NetWare to be a player in the UNIX world, and its new NFS

Gateway is a tremendous step forward. With this program, a NetWare client can access NFS file systems anywhere on the network, exactly as if they are NetWare volumes. Once again, Novell is two generations ahead of the other PC LAN vendors.

ELECTRONIC MAIL SERVICES

One serious shortcoming of NetWare and PC LANs in general is the lack of electronic mail (e-mail) standards. Years ago, UNIX established an entire protocol, called SMTP (Simple Mail Transfer Protocol), just to make sure disparate systems could communicate. Once again, the fractured and fractious PC world is holding itself back.

The e-mail standards proposed to date have less to do with a spirit of cooperation than with certain vendors trying to gain advantage. Publishing internal Application Program Interfaces (APIs) from a proprietary application and hoping the world writes to your specifications is self-serving and shortsighted. So far, however, that's about all there is for e-mail sharing in the current world of PC LANs. Perhaps soon one of the proposed sets of standards will take the lead, and e-mail will move into high gear.

CHAPTER 3

Connecting the Networks

As in most projects, there are an amazing number of petty details to conquer before you can integrate NetWare and UNIX installations. The problem with petty details is that they're only petty when they're taken care of properly.

If you don't believe small details can become huge, try this little exercise. Pick up a pebble and hold it at arm's length. Does it impact your ability to see the world around you? Of course not. Now hold that same pebble right in front of your left eye, while closing your right eye. Does that very same pebble block your view of the rest of the world? Of course it does.

"Little" details in an integration project work in the same manner. If you handle them properly, no one knows or cares what they are. When they're handled improperly, the phone will ring constantly, with angry users on the other end.

"Selling" Your Integration Project

You know that the NetWare users and the UNIX users need to share files. You know that the UNIX system administrator is drooling over the NetWare Post-Script printer. You know the ancient PC database needs to be upgraded and the LAN administrator is going to seminars touting UNIX SQL databases as the back-end for PC clients. You know all these things, but how do you put it on paper to convince the nontechnical boss?

Even if your management is sold on this grand and noble integration project, it doesn't mean that they have allocated proper resources (time, money, and personnel) to get the job done. Don't underestimate the need for continued selling and reselling of your project.

As a network specialist, I became successful only when I realized that no one makes a decision like this in a vacuum. Networking by definition involves multiple people and departments. Even managers who officially have the authority to sign the capital requests need positive peer-group feedback before doing so.

Don't drop your persuasion level after the project is approved. Every manager wants to know that he or she is making the right decision, especially in areas that overlap with other people and departments. Doubts can creep in and sour the decision. Keep reminding management that the decision was good, things will be better in the near future, and that they're smart, wise, and well-respected. The project will roll smoother once you learn to grease the wheels properly.

Benefits of Connecting NetWare and UNIX

Unfortunately, many of the best benefits from an integration project can't be listed ahead of time. The synergy between two good systems made better by proper integration can only happen after the fact. Just remember that UNIX is not Utopia, and NetWare is not Nirvana. Don't promise too much; management always remembers the promises you make, but rarely the fine print of those promises.

The following sections cover some of the most obvious advantages of integrating NetWare and UNIX. Of course, the ones that will convice your management depend on your particular project (and your particular management).

THE JOY OF INFORMATION SHARING

The 90's may be known as the Decade of Data Independence. Watching the fight over client-server technologies may be reminiscent of mud-wrestling, but the idea is to share information. Vendors for various front-end and back-end data services scramble to make their products work with everyone else's yet still be special. Although the fighting is not pretty, the goal of sharing data everywhere is a good one.

Yet data is not information until intelligence is applied. This means some person or persons must have access to that data. The easier the access, the more likely data will become information on a timely and usable basis.

In the past, companies had separate pools of data scattered around. In the past, middle managers could take a few weeks to retype reports from the different systems into a Lotus 1-2-3 spreadsheet. The past is gone. Today, there are fewer middle managers in most companies. Today, higher-level managers don't want to wait for their information. Today, retyping reports is considered technologically backward and embarrassing. Today, every system must be able to reach every other system.

The new lean and mean corporate structure relies on the availability of information to more people than in the past. Increased automation requires fewer middle managers to massage data into some form of information for the next management layer. The remaining managers must be able to quickly retrieve data from disparate sources and try to make it into information themselves.

Justifying better interdepartment sharing can be difficult. The time being wasted in making data from different departments usable is often hidden in standard work procedures. Here are some examples of information flow bottlenecks in a typical company:

- ▶ Reports are retyped into different systems.

- ▶ Updates and reports have long delivery times.

- ▶ Managers can't make decisions without more information.

- ▶ Information takes forever to move around the company.

- ▶ Employees and entire departments feel left out and isolated.

- ▶ "The System" eats orders, files, and records.

- ▶ No single electronic mail system connects all employees.

This is not a pretty picture, but it's all too common. Things have gotten so bad that an entire discipline, Organizational Development, has sprung up to address information flow bottlenecks. An enormous effort is being made to help people work together and solve problems rationally. The least those of us in the computer business can do is make our computers work together.

SHARING CAPITAL RESOURCES

It's unfortunate that information is an abstract concept to many people. If data were something that you could hold in your hand, people might feel much more inclined to treat it with the respect it deserves.

Until that day when we can see data and touch it, people (read managers) will treat hardware and packaged software with more respect than data. Hardware is important and worthy of respect, so use that to your advantage in getting your integration project started. While information may be difficult to track, dollars spent on equipment aren't.

Printers are the most popular shareable resource, but companies also benefit from sharing other devices. Plotters, cable hubs and physical network management equipment, hard disks, and tape systems are examples of other resources that can be shared by NetWare and UNIX users.

Printers

After nearly 20 years of networking, companies still buy networks to share printers. Not only companies with hundreds of thousands of dollars invested in mainframe typesetting printers, but also those with standard laser printers. No matter how many printers there are, every user feels that the printers are too far away. Being able to send jobs to any printer in the area, regardless of its controlling operating system, is attractive to every company.

For example, I know of one organization that bought a NetWare package solely for the purpose of sharing printers. Admittedly, it had a special situation, with a multitude of expensive printers attached to a Data General (DG) mainframe. Being a hospital, it had plenty of custom forms designed for Medicare and other government agencies and insurance companies. These were all mounted on DG mainframe printers, scattered around the hospital.

The solution was to use Portable NetWare (now called NetWare for UNIX) from DG as a front-end for the PC users to the host printers. PCs sent particular forms to particular print queues, and each print queue had the proper formatting codes built into the forms definitions.

Most people don't have such an interesting application, but don't underestimate printer sharing when selling your integration project. Even when the networking components add up to many thousands of dollars, management may not count those dollars the same way as you or I. The $3,000 that might be spent for more laser printers adds up to hard dollars that come directly from the budget.

The moral of this story is to include printer "savings" in your proposals. Don't ask me why, but managers love this.

Hard Disks

Less common than sharing printers, but often important, is the ability to share hard-disk storage space among various platforms. Several years ago, it was always true that a megabyte of disk space on a midrange system cost five or more times as much as a megabyte of PC hard disk. With the increase in disk size for PCs and NetWare servers, the price per megabyte is even lower today.

The downward trend in disk pricing has hit the UNIX world as well. Since many of the disk makers use the same physical disk in multiple systems, the volume pricing for PCs is having a positive effect on the midrange pricing world.

Many UNIX systems today run on the exact same hardware as a PC NetWare file server. This also helps level the costs of the actual disk hardware.

While all these things are true, it's also true that open disk space is never where you want it when you want it. With the increase of disk-eating programs in the PC world, such as new graphic interfaces and industrial-strength relational databases, open megabytes are always welcome.

Sharing disk space can be done so the user has no idea it's happening. By copying critical files to other hardware platforms and operating systems in the network, you can ensure data integrity. This keeps these files safe yet easily accessible.

Tape Systems

The ability of UNIX tape systems to back up and restore data without impacting performance of the system is way ahead of what is available with NetWare tape systems. Using the higher bandwidth buses available in UNIX systems makes for more efficiency as well. Most NetWare tape products are simply enhancements to stand-alone PC backup products.

Companies will invest in tape-tracking and file-locating procedures for large systems well before they will do so for LAN systems. Proper tape rotation and off-site storage procedures are in place for virtually all large systems as a matter of course. However, NetWare administrators often don't have any products to help them or time to develop their own systems.

We welcome the UNIX tape vendors into the NetWare marketplace. There's no sense in reinventing the wheel for NetWare tape systems. Looking outside the PC LAN world for better products is smart.

If your management is big on security and uptime, the improvement in tape backup and restoration procedures may be a big hot button. Push it hard. If it's not important to your management now, it will be when someone erases the wrong directory while the corporate auditors are in the lobby.

RIGHTSIZING PLATFORMS

In the Buzzword Wars, *downsizing* was the first winner. This meant taking critical applications from the old, mainframe dinosaur and putting them on the fleet, nimble, midrange (often UNIX) systems. This was in the '70's, and people declared the mainframe dead.

In the 80's, downsizing meant taking critical applications from the old, midrange dinosaurs and putting them on the fleet, nimble PC LAN systems. The same people that wrongly predicted the death of the mainframe declared the midrange system dead.

In the 90's, downsizing has been replaced by *rightsizing*, because there aren't any smaller platforms than the PC LAN's to migrate down to. This is a much more intelligent attitude, especially since both mainframes and midrange systems are still around.

This new attitude places a premium on putting applications on platforms that best support them. In most companies, there is no budget to move working applications from one platform to another. What little resources are available tend to be used to make new applications work as well as possible. During design time, applications should be matched with platforms, and that's happening. Making it easy to connect to that right platform from any desktop is one of the advantages of integrating NetWare and UNIX.

Database Engines

UNIX systems, with their multithreading operating system and strong multiprocessor support, make great database engines. Sorting and massaging huge data files works best under UNIX. However, UNIX presentation at the user level sometimes leaves something to be desired.

PCs running NetWare can present a multitude of friendly faces to the user. However, sorting and massaging huge data files taxes the network. Furthermore, this work is done by a single DOS PC client, which is not known to be a high-performance database engine.

By combining UNIX and NetWare, you can cover both sides of the database issue intelligently. You can let NetWare be the friendly face to the user and let UNIX be the background workhorse.

Graphics Processing

A hot topic today is graphics and GUIs. In the PC world, this means Microsoft Windows or IBM's OS/2. In the UNIX world, this means the X Window System.

As many PC users discovered to their dismay, even minimal GUIs like Windows require huge amounts of processing power, disk space, and network bandwidth.

One area of new programs attempts to turn PCs into X terminals, often using Microsoft Windows as the starting point. A few GUIs, such as DESQview/X from Quarterdeck Office Systems, even attempt to turn the PC into an X server for other PCs.

You can guess where this is heading: X services require horsepower by the bushel basket. If graphics imaging or manipulation is important in your business, a combination of UNIX and NetWare platforms will be the most cost-effective and flexible solution.

Document Imaging

Companies investigating document imaging, especially those trying to reduce paper to electronic images, will find UNIX as the platform of choice. Many systems have a UNIX system as the primary storage and retrieval engine.

Even companies that use strictly NetWare often work with images provided by UNIX-based scanners. Several document-management programs running on NetWare either communicate with modules on UNIX systems or with SQL databases. This ties in directly with the idea of UNIX as the database engine of choice, with the user presentation handled by NetWare.

Planning Considerations

Every journey begins with that famous "first step," and your integration project is no exception. As with any other journey, remember the five P's: Proper Planning Prevents Poor Performance. Proper planning is more important in this type of project than many others because of the wide differences between the two connected networks.

CONNECTING DIFFERENT WORLDS

To go between NetWare and UNIX is really saying, to borrow from Monty Python, "And now for something Completely Different." Don't let the surface similarities blind you to the multitude of differences.

In many ways, combining NetWare and UNIX is a translation project. If you were to come upon two gentlemen, one French and one German, wanted to communicate, you would have three options: teach the Frenchman some German, teach the German some French, or find a third person to translate between the two.

This example isn't random: the French and Germans have been more or less hostile toward each other for hundreds of years, with periods of friendship in between. Likewise, UNIX and NetWare people have been hostile to each other for some time, with pockets of friendliness. And as Europe is forcing itself to become better integrated, so is the computer business, and we also have three choices:

- ► Teach UNIX systems to speak NetWare.

- ► Teach NetWare systems to speak UNIX.

- ► Provide a "black box" translator between the two.

Teaching UNIX to Speak NetWare

This approach takes the position that the PC is a fragile environment, limited in memory and horsepower. UNIX is a strong environment, with much better memory management and horsepower available (even when running on the same Intel hardware). It's better to make the strong side (UNIX) change rather than the weak side (NetWare).

There is a lot to be said for this approach, especially if the NetWare crowd is installed long before the UNIX crowd. Speaking practically from a network manager's viewpoint, it's easier to change one system than hundreds. This approach is the rationale for all the NetWare for UNIX products.

Here are the advantages of getting a UNIX system to communicate in NetWare language:

- ▸ No PC client changes

- ▸ Single point of administration

- ▸ Good local performance with IPX/SPX

- ▸ Low RAM impact on clients

And here are the disadvantages of this method:

- ▸ May slow the rest of the UNIX system

- ▸ Poor WAN connections with IPX/SPX

- ▸ More expensive administration talent

- ▸ Dual UNIX administration for users

Teaching NetWare to Speak UNIX

If the UNIX side predates the NetWare, this approach has probably been the default choice. It's popular because our first option (teaching UNIX to speak NetWare) is a fairly recent phenomenon. It's also less expensive if only a few of the NetWare clients or users need access to UNIX data and resources.

This approach is behind all the NetWare NFS and FLeX/IP products. It's also behind all the various stand-alone PC packages that add TCP/IP or NFS to DOS and Windows. Most of these stand-alone PC packages will function inside a client computer also running NetWare. Four years ago, before Network Device Interface Specifications (NDIS) and Open DataLink Interface (ODI) drivers became available, it was nearly impossible to run IPX/SPX and TCP/IP concurrently on a PC. Now every TCP/IP vendor must offer this capability or face the wrath of the market.

Teaching NetWare to speak UNIX has the following advantages:

- Spreads the conversion overhead among all clients, so that the cost is less noticeable

- Customizable per user

- Easy to prototype with a few users

And here are its disadvantages:

- IP addresses to manage for every PC client

- High RAM impact on PC clients

- PC users must learn UNIX

Using a Translator

The "black box" for UNIX and NetWare is the TCP/IP gateway. In this book, we will examine three TCP/IP gateways, two of which require a dedicated PC and one of which runs in the NetWare file server itself. These all work in similar fashion: a PC client runs software at that PC to make connection to the TCP/IP gateway, and then software makes the connection from the gateway to a requested UNIX host. Telnet (terminal emulation) sessions are opened, and you then have the ability to transfer files and share printers.

Here are the advantages of the translator method:

- No impact on either system

- Central administration

- One IP address to manage

- Some extra security options

And here are the disadvantages of the approach:

- Lower performance under load

> ▸ Dedicated PC expense

> ▸ Less flexible than the second option per PC user

> ▸ Doubles traffic on the network (packet to gateway, then packet from gateway to host, then vice versa)

THE PERFORMANCE ISSUE

Most people are optimistic and ask questions like "which is the best option?" Although *best* has multiple meanings, *fastest* is always toward the top of the list.

Native NetWare will always perform better per dollar spent than any NetWare for UNIX implementation. However, some of the UNIX platforms running Net-Ware for UNIX are approaching the performance of Native NetWare. Before the cheers ring out, remember that this is possible only on large and seriously expensive UNIX hardware platforms. Few people believe it's better to spend $100,000 on UNIX hardware to get 10 percent better performance than is possible with a $12,000 Intel-based server.

To decide which option provides the best performance, you must consider several variables. Speed alone is seldom the limiting factor in successful network computing.

SCALABILITY

Big buzzword, *scalability*. The UNIX world has used it for years. Since UNIX can run on hardware platforms ranging from notebooks to mainframes, it's very scalable. Database too slow? Put it on a faster box or add another half dozen processors. No need to change a line of code or convert a digit of data.

Novell provides some of that same scalability. NetWare now supports more users and offers more features. In 1987, 30 users was a good upper limit for a single NetWare server. Today, many companies routinely support hundreds of users per server.

One of the reasons that NetWare and UNIX are the winners in the computer world is that both systems provide ways to maintain the software investment over a variety of hardware platforms. This goes both ways: up for larger user populations, or down for smaller departments or branch offices.

EXPANDABILITY

The ability to expand when needed is another important feature to consider. Normally, expansion is related to the number of active users, but active processes and pure number crunching count as well.

Both NetWare and UNIX systems can be expanded without obsoleting any prior purchase. Novell uses tiered pricing for NetWare (5, 10, 20, 50, 100, 250, 1000 users), and many products that work with NetWare adopt that tiered pricing. The procedure to expand from 20 users to 50 is generally a software update only. You don't need to change or convert data.

UNIX systems work in the same manner. Again, a software update is all that is required to increase the number of users.

For the hardware-based systems, such as gateways, expansion is not so easy. Many gateways now support the ability to run multiple gateway functions in the same PC client, but many do not. All of them allow multiple gateways to exist on the same network. If one is not enough, add another. The procedures for users will remain the same, except it will take administrators twice as long because there are twice as many physical gateways. Aren't computers wonderful?

MANAGEABILITY

Management of both NetWare and UNIX remains too difficult and time-consuming. Fortunately, NetWare for UNIX doesn't add much to that burden, but neither does it diminish it.

Common management of both NetWare and UNIX users in these mixed environments is a high priority for all the NetWare for UNIX vendors. The ability to control, monitor, and administer a hybrid user (one with access rights to both systems) from one platform is a shining trophy yet to be earned.

One of the difficulties in integrating NetWare and UNIX is the different skill sets each operating system requires. Many of the concepts are the same, but the vocabulary is not.

In many cases, it's suggested that a NetWare and a UNIX administrator configure an installation together. This may seem a bit labor-intensive, but it actually saves time. When something is being installed, people are usually waiting for it. That is not the time for the NetWare administrator to try to decipher the mysteries of IP addressing, nor for the UNIX administrator to delve into the PRINTDEF utility.

For every integration project, there is both a NetWare and a UNIX side, so both angles must be considered. System administrators, the people that most enjoy a lack of change, must regain some enthusiasm and curiosity. This project of integrating NetWare and UNIX will change your view of the world. The world may not initially be better, neater, cleaner, or less aggravating, but it will be different.

Protocol Choice Considerations

In the old days (four years ago), the idea of choosing a protocol was unheard of; customers used the protocol that came with their system, period. As in much of the computer business, more power has made for more choices. Protocols are included in these choices, although the traditional choices hold sway. If you run UNIX, you run TCP/IP. If you run NetWare, you run IPX/SPX. The new part is in mixing these protocols whenever you want.

Today, there are options for putting Novell's IPX/SPX protocol on PC, Macintosh, NeXT, SCO, SVR4 UNIX, Solaris, UnixWare, LAN Manager, LAN Server, Banyan, and even IBM 370 mainframe systems. For a humble little local protocol, IPX/SPX has come a long way.

Conversely, TCP/IP started as the protocol of UNIX systems only, and it's now available on all the above-mentioned platforms and many more. Suffice it to say that both IPX/SPX and TCP/IP can be loaded on every conceivable computer platform in one way or another.

Some LAN systems have embraced TCP/IP as a viable transport protocol for the PC-only LAN. The primary example is LAN Manager from Microsoft, although TCP/IP is used as a transport layer for Server Message Block (SMB) and NetBIOS. The licensees of LAN Manager, such as StarGroup from ATT/NCR, now use TCP/IP in place of Open Systems Interconnect (OSI), the protocol that is destined to replace TCP/IP at some indeterminate time in the future.

TCP/IP (FOR NETWARE PEOPLE)

NetWare people often believe TCP/IP is some bloated, RAM-stealing, old-fashioned protocol, built for slow WAN connections and good for nothing else. If this is what you think, here's some advice: get over it.

TCP/IP has almost single-handedly built up the world of networking. TCP/IP has some features that NetWare may never match. IPX/SPX came from a subset of XNS, which is a subset of TCP/IP. There are differences, but IPX/SPX is two or more generations behind.

Here are some of the features of TCP/IP as they apply to LANs today (from "TCP/IP and TN3270," a White Paper by DCA):

- ▶ It can route data between different networks or subnetworks.

- ▶ It's independent of technology used for subnetworks (such as Ethernet, Token Ring, and X.25).

- ▶ It's independent of the host hardware.

- ▶ It can tolerate high error rates in subnetworks.

- ▶ It has a robust recovery from failures.

If nothing else, TCP/IP is a valuable foundation and fountain of knowledge for future development of IPX/SPX. The method of enhancing TCP/IP and the amount of input from concerned users is a model of "co-opetition," one of Novell's favorite concepts. To paraphrase Ray Noorda (Chairman of Novell since 1983 and widely credited with making Novell what it is today), rising waters raise all boats. Nowhere is this attitude more in evidence than in the Internet (UNIX) community.

Don't make the mistake of thinking an understanding of TCP/IP is unnecessary since OSI will replace it Real Soon Now. OSI was developed as a way to solve the problems that have developed in TCP/IP as networking exploded globally. TCP/IP is not broken; the world of computing is simply asking it to do much more than was ever imagined. The points of breakdown are being fixed both within the TCP/IP community and by the committees dedicated to bringing OSI to the world. However, the committees are losing; TCP/IP will live forever.

IPX/SPX (FOR UNIX PEOPLE)

If you believe IPX/SPX is some brain-damaged, limited, local, baby PC protocol, get over it. IPX/SPX mirrors what some new high-speed protocols are trying to do: specifically tailor a protocol for the new job at hand.

For IPX/SPX, Novell enhanced Xerox Network Services (XNS) to perform better in a local, highly reliable LAN, consisting of not-too-intelligent early PCs. By condensing the protocol to run in this environment, IPX/SPX delivered outstanding performance with little RAM overhead. This was much more important in the time of a 640K PC with no memory management techniques than the ability to recover from a sliding window packet being delivered out of sequence.

Here are some of the features of IPX/SPX as they apply to LANs today:

▶ It's consistent with XNS protocol.

▶ IPX is the workhorse: connectionless and identical to XNS Internetwork Datagram Packet (IDP) protocol.

▶ IPX provides addressing and routing functions.

▶ SPX adds Transport layer functions, providing a guaranteed delivery, connection-oriented link between nodes.

▶ SPX is often bypassed for workstation-to-server links.

Many UNIX people carry a grudge against IPX/SPX because they carry a grudge against DOS. "What a stupid operating system," they say, "networking has to be grafted on as an afterthought." The new world of desktop operating systems is changing that tune, however. A standard DOS package, DR DOS, now (since its purchase by Novell) includes networking protocols within it. Microsoft Windows comes with IPX/SPX built in, as does Windows NT, OS/2, SCO, NeXTstep 3.0, Solaris 2.0, UnixWare, and almost every other desktop system.

Numerically, IPX/SPX has been outshipping TCP/IP for years. New NetWare IPX/SPX nodes number over one million per month; TCP/IP less than a tenth of that. In the corporate world, NetWare, and by extension IPX/SPX, has about 70 percent of the market. If UNIX is going to expand into corporate America, it will do so in cooperation with IPX/SPX.

Yes, Novell controlled IPX/SPX for many years, and a proprietary protocol has little chance of winning hearts and minds in the UNIX community. In the fall of 1992, Novell addressed this issue by licensing IPX/SPX inexpensively to all takers. But it's still technically proprietary, in the sense that Novell controls future development. It's hard to reconcile *capitalistic* and *open*; companies and products are always weighted to one side of the equation or the other.

But the market has spoken: IPX/SPX is the transport protocol of choice in corporate America. Say what you want about TCP/IP as a better protocol; the battle is over and IPX/SPX won. TCP/IP will live forever, but IPX/SPX will dominate and control the PC-oriented desktop through the end of the century.

NETBIOS (FOR EVERYONE)

The PC people are wondering where NetBIOS is in a discussion of network protocols? Isn't it one? Well, actually, no it isn't.

Technically speaking, NetBIOS (for NETwork Basic Input Output System) isn't a protocol or an API—it's a low-level software interface. It's language and protocol independent, leaving it outside the definitions of protocol or API. But don't be rude to people that insist NetBIOS is a protocol developed by IBM; their confusion is understandable.

Appearing in 1984 with IBM's PC Network program and broadband-based network interface card, SMB servers and REDIRECTOR software clients became available on a PC-only platform. Much of the NetBIOS code ran on the card itself, since the PC platform was underpowered. It became truly important (and noticeable in the market) when IBM shipped Token Ring adapters in 1986, again supporting NetBIOS.

NetBIOS has more in common with a PC BIOS than with traditional networking. Software interrupts from the CPU deliver a Network Control Block (NCB) through NetBIOS to the low-level network software. The NetBIOS functions are protocol independent because IBM's competitors figured that supporting NetBIOS functions would allow software written for the IBM network to run on non-IBM hardware and software. NetBIOS commonly runs over IPX/SPX, TCP/IP, or OSI today. See RFC 1001/1002 for the specifications of NetBIOS over TCP/IP.

Despite the fact that NetBIOS has some good features and many admirers, Net-Ware users generally avoid it. Novell has not spent the time making NetBIOS an important part of NetWare, since most functions provided by NetBIOS are also covered by various features of IPX/SPX and NetWare itself. Also, NetBIOS is touchy about interoperability. The same NetBIOS must be used everywhere to guarantee communications.

NetBIOS counterparts are available for many of the products mentioned for NetWare-UNIX integration, especially TCP/IP gateways. Several companies, most notably Performance Technology in San Antonio, Texas, and Micro Computer Systems (MCS) in the Dallas area, add NetBIOS to UNIX systems. This does all the same things that adding IPX/SPX to a UNIX system does: allows a PC client to run terminal emulation to the host without TCP/IP.

Using Routers or Bridges

The safest way to connect two existing networks (assuming UNIX and Net-Ware are both functioning in your site already) is by placing a router or bridge at the intersection point. This method provides a way to plug them together without disturbing the existing networks. It also gives you a quick way to unplug the connection if things go south.

If a device makes decisions based on the physical addresses of the source and destination nodes within the packet, it's a *bridge*. If the decisions are made by examining a higher level protocol, the device is a *router*.

Routers are becoming more popular on the local level, taking over much of the territory that used to belong to the simple bridge. Part of the reason is that the costs for intelligent network hardware are going down, taking away much of the bridge's price advantage. Another part of the reason is the increasing need for control, security, and management in networks today—routers generally do a better job of these functions than do bridges.

THE NOVELL SERVER AS ROUTER

Novell added the capability for NetWare to bridge multiple LAN segments in the file server in 1986. Novell called this a bridge for several years, but since the "bridge" looked only at IPX/SPX addresses for packet-routing decisions, it was officially a router. Novell refused to acknowledge this, even after NetBIOS packets running over IBM's early Token Ring interface cards could not be "bridged" by NetWare.

Things have gotten much better in the NetWare router world, and Novell now calls the router a router. However, there are several reasons why you should not trust the NetWare server to be the primary router in your network.

In a server, the most important functions are file and print services. Routing is far down the priority list in a NetWare server. This means that using the server for routing will degrade file and print services, and the server won't perform well as a router either.

Large networks today require solid management. Yes, the TCP/IP NLM includes a Simple Network Management Protocol (SNMP) agent, but it's of limited functionality.

If your network consists of one or two NetWare servers with multiple physical LAN segments from each one, the server router will perform well. If your network is beyond that, look for something outside the NetWare server to perform your routing functions.

THE NOVELL STAND-ALONE ROUTER

To capitalize on what it has learned about routing software, Novell has released their Multi-Protocol Router as a separate product. Running in a stand-alone PC with the NetWare Runtime operating system, it supports IPX, IP, Apple-Talk, OSI, and Novell's NetBIOS. Routing protocols supported are IPX RIP, IP RIP, AppleTalk RTMP, and OSI IS-IS.

Placing this software into an 80386 PC with 8MB of RAM and a 40MB hard disk results in a good performance per dollar ratio, without any degradation of file and print services. It's a good choice for the connecting point between a NetWare and UNIX network. If you're a NetWare person, this is the router you're most familiar with. If you have a counterpart on the UNIX side, arrange a meeting and discuss some non-NetWare solutions.

THIRD-PARTY ROUTERS OR BRIDGES

The Internet was built on routing (primarily WAN routing, but routing nonetheless). The best LAN routers are from companies that learned their lessons on UNIX networks, particularly the Internet vendors.

The biggest names in TCP/IP routing are Cisco Systems and Wellfleet, with companies such as Vitalink, Proteon, CrossCom, 3Com, and IBM coming on strong. The Features War is fierce, and all these companies have strong local routing options as well as WAN routing.

Since UNIX has been more complex than NetWare from the beginning, network management has progressed farther in the TCP/IP world than in the PC LAN world. Management of routers is one of the priorities in this world. In fact, SNMP was developed to expand on Simple Gateway Management Protocol (SGMP) and to control gateways and routers network administrators need to manage.

For the NetWare side of the network, less is available in the way of comprehensive management tools. For that reason, if you're a NetWare administrator and have a chance to just buy a port for an existing router rather than buy your own, do it. It will cost less, and your UNIX administrator friends will probably already be able to manage and monitor your new port better than you could yourself.

## CHAPTER 4

Portable NetWare or NetWare for UNIX

NetWare for UNIX was originally labeled Portable NetWare. The product is a C source-code version of NetWare, licensed to Original Equipment Manufacturer (OEM) customers only. Great care was taken to preserve the same NetWare client interface that the client sees in Native NetWare. The early versions required management contortions at times, but the NetWare user was protected from the differences.

NetWare has become so popular that NetWare for UNIX-type products is now available from companies that have not licensed the code from Novell. Recreating the code seems like an enormous amount of extra work, but several small companies are doing this. In a tribute to what UNIX programmers can do when challenged, these implementations are actually pretty good.

History of NetWare for UNIX

Although NetWare for UNIX is not old, it has an interesting history. The work that went into porting NetWare to UNIX platforms was extensive. But the project was also a catalyst for a number of other changes that needed to be made. If this porting activity continues, people may never believe it when we old-timers tell them about the days NetWare was limited to a single microprocessor.

NETWARE FOR VMS

The first nonnative NetWare was built on the VMS (Virtual Management System) platform, aimed at the DEC MicroVax systems. It was slow and awkward to administer, but it was a start.

At this time in the development of Portable NetWare, vendors thought its performance would be a big advantage over Native NetWare. Real-world testing, including exhausting trials such as a login or a file copy, showed performance to be putrid compared to Native NetWare. Much retrenching of marketing thought was undertaken, and the integration of NetWare to VMS became the focal point.

NetWare Virtual Terminal (NVT) made its appearance, in its early incarnation of TES (Terminal Emulation Services, now sold by Interconnections), allowing a NetWare client running only IPX/SPX protocols to connect to a non-NetWare host. This may be the first instance of Novell's protocol beginning to expand beyond the PC-only world that gave it birth.

NetWare for VMS was unique in that Novell itself attempted to sell the product. Every other NetWare for UNIX program since has been sold by the UNIX host vendor. Novell learned a lesson concerning reaching into new worlds before being ready.

The new NetWare for VMS, cleaned up and much faster now, is sold by other vendors, not Novell.

NETWARE FOR UNIX CODE RELEASE

Much work went into NetWare to separate the file and print services from the operating system. That required a basic overhaul of NetWare, since the idea of hardware independence was not considered in the early 1980's as NetWare grew and developed.

Early NetWare was written in assembly language, for speed but not portability. For NetWare 386, part of the code was rewritten in C. The Runtime operating system, the part that controls the hardware of the server, has stayed mostly in assembler for speed purposes. The code given to the NetWare for UNIX vendors is all in C.

Now hardware independence is part of being "open," so most software companies are rapidly porting their products to run on hardware with different labels on the front. These systems may have an Intel processor, or a SPARC, Motorola, Alpha, or whatever. The important point to customers is that they now can choose hardware from different vendors and with various levels of performance.

Marketing of NetWare for UNIX

The marketing of NetWare for UNIX is the concern of each of the licensees. This has been one of the major limitations of the product. All too often, the salespeople responsible for the product see NetWare for UNIX as competition to the UNIX host system they normally sell. Even those salespeople that understand

and appreciate the product have obstacles; the MIS contacts for UNIX hosts are not the contacts for departmental NetWare networks.

The benefits and use of NetWare are different than the benefits and use of UNIX systems. The philosophies of both systems are different, the user communities are different, and the sales process is different. With all this working against them, it's amazing those sales representatives have sold anything.

Only SunSelect, the PC and UNIX integration division of Sun Microsystems, has released its NetWare SunLink (NetWare for UNIX) product for distribution outside its internal sales force. Some Sun dealers and NetWare resellers offer the product, and the SunExpress mail order/telemarketing division pushes it as well.

Benefits of NetWare for UNIX

Since raw speed has been dismissed as a reason to buy NetWare for UNIX, what are the benefits? Why would a company buy NetWare for UNIX when it may cost more than Native NetWare? According to Novell, these kinds of companies will benefit from NetWare for UNIX (from "Inside NetWare for UNIX v3.11," a research paper):

- ▶ Companies that require integration of existing PC LANs with existing systems running business-critical applications

- ▶ Companies that want to share file and print capabilities of their UNIX-based systems with NetWare clients

- ▶ Companies that are committed to open systems and have decided to use UNIX as a standard

- ▶ Companies that are prolonging the investment of computer hardware by providing NetWare access to these existing systems

This is all well and good, but I don't buy it. Companies are made of people, and people read these types of marketing reports with glazed eyes. People buy NetWare for UNIX for a variety of reasons, but the list above misses the most important points.

People buy NetWare for UNIX to share data. Is the accounting report on a Sequent? Go get it. Is the manufacturing bill of materials on an HP? Go get it. Is the shop floor work schedule on a DEC? Go get it.

If information is a river, NetWare will be on one bank and UNIX will be on the other. Unfortunately, the side you're on is never the right side for the job at hand. There must be an easy bridge across the data river. In many situations, that bridge is a NetWare for UNIX system.

People also buy NetWare for UNIX to share printers. As noted in the previous chapter, sharing printers is still a big deal for many companies. And there are other resources, ranging from tape systems to routers and bridges, that companies need to share.

How NetWare for UNIX Works

The goal of NetWare for UNIX is simple to state but difficult to achieve: make NCP and other NetWare file and print services run under other operating systems. Native NetWare, running on Intel processors in a PC platform, consists of two pieces: the Runtime operating system and the NetWare services. Here is the division of functions between Native NetWare and NetWare for UNIX:

NATIVE NETWARE	NETWARE FOR UNIX
File and print services	File and print services
Runtime operating system	UNIX operating system
Hardware (PC)	Hardware (UNIX minicomputer or PC)

As you can see, NetWare for UNIX layers the file and print services on top of a different operating system. In this case, it's UNIX. Rumors of a working but unmarketed NetWare for OS/2 have been around for two years. In fact, the name of Portable NetWare was changed to NetWare for UNIX just about the time OS/2 was announced. It's easy to believe that the NetWare Runtime operating system is a better server platform than OS/2, since Novell began working on it 8 years before OS/2 was released.

Following the spirit of "openness," NetWare for UNIX runs on (at last count) over 25 different UNIX systems. Every major UNIX vendor either has a product or has announced one.

FOCUS ON THE CLIENT

Care was taken in design so that a NetWare for UNIX server looks exactly like any other file server to a NetWare client. Nothing seen by a user will indicate whether a server is Native NetWare or NetWare for UNIX. Because of this, NetWare for UNIX servers can be dropped into an existing NetWare environment without client disruption. Which server shown in the SLIST program screen in Figure 4.1 is the NetWare for UNIX server?

▶ · ◀

F I G U R E 4.1

Which is the NetWare
for UNIX server?

```
F:\LOGIN >slist
Known NetWare File Servers                 Network   Node Address
--------------------------                 -------   ------------
ACS4500                                    [    99] [          1] Default
GCS                                        [   100] [          1]

Total of 2 file servers found

F:\LOGIN >
```

This design limits changes to as few computer systems as possible. The early versions of LAN Manager for UNIX (LM/X), as an example, required a different protocol for PC-client-to-UNIX-server communications. Instead of the normal NetBEUI and SMB communications, the LM/X clients added TCP/IP for their host communications.

Using the LM/X idea, a PC client can make connections not only to the LM/X server, but to any TCP/IP host on the network. If the network is weighted toward UNIX hosts, that makes sense. However, the penalty is the work necessary to update each and every client with the new protocol. That work includes assigning and managing IP addresses for every client.

Novell's attitude is 180 degrees different. By leaving the client exactly the same, each client using NetWare can immediately start using the new UNIX-based server. You don't need to assign or manage any IP addresses. If something of interest is placed on the new UNIX-based NetWare system, just have a client attach the server as it would any other NetWare server.

For those sites with multiple UNIX or TCP/IP hosts, NetWare for UNIX provides a way to allow every client to access any host. The NVT program lets a client communicate with a UNIX server. From there, it can reach any other system, as explained later in this chapter.

PACKET TYPE SUPPORT

NetWare uses what is commonly referred to as "raw" Ethernet packets, or 802.3 packets. This is a reflection of Novell's adaptation of Xerox's older XNS protocol in the early 1980's. The company decided on using these packets just a year or two before the UNIX world moved to Ethernet_II packets.

These packet types are very similar, and they can coexist on the same physical network without problems. However, there is a 2 byte difference in the packet types, and this can cause all sorts of headaches when not handled properly.

Again, the decision was made to change the one rather than the many. Novell changed the host to accept 802.3 packets rather than reconfiguring all the clients to use Ethernet_II packets. All NetWare for UNIX programs support both types of packets, but the default is 802.3 in deference to the huge IPX/SPX installed user base.

THE UNIX *SCONSOLE* UTILITY

From the UNIX host, all NetWare parameters can be controlled through the *sconsole* utility. This is the official link between the host UNIX system and the NetWare for UNIX file server.

All parameters changed in *sconsole* are stored in the *NWConfig* and *NPSConfig* files in the */etc/netware* directory. Only the owner of the NetWare system (*nwadmin*, by default) or *root* can run *sconsole*.

Everything happens in *sconsole*: NetWare for UNIX is started and stopped, error logs are read and reset, printers are set up, and users are configured.

The *sconsole* utility is one of the few areas NetWare for UNIX vendors have a place for specialization. Some are more elaborate than others, with lots of menus and submenus for various functions.

PRINTING WITH NETWARE FOR UNIX

Much of NetWare's printing is similar to that of UNIX: there are printers, there are queues, and both can be pointed in a variety of directions. Both can have default printers that prioritize and print everything not specifically routed elsewhere. Both support printers attached to the host server and printers connected to the individual client. Remember CAPTURE for one and *lp* for the other, and go for it.

Well, it might not be quite that easy. With UNIX, it's more difficult to make a particular printer work because of the baggage of tradition; hundreds of arcane printers and terminal types can still be used, and that morass must be conquered. NetWare has more up-to-date drivers, since the choice is restricted to PC-supported printers and not ancient teletype devices. However, many feel that defining the printers for NetWare is more complicated and confusing than defining them for most UNIX systems.

NetWare for UNIX systems handle printing fairly logically. The NetWare printing utilities, such as PRINTCON, PCONSOLE, and PRINTDEF, are all there. However, they map to remote printers, even when the printers are physically attached to the host system. Sound strange? It's not, because the printers *are* remote to NetWare.

In a two-step process, NetWare print queues are aimed at UNIX spoolers. Those spoolers are configured to take input from remote systems. Once both sides are adjusted, all NetWare print jobs route to a UNIX spooler and appear on a UNIX system printer.

Using the RPRINTER (Remote PRINTER) Novell utility, a PC can make a lo-cally attached printer available to everyone on the network. The printer must be defined on the server, and the RPRINTER TSR (terminate-and-stay-resident) program must be run on that PC, just as with Native NetWare.

This is similar to using a printer attached to a UNIX system terminal in pass-through or system printer mode. With a bit of work, any printer can become available to any user from any of the connected systems. Nothing stops a remote NetWare server from using the NetWare for UNIX print queues, or a UNIX spooler from aiming at a remote NetWare printer. In fact, it's possible to route and reroute printers back and forth so much that everyone involved will become helplessly confused.

FILE SHARING WITH NETWARE FOR UNIX

The biggest advantage of using a NetWare for UNIX system is the integration capabilities. The early claims of superior performance have now been run through the truth filter; the proper claims are for NetWare and UNIX integration.

The easiest way to share files is to allow both the NetWare for UNIX users and the traditional UNIX clients to access the same files. Since NetWare files are stored as UNIX files on the host system, this is easy to accommodate. Figure 4.2 diagrams a typical NetWare for UNIX file structure. All of these files are available to the UNIX user, as long as proper access rights are granted.

This type of file sharing is great for applications that use the same file format under both UNIX and DOS. An example of a program using this method is WordPerfect's word processor. Every WordPerfect program on every platform can read any WordPerfect file from any other platform. A WordPerfect DOS file can be used by any WordPerfect UNIX version and vice versa. The appropriate WordPerfect license is needed for each platform, of course.

Text files are a bit more trouble. DOS and UNIX store these files in different formats. DOS uses a carriage return/line feed sequence at the end of a line, where UNIX uses only the line feed. DOS text editors have a hard time formatting UNIX files that haven't been run through a conversion program. For conversions, use the DOS2UNIX.EXE and UNIX2DOS.EXE files (or U2D.EXE, or something along these lines).

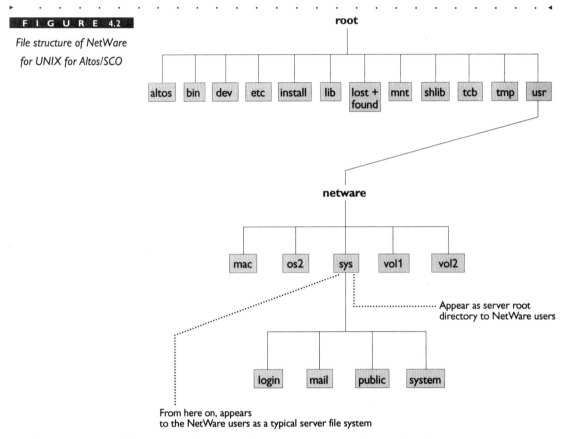

FIGURE 4.2

*File structure of NetWare
for UNIX for Altos/SCO*

The other main difference is that DOS file names are limited to eight characters plus a three-character extension. NetWare for UNIX versions and file-transfer software will change UNIX file names that don't fit into the DOS convention. Some products truncate the name, and some add an incremental counter number to differentiate file names that are the same within the DOS parameters (*income.dec92* and *income.dec93* may become INCOME.DE0 and INCOME.DE1).

NVT FOR NETWARE CLIENTS

Each NetWare for UNIX version comes with a program named NVT.EXE. It will most likely be in the */usr/netware/sys/public* directory. It usually gets loaded when the NetWare for UNIX software is loaded.

The purpose of NVT.EXE is to allow terminal-emulation programs to connect to the UNIX host over IPX/SPX rather than needing TCP/IP. Novell's IPX/SPX protocols are loaded on the UNIX host as part of the NetWare for UNIX software, so NetWare clients can communicate with this server in the same way that they communicate with every other NetWare server.

Some customers buy the software and hardware necessary for NetWare for UNIX for this function alone. Look for more companies to start selling just the means to connect IPX/SPX PCs to UNIX systems, without all the rest of NetWare for UNIX. To a manager in a company full of NetWare clients starting to get into the UNIX integration business, NVT.EXE is nirvana.

The advantage of putting TCP/IP on a PC is that a PC so equipped can connect to any UNIX host in the network. Most terminal-emulation packages available today can use INT14 in the PC to route across the network rather than through the serial port. TCP/IP is the typical network transport for these terminal emulators, but they don't care; they just need to find INT14. Once the client PC loads NVT.EXE (IPX/SPX must already be loaded), the terminal emulator will be satisfied.

Big deal, you say, all we've done is connect the NetWare PC client to a single UNIX host, the one running NetWare for UNIX. How does that get that same PC connected to anything else on the network? Well, simple: *telnet* and *rlogin*. Remember them? Sure, they are for terminal users to connect and log in to remote systems. But isn't that what our NetWare PC client is now, a terminal? Using some standard emulation, such as vt220, the client looks to the first UNIX host, the one with IPX/SPX, like any other vt220 terminal. From the UNIX host, the client can open a remote session in exactly the same manner as any other terminal.

Visualize a fence in the UNIX host running NetWare for UNIX. On one side of the fence is UNIX, and on the other is NetWare. Once a NetWare client jumps that fence, it's a UNIX client. Once that fence is hopped, the rest of the TCP/IP network is available. Subject to proper security and access rights, of course. Figure 4.3 illustrates this concept.

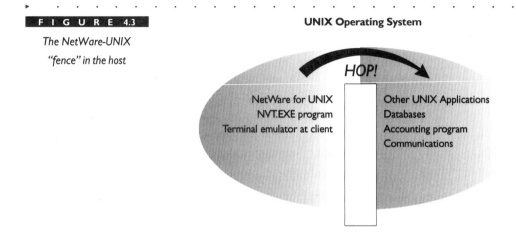

F I G U R E 4.3

The NetWare-UNIX

"fence" in the host

USERS AND HYBRID USERS

Once the NetWare clients have jumped that fence, they may want to run typical UNIX applications on the host. Once the applications are started, those clients may want to access files previously created in the NetWare server portion of the disk. If those clients are set up as hybrid users, they will be able to open NetWare files from UNIX applications.

To make a hybrid user, the UNIX administrator must create a user on the UNIX side of the host, then run the *hybrid* utility. This will link the NetWare and UNIX user identifications. The format is

    hybrid -b NW*username* HOST*username*

The -b is for bind (use -u to unbind, or delete, an existing hybrid user). The NetWare *username* and HOST *username* do not need to be the same.

When NetWare for UNIX is installed, two UNIX users are created behind the scenes. Normally named *nwuser* and *nwgroup* (or *pnw* or *nwadmin* or the like), these two are the owners of all the NetWare files created during installation. These users are also the owners of all files created by any NetWare client, if that client is not a hybrid user.

NETWARE RIGHTS AND UNIX PERMISSIONS

The NetWare file system is a guest of the UNIX host file system. Each NetWare file right must be mapped to a UNIX file permission. This part of NetWare for UNIX will vary according to the UNIX vendor, but the basic outline is the same for all systems.

UNIX controls access on the basis of the permissions (*rights*, to NetWare people) of the file itself. NetWare controls access on the basis of the security rights of the user. Even more fun, NetWare has more rights than UNIX has permissions. Here is a general idea of how the NetWare rights and UNIX permissions correspond:

NETWARE RIGHT	MAPPED UNIX PERMISSION
Read	Read
Write	Write
Erase	Write
Create	Write
File Scan	Read
Modify	Write
Access Control	n/a
Supervisory	n/a
n/a	Execute

UNIX file permissions are always listed at the beginning of *ls -al* output. When you see *drwxr-x---* or *drwxrwxrwx*, the meaning of each letter in the group of ten letters is as follows:

CHARACTER NUMBER	MEANING
1	Type of file; the most common are - (regular file) and *d* (directory)

CHARACTER NUMBER	MEANING
2–4	Permissions for the file's owner
5–7	Permissions for the file's group
8–10	Permissions for all users (not the file's owner or a member of the file's group)

The default permissions of *nwuser* for files are -rw-rw---. The default permissions for directories are -rwxrwxr-x. These permissions are set in the */etc/netware/NWConfig* file through the *sconsole* utility.

If the NetWare and UNIX user rights conflict, the UNIX host rights prevail. Most administrative problems with hybrid users are due to inconsistent rights and access control setup on the UNIX side. Check your UNIX groups carefully, and grant most of the rights for the group rather than for individual hybrid users.

MANAGEMENT

You use the *sconsole* utility to manage all the NetWare for UNIX parameters and services controlled by the host UNIX system. The standard NetWare utilities, particularly SYSCON, are included as part of the NetWare for UNIX system.

Currently, there is no single point for managing both UNIX and NetWare-only clients. This would require an effort above and beyond that expected for porting NetWare to a UNIX platform. Also, a common user-management utility would go against the philosophy of NetWare for UNIX. A NetWare administrator should feel that the NetWare for UNIX installation is exactly the same as a Native NetWare installation.

The supervisor (*root*) for NetWare can control all the NetWare users on the UNIX host system without having any privileges whatsoever on the UNIX host itself. In fact, the NetWare supervisor doesn't need to be a hybrid user in order to perform all of his or her administrative duties.

Remember that the *sconsole* program can be executed only by the UNIX *superuser* or defined *nwadmin* user. Remember also that NetWare-only clients will have no reason to use or be directly affected by any of the *sconsole* utilities.

## CHAPTER 5

NetWare-Based
Terminal Emulation

On the face of things, turning an intelligent PC with a powerful processor into a "dumb" terminal is, well, dumb. If this is your attitude as a PC person, reorient your thinking just a bit. Convince yourself that terminal emulation from a PC is an easy way to limit the number of variables for the host system.

Why use terminal emulation when client-server computing is the hot trend? Why use the intelligent PC strictly as a keyboard and monitor for the UNIX system? To get work done today. Billions and billions of lines of code must be changed or created before the world is client-server, and your boss probably won't wait.

The Terminal Emulation Option

As the LAN has taken hold in corporate America, it makes sense to have all data communications go across those networks. In the past, companies had network coax snaking under desks right beside serial cables. Today, the balance is strongly tipped toward using the network for terminal emulation because this approach provides increased performance and manageability.

The terminal emulation option is used to allow PC users to run applications, usually character-based, on the host UNIX system from their PCs. Anything a basic serial terminal can do, a PC using terminal emulation can do just as well. The terminal emulation program is "fooled" into running across the network instead of running out the serial port. This is done by redirecting the program output through INT14 (generally) and out to the network. Figure 5.1 illustrates the typical terminal emulation software route through a serial port and the route through the network.

On the host side, the system must be configured to accept *pseudo* terminals. These are terminal IDs coming from the network interface rather than the serial ports. Most host systems today come configured for pseudo terminals if there is a network interface card installed.

Yes, 9600 bps serial terminal emulation is fine today, but that's just for older character-based systems. Imagine the pain of waiting for X Windows or any other GUI at those speeds. This is an excellent reason to upgrade your terminal emulation to a network-based system. The products of tomorrow require enormous

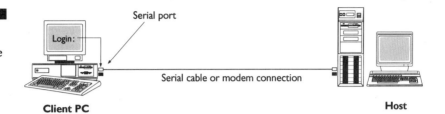

F I G U R E 5.1

Terminal emulation
software route through the
serial port versus through
the network

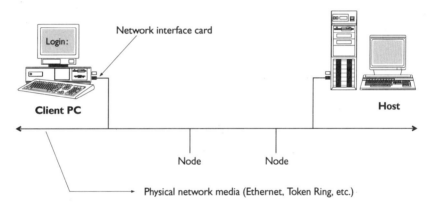

bandwidth, and network terminal emulation is the first of many steps in providing that bandwidth.

Today, every PC terminal emulation program worth the diskettes it's shipped on runs concurrently with NetWare. All use TCP/IP as the UNIX transport layer, as you would expect, but they will run in the PC at the same time as the NetWare shell.

This wasn't true in 1988, unless you spent big dollars on network interface cards for your PCs that had a coprocessor to support TCP/IP. The development of NDIS by Microsoft and 3Com and the ODI specifications from Novell made the coprocessor cards obsolete. Now these intermediate software layers are able to juggle up to four protocols concurrently, and life is much simpler for the PC user on this front.

Dozens of terminal emulation programs exist for individual PCs, but this book focuses on those that are available as a *network* service. There's nothing wrong with these stand-alone packages for PC to UNIX connections, but we're looking at NetWare to UNIX connections. Several network products are introduced in this chapter. Instructions for installing these packages, as well as the other products covered in this book, are included in Appendix D.

Telnet: Basic Terminal Emulation

Telnet is the standard Internet application protocol for remote login. Telnet is the foundation of all terminal emulation, and it was developed along with the Internet. Complete details are available in RFC 854, but dozens of other RFCs detail the development and options of Telnet.

Telnet is the lowest common denominator for remote UNIX connection. Since the UNIX host must interpret and echo each and every keystroke from every terminal, there is a limit to the number of terminals supported. Every terminal emulation package you examine will have more flexibility, flash, and features than Telnet.

The most common terminal emulations built on top of Telnet are vt52, vt100, and vt220. The *vt* stands for video terminal, acknowledging the great technical strides made by DEC to upgrade the vacuum-tube teletype terminals to transistor technology. As in everything else in the funny world of computers, this feeble old stuff was state-of-the-art at one time.

The basic list of terminals emulated vary from package to package, but at least one or two of the above three are always available. vt220 is the default terminal for many of the more expensive packages, but vt100 or even vt52 will usually be available. Occasionally, Wyse50 or Wyse60 emulations are included in deference to the many PC-type terminal keyboards sold over the years.

Some of the aggravations for PC users using vt terminal emulations will be the lack of "extra" keys available. You can compare the standard vt220 keyboard shown in Figure 5.2 with the standard PC keyboard shown in that figure. Not only are all the function keys useless, but often the Backspace, Delete, Page Up, Page Down, Home, and End keys are worthless as well. The lowest common denominator is rarely much fun, but remember these terminals were around long before the PC.

FIGURE 5.2

*The standard vt220
keyboard versus the
standard PC keyboard.
(vt220 keyboard courtesy
of Walker Richer & Quinn,
Inc.; PC keyboard courtesy
of Key Tronic Corp.)*

When you as a PC user start complaining about the cryptic and confusing commands in the text editor vi, remember the keyboard problem. vi is a complete text editor without the benefit of any special keys; everything must be done with the Control key and alphabetic characters. It might help control your aggravation during the learning phase.

LAN WorkGroup from Novell

In early 1986, Excelan released the first version of LAN WorkPlace for DOS. Not only was it one of the early PC-based TCP/IP packages, it was just about the only one that could coexist with NetWare on the same client.

The version of the program that goes on the file server is now called LAN WorkGroup, although little else has changed in the program. In the world of functional but not overly fancy emulators, LAN WorkGroup holds a good reputation. The performance of the emulation is quick and predictable, and multiple keyboard remapping options are available. The program also includes file transfer and printer redirection options.

THE DEVELOPMENT OF LAN WORKGROUP

LAN WorkPlace began life as TCP/IP for PCs. This allowed PCs to emulate UNIX terminals and become integrated, however minimally, into the world of UNIX networking. Later, a Macintosh version came out, but the thrust has always been on the PC.

Using its own proprietary Ethernet board with a coprocessor, Excelan executed the code for most of LAN WorkPlace's TCP/IP support on the board itself. Along with raising the cost of the TCP/IP support by using an intelligent network interface, this approach performed two important functions: it was the only way at the time to support two protocols at once on a PC, allowing IPX/SPX to accommodate TCP/IP, and it worked without much RAM on the host PC. Remember, this was before memory management techniques allowed pushing programs above 640K.

When Novell purchased Excelan in early 1989, the hardware lines were gradually sold off. The software group, however, became the raging fire within Novell and pushed The Big Red Horde into UNIX.

One strong product Novell inherited was the LANalyzer. Originally a hardware/software combination, Novell has pushed the software development to support high-powered DOS machines. A Microsoft Windows version has been customized for NetWare monitoring.

Multiple PC Protocols: ODI and NDIS

Separating the TCP/IP software from the intelligent Ethernet board became possible with the development of ODI. This software interface enables a single network interface board inside a PC to support up to four protocols concurrently. Figure 5.3 illustrates the architecture of ODI.

Novell actually proposed ODI before Microsoft and 3Com published details about NDIS. The announcement timing was probably too close to accuse one company of stealing the idea of another, although some have tried pointing

FIGURE 5.3

Novell's ODI architecture

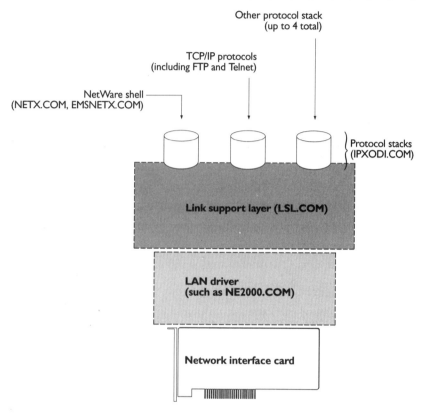

fingers. Most likely, this was an idea "whose time has come," and the technology was in place to support multiple protocols within DOS.

Unfortunately for Novell, NDIS code and developer's kits were released long before those for ODI. This meant Novell watched as NDIS products were released more than a year sooner than ODI products. Sometimes PR outruns a product, and that seemed to be the case here.

Although NDIS started with a big lead, two things worked against it. First of all, 3Com quit the LAN operating system business after only a couple years of selling 3+Open, which was really LAN Manager from Microsoft in a 3Com box. 3Com had been locked in a grudge match with Novell for almost 10 years, and finally with 3+Open, it had an operating system that was nearly comparable to NetWare. The work 3Com did with HP in developing TCP/IP support using NDIS made 3+Open stand above generic LAN Manager. Its Demand Protocol Architecture (DPA) TCP/IP client for PCs was an excellent product, and it made dual PC LAN and TCP/IP concurrent connections a reality a full year before Novell's product. Had 3Com kept on course, Novell may never have gotten such a grip on the PC LAN to UNIX marketplace.

The other strike against NDIS has been the continued weakness of LAN Manager as a competitor to NetWare. When 3Com folded 3+Open, Microsoft took more than a year to get a grip on the DPA products. By that time, Novell had ODI rolling and LAN WorkPlace rolling along with it. Before Microsoft reorganized its LAN Manager sales efforts, the NT noise was beginning. The desire on Microsoft's part to make NT a server, especially for Windows PCs, emasculated LAN Manager even more. This is just another example in computer industry history of good products being killed by poor marketing and management.

LAN WorkPlace Becomes LAN WorkGroup

Since LAN WorkPlace started at Excelan before that company was absorbed by Novell, there was no "NetWare-ness" in the product. As Excelan and Novell started moving toward the merger, LAN WorkPlace became as NetWare-friendly as any of the other PC TCP/IP packages.

When ODI became a reality, LAN WorkPlace was a Novell product, and it became one of the prime proponents of the ODI technology. This made it easier for the product to work in a NetWare environment, but not any worthier of inclusion here as a "network" product than the other two dozen PC-to-TCP/IP offerings.

When Novell hit on the idea of making the NetWare file server a BOOTP server, LAN WorkGroup became more of a network resource and less of a PC-only resource. BOOTP (BOOT Protocol) is the UNIX protocol that dictates how a diskless UNIX workstation can get system and network information from a BOOTP server.

LAN WorkGroup doesn't supply the operating system information as does a UNIX BOOTP server, because diskless PCs have had the ability to boot from the NetWare server, and get all the same DOS startup information from the server as they normally do from their local boot disk, for many years. If a diskless PC boots from the server and needs TCP/IP information, LAN WorkGroup will pick up where the DOS side of the boot process leaves off.

LAN WORKGROUP TERMINAL EMULATION UNDER DOS

The primary program LAN WorkGroup uses for terminal emulation access to a UNIX host is TNVT220.EXE, in the \NET\BIN subdirectory on your server. Since the installation routine added \NET\BIN to your search paths, the program may be launched from anywhere. As is common in programs such as this, typing **TNVT220** *hostname* will connect to the host and present a host login prompt.

The terminal emulation is clean but not fancy. That's the trend in terminal emulation products that come along with their transport layer. For some reason, the world of client TCP/IP for PCs has created a line between those that provide transport and those that provide feature-rich emulations. Only since late 1992 has a provider of fancy emulation packages (Walker Richer & Quinn) started offering the transport for those emulations.

OTHER LAN WORKGROUP DOS PROGRAMS

The UNIX command *ping*, ported to DOS for every TCP/IP package for use in network setup and testing, performs a simple but vital function. According to SunOS 4.1.3, *ping's* function is to send ICMP ECHO_REQUEST packets to network hosts.

The packet goes to the named host and forces that host to reply. Again in UNIX tradition, if the host is active, a response is printed to the standard output device (the monitor). If the host is not active, or there is something blocking traffic to that host, no response is given. Once the *ping* request times out, usually 20 seconds, the prompt returns, and that is the only failure indication. No news is bad news, another UNIX tradition, except where no news is good news.

To test the network connection, use PING.EXE. The format is PING *hostaddress*, as in

    PING 192.9.200.1

If the command works, your network connection is viable. If it doesn't, the troubleshooting begins. Start by making sure the network is up and the host being pinged is up as well. No sense getting all worried until you need to. Always postpone panic until the cables are connected and the power is turned on.

Multiple utilities deal with printing (which we deal with later), file transfer (ditto), and allowing remote users to take over the PC running LAN WorkGroup (XPC.EXE). One other utility of interest is TelAPI (Telnet Application Program Interface), which provides support for third-party terminal emulators to ride the network transport provided by LAN WorkGroup. For systems using the emulations included with LAN WorkGroup, it's hard to imagine needing more features. There are many systems that speak TCP/IP but not vt220, and those can be accommodated easily.

RUNNING LAN WORKGROUP UNDER WINDOWS

If there weren't any error messages concerning Windows during installation, the next time Windows starts, the LANWG Group should appear. Eight Windows-specific programs are arranged at the top of the group window (the ninth, Script Director, is located inside the TNVT220 program), and all the DOS programs have an icon as well. Many are surprised at the size of the group window the first time it opens. Feel free to prune this group for your own purposes. It's not unusual for a system administrator to limit the utility list for the users.

The Windows program integration is good. The primary Windows programs, Host Presenter and Rapid Filer, are excellent examples of Windows programming (well, Rapid Filer a little more than Host Presenter). Since Rapid Filer is a file-transfer program for multiple hosts, we will examine it later.

Host Presenter

To make life easier for the casual UNIX user, Novell has provided a program that stores profiles of UNIX host names and addresses and the terminal emulation parameters for that host. The user can recall the profiles from Host Presenter. Figure 5.4 shows the dialog box for opening a session with a host. The user can attach a UNIX host simply by pointing and clicking; IP addresses or host names aren't required.

FIGURE 5.4

The Host Presenter Open

Session dialog box

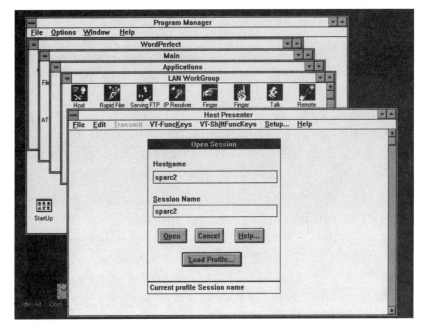

The advantage is clear for the administrators supporting a large group of UNIX neophytes. You can load the profiles so each user sees the same description, then let the user click on Accounting Programs rather than on TNVT220 192.9.200.8. Host Presenter lets users perform the following tasks:

▸ Open multiple sessions with one or more hosts.

▸ Copy text between session windows.

▸ Capture data from a session in a file.

▸ Print text that is displayed on the screen.

▸ Change the displayed fonts, text colors, and display characteristics.

▸ Restore the default profile settings.

▸ Create a profile.

> ▸ Select a transport service.

> ▸ Use national terminal types.

Using some standard NetWare commands, you can make the profiles read-only, so users can't overlay a carefully crafted session profile with lurid text colors and strange fonts. The extra step required to be able to write to these profiles again before making any changes is worth the effort.

A series of script commands is available to handle any other connection details. Using Script Director, the Host Presenter scripting utility, the user can run script files and attach and detach scripts from keys with simple mouse clicks.

TNVT220 Differences under Windows

The performance of TNVT220 under Windows is slower than under DOS, but don't get mad at Novell for that. Every emulation product on the market is slower under Windows than under DOS. The overhead of Windows in reformatting and writing text characters to the screen takes a huge toll when the entire job of the program is to write text characters to the screen. You can see noticeable performance differences with some products when you change the font used inside the emulation window, which indicates some fonts are easier for Windows to handle than others. If users will use LAN WorkGroup simply to replace ASCII terminals with PCs, don't give them Windows machines. Drag the old XTs and ATs out of the closet; they'll do a better job for a lot less money.

This is not to say that TNVT220 under Windows doesn't work. The performance is as good as any other Windows emulator, and better than some. For the casual and moderate user, the performance will be perfectly acceptable. Head-down UNIX programmers are probably not going to use Windows, so they won't be complaining about performance.

The ability of Host Presenter to make connections quick and simple even for the most UNIX-phobic user may well be worth the extra administration and expense of Windows. Computers aren't much good if people don't use them, and Windows often has a soothing effect on the scared computer user. Besides, if users have trouble dealing with DOS and prefer Windows, they will certainly need the help of Host Presenter rather than raw Telnet.

Although TNVT220 is only a DOS program running under Windows, its window, shown in Figure 5.5, is configured correctly during installation and is scalable. This allows the emulation window to stay on the screen along with other application windows. Font choices can allow the window to shrink even more. While this may cause eyestrain, it's also a handy way to move the emulation window out of the way while a job is being processed on the host and the user wants to focus on other applications. If you minimize a window, there is no way to know when the host job has finished.

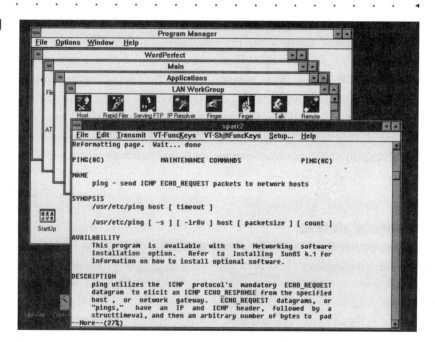

FIGURE 5.5

*TNVT220 under Windows
to a Sun SparcSTATION 2*

Other Windows Utilities

Other Windows utilities in LAN WorkGroup include Serving FTP, which allows multiple FTP clients to log in to the PC running LAN WorkGroup and access files and directories. Four other network information utilities are also full

Windows programs: IP Resolver, Finger, Finger Daemon, and Talk. These identify hosts from an IP address or the reverse, provide details about a particular host user, handle Finger requests from other hosts, and allow interactive communication with users on remote hosts.

Third-Party TCP/IP Gateways

The computer business being what it is, every vacuum, real or imagined, is filled quickly. Several vendors are taking advantage of NetWare users' natural distrust of TCP/IP stacks on the client by selling TCP/IP gateways.

The function of the gateway is to translate the IPX/SPX packets coming from the NetWare client into TCP/IP packets the UNIX host can understand, as illustrated in Figure 5.6. This means that no extra protocols need to be added to the NetWare client. Unlike with LAN WorkGroup from Novell, there is no need to configure the TCP/IP details for each PC, since they don't execute at the PC. Because of this, the configuration of the individual PC doesn't matter, only the configuration of the program executing at the gateway.

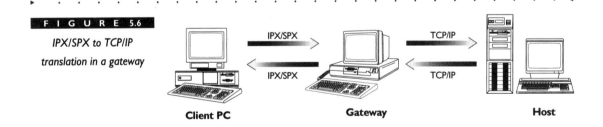

FIGURE 5.6

IPX/SPX to TCP/IP translation in a gateway

Client PC   Gateway   Host

Novix for NetWare from Firefox

The first NetWare server-based terminal emulation package, Novix for NetWare from Firefox Communications, works cleanly and quickly. The subtitle is "The Integrated TCP/IP Communications Solution" and the product can make that claim honestly.

Headquartered in England, Firefox developed its product in response to customer needs for better emulation services to UNIX systems, covering both the TCP/IP and OSI protocols. The founders have many years of engineering experience for various companies in the UK and bring a strong engineering focus to the product. Their considerable expertise in OSI has helped them develop a strong working relationship with Novell. The product shows evidence of this close partnership.

Examples of the company's European heritage include support for BICC Ethernet interface cards (big in Europe) and ICL's OfficeServer terminal emulation software. In addition, the early version's default language module comes up in UK English, decidedly different from English as used in the States. To see the # prompt for the *superuser* come up as a £, the English pound sign, is very continental but a bit confusing.

Firefox is one of the companies that still supports the older NetWare versions, and Novix is available with either NLMs for NetWare 386 or VAPs for NetWare 286. firefox has been a member of Novell's Professional Developer program, and has signed on as an OEM partner as well, integrating the LAN WorkPlace programs into Novix.

The use of NLMs allows the program to run on regular NetWare or any NetWare Runtime version. Placing the software in a NetWare router or bridge allows great flexibility in network design. This arrangement also makes it easy to support users from multiple file servers and multiple types of network interface cards with minimal fuss.

The IPX/SPX to TCP/IP translation happens quickly and with little impact on the NetWare 386 server because of the efficiency of the NLM process. Older systems using VAPs may suffer more performance penalties because of the limitations of VAPs and the fact that many of these older servers have less horsepower.

An advantage of Novix is that it imports its own TCP/IP stack for the file server. In fact, the Novell TCP/IP stack can't be running on the same network interface card with Novix, although it can be resident on another card in the same server. Novell supports only TCP/IP on server versions 386 3.11 and above. Older servers equipped with Novix can become players in the TCP/IP world rather than being put out to pasture.

One detail no longer a concern for the network administrator is individual TCP/IP addresses for each client. The gateway software runs on a NetWare server that has its own TCP/IP address, and that address is used to support multiple active connections to the host. The client suffers no consequences of this action, and it certainly makes for streamlined management. This is one reason that TCP/IP gateways are exciting for those companies running low on IP addresses (or running low on network administrators).

THE NOVIX PROTOCOL

The fact that the TCP/IP protocol does not execute at the client is not a concern to the UNIX host in any way. As long as a legitimate TCP/IP client comes knocking at the door with the proper socket numbers, the host is happy to accept the connection.

To the host, the packets coming from Novix will be no different than those coming from clients running LAN WorkGroup. TCP/IP is the standard protocol suite in the UNIX world, and the ability to make TCP/IP packets is common. All the normal TCP/IP functions are included inside Novix—enough to satisfy any TCP/IP host.

In some ways, Novix configuration is more flexible than LAN WorkGroup configuration. The individual configuration files for Novix allow setting different Telnet port numbers. Some systems don't use the standard port (23) for Telnet. In these cases, the flexibility of Novix will be greatly appreciated.

For those wanting a fancier interface than a basic vt220 emulation, the client portions of LAN WorkPlace (the stand-alone PC client TCP/IP software that forms the basis of LAN WorkGroup) will run on top of the transport provided by Novix. This capability is new with version 2.0, and it turns a solid product into a truly flexible and powerful one.

NOVIX SECURITY

One of the advantages of using a gateway TCP/IP product is the extra security offered. A PC-based TCP/IP package has no security; any host can be attached by Telnet or FTP. The only security involved is that of the UNIX host. Many corporations feel the words *UNIX* and *security* don't belong in the same sentence.

Leaving the entire security system based strictly on the UNIX /etc/passwd file makes corporations uncomfortable. Remember that large corporations often have IBM mainframes, and security there is much tighter than any UNIX administrator ever imagined. They are reluctant to downsize to a less secure platform than their IBM. The extra security in Novix may help calm some nerves.

The Novix gateway is part of the Novell file server, and as such integrates well with the security concepts in place with NetWare. By using NetWare groups as the principal security mechanism, Novix provides a strong level of security without making that security obvious to the users. If a group is not allowed to see certain functions, those functions will not appear on any menus for the group members. The best security is hiding that which should be secure, and Novix does that.

UNIX user security is rarely this tight, for a variety of reasons. Primarily, the whole philosophy of UNIX is a sharing philosophy, and strong security violates that philosophy. Beyond that, the UNIX host will probably be supporting multiple users needing access to the same list of applications. In that case, security features may appear of little benefit. However, in the new role of corporate workhorse, UNIX must learn some new behaviors. Among them is the flexibility to configure as tight a system as the company desires.

There are practical reasons for restricting access to certain hosts. UNIX is often used in a distributed environment, and some of the hosts listed may be remote hosts. Access to these hosts is more expensive than access to local hosts, since the connection incurs remote connection costs from the long-distance carrier. Keeping users from attaching to and trying to log in to the wrong host will also keep the expensive remote links clear of nonessential traffic.

The first piece of security comes when trying to run NVCONFIG, the configuration program for all of Novix. The program can be executed only from within the \TCPGWAY directory by the NetWare SUPERVISOR.

During the initial installation process, the default for user access to Novix is EVERYONE, but that means every NetWare user, not the group EVERYONE. For tighter security, you can limit access to each host to certain groups and withhold access from all other groups. See Appendix D for details on setting up group, user, and exclusionary security for Novix.

NOVIX REMOTE CONSOLE MANAGEMENT

Once the Novix TCP/IP gateway product is running on the NetWare server, some commands and procedures may need to be executed from the server console. Using Novell's RCONSOLE utility is the traditional way of doing this type of configuration, but Novix also offers an NVHCM program to perform the same functions. If the TCP/IP administrator is not the NetWare administrator, using NVHCM allows control over the gateway without allowing access to all the other NetWare server console commands.

Eighteen commands are available, not including the on/off settings for seven of those commands. The most useful in setting up the initial gateway is PING. Other useful commands are READ, which forces the software to read the configuration files without bringing the system down; DNS, which lists the domain name servers defined inside Novix; GATE, which lists the defined gateways; and ARP, which lists the current Address Resolution Protocol table. Through NVHCM, status monitors and logs can be started and stopped. Various trace facilities are also included.

USING NOVIX

Although it appears a ton of things must happen before a connection is made between a NetWare user and a UNIX host, in reality, the connection is quick and seamless. Users configured with session files and login scripts will never know the circuitous route every keystroke must make. Even those users going through the Novix screens will be happy with the ease of connecting.

There is no apparent strain on the file server, and some actions actually seem faster than in LAN WorkGroup. Since LAN WorkGroup makes direct connections between the PC client and the UNIX host, this speaks well of the performance of Novix.

In testing, the flexibility of the vt220 emulation was sufficient to overcome several nagging problems with strange host combinations. By tweaking the emulation to use vt220 7 bit, I achieved proper screen formatting for a Pick application running under AIX on an IBM RS/6000. Once I discovered the combination, saving the configuration file made it easy to recall.

NOVIX SUPPORT FOR LAN WORKPLACE

In a move that benefits both Novell and Firefox, Novix provides strong support for LAN WorkPlace for DOS. In fact, it goes so far as to bundle LAN Work-Place with its own product as an option. Use of LAN WorkPlace provides UNIX sockets (programming interfaces for communications), which support more programs and applications than the INT14 PC BIOS hooks already in Novix.

The socket driver presents an interface in a NetWare PC workstation compatible with the top of the TCP/IP stack in LAN WorkPlace. It includes support for the Berkeley Socket Library (BSD4.3) and the Dynamic Link Library (DLL) for Microsoft Windows programs.

With LAN WorkPlace software, Novix uses the IPX/SPX transport protocol from NetWare between the client and the NetWare server. Between the NetWare server and the UNIX host, TCP/IP is used. Although the LAN WorkPlace applications normally require TCP/IP for the entire trip, they work well with the Novix product.

All the LAN WorkPlace functions will perform exactly as they do in LAN WorkGroup. You must run the Novix TelAPI redirector, which provides commands in the format of LAN WorkPlace for DOS. The socket driver allows any product written to support LAN WorkPlace for DOS to function over Novix.

In this arrangement, Firefox gains access to an entire new world of application programs supporting LAN WorkPlace. Novell gains a platform for LAN Work-Place in areas previously difficult to reach, including non-Ethernet NetWare clients and older PCs without memory management to minimize the TCP/IP stack requirements. In addition, the security aspects of Novix carry forward in support of the LAN WorkPlace product. When running on top of Novix, LAN WorkPlace is a much more secure product than when running alone.

NOVIX SUPPORT FOR OTHER THIRD-PARTY EMULATORS

Not forgetting the rest of the terminal emulator world, Novix also supports INT14, the Hayes INT14 Redirector, and INT5B (used in Europe to support BICC interface cards). The redirectors are initially placed into the \NOVIX\REDIRECT directory on the NetWare host server. When they are installed, only the SUPER-VISOR has access to them—another good security feature.

INT14 is now available in all good terminal emulation programs, allowing the emulator to run over the network rather than through the serial ports. Existing network modem software will generally work over INT14. Many companies can use Novix or a similar product to reroute host connection traffic without changing the client software and confusing the users.

The Hayes INT14 Redirector allows modem software to initiate and control the host connection. Unlike the regular INT14 Redirector, the Hayes INT14 Redirector doesn't require an active host connection before functioning. Modem commands are interpreted as TCP/IP addresses for connection; the modem software happily continues as if an actual modem were attached.

INT5B is designed primarily to support programs written to run on OSI systems. BICC Data Networks made this popular as an API into an OSI transport layer on its multiprotocol Ethernet card. This is rarely used in the U.S. but it's important in areas more advanced in OSI.

The redirectors support single and multiple connection sessions, and they are invoked from the command line. All commands can be listed in batch files. You can connect to the host before or after the emulation software is started, and map multiple sessions to multiple emulators for real confusion. Try to avoid the multiple emulators scenario if possible, but if you must do it, Novix will provide plenty of rope to hang yourself.

RUNNING NOVIX UNDER WINDOWS

Novix runs as a DOS session under Microsoft Windows, but it will function inside a scalable window if it's run in Windows 3.1 Enhanced mode. The Windows features of Novix are limited to this.

Using the LAN WorkPlace optional software, however, starts a new Windows game. The Novell product is one of the better Windows terminal emulators, and all the features in the standard LAN WorkPlace product work over Novix.

Host Presenter gives an excellent front-end for users to pick a host using descriptive English and log in painlessly. Although the Novix programs do a good job of settling down scared users, the Windows-maniacs will feel more comfortable with the addition of LAN WorkPlace.

Catipult from Ipswitch

A company taking a slightly different approach to the IPX/SPX to TCP/IP gateway is Ipswitch, with its Catipult product. Rather than running the software inside the file server, it executes on a separate PC running OS/2 (version 1.3). The gateway concept is still viable, and all the earlier advantages mentioned for the Firefox product apply.

Microsoft Windows support is planned and should help broaden the appeal of the product. Catipult already supports INT14 and INT61 for third-party products.

Mail programs for communicating with standard UNIX mail systems are included, along with various utilities and a game (ah, where would UNIX be without those game players?). The mail and file-transfer options are covered in later chapters.

WHY OS/2?

The reasons for choosing OS/2 as a gateway platform are simple: it's powerful, it's multitasking, it supports multiple protocols, and it's cheap. The cost to the end user for OS/2 is in the $150 range. This is much less expensive than making UNIX the gateway operating system. Beyond that, many companies feel OS/2 is like an extended DOS, while UNIX requires much more care and feeding (not to mention training).

The success or failure of OS/2 as a desktop operating system matters little in this situation. Powerful programming tools are available for OS/2, allowing developers to perform quite amazing feats of software magic. Perhaps if IBM had done a better job of positioning OS/2 with a desktop version and a server version (like UnixWare from Novell and Windows NT from Microsoft), using OS/2 as a gateway between NetWare and UNIX wouldn't seem so strange. But strange as it may seem, it works well.

THE CATIPULT PROTOCOL

The gateway concept of using IPX/SPX to reach the gateway, convert to TCP/IP, then continue on to the host is still valid. One disadvantage of using OS/2 for the gateway platform in Catipult is the requirement for NetBIOS in addition to

IPX/SPX. Novell and IPX/SPX have just about driven a stake through the heart of NetBIOS, but for OS/2-based gateways, NetBIOS is required.

Unlike Novix, Catipult is not tied to any particular NetWare file server. In a large network of several file servers, even mixed with NetWare 2.*x*, 3.*x*, and 4.*x*, the client list of the gateway is separate from that of any one server. As long as the IPX/SPX software on the client can connect to a NetWare server, the client will be supported.

The UNIX host cares nothing about the other side of the gateway. As long as valid TCP/IP packets with valid socket number requests present themselves to the host, all is well. Life would be better with rules such as this.

NetWare TCP/IP Gateway 386 from NCM

The NetWare TCP/IP Gateway 386 product has a long and varied history, going back two or three companies. First seen at InterOp 90 (many products are first seen at InterOp) under the Racal banner, it's now sold by NCM (Network and Communications Management, Inc.).

This isn't the result of some corporate piracy. NCM developed the product for Racal and provided most of the customer support. When Racal reorganized and placed more emphasis in other areas, NCM regained the rights to market the software itself. Now it still markets with Racal and InterLan, but also under its own label.

NetWare TCP/IP Gateway 386 is a separate gateway PC, running OS/2 as the operating system. New is the fact that much of the TCP/IP processing happens on an intelligent Ethernet interface card (a Racal card) provided by NCM.

THE TCP/IP GATEWAY 386 PROTOCOL

The gateway scenario is repeated in this product: IPX/SPX carries NetBIOS to the gateway, using any type of physical network, and TCP/IP goes out to the UNIX host. The UNIX host isn't changed, and the PC client doesn't need to run TCP/IP or have its own IP address.

The network coprocessor (the intelligent Ethernet card) provides several advantages. Since much of the processing happens on the card, the CPU of the PC is less involved. This gives both better performance and the ability to support more users than a purely software solution. Code that deals with the TCP/IP network, a stable and reliable environment that has standards documentation to follow, can be put in the card's memory. Code that deals with the more changeable NetWare and user interface environment can stay on the gateway PC itself for easy updating.

USING TCP/IP GATEWAY 386

A NetWare-style menu system called by TCPWS.EXE controls access to the gateway and other utilities. The inclusion of mail and file-transfer utilities will entice some users to get involved, even if they never see an actual UNIX login prompt.

The Softronics emulator software included as part of the system provides Telnet functions to the host. Telnet can be started through the menu or on the command line. The product also supports INT14, and a third-party terminal emulator can be made the default choice for any user.

IPX/SPX on UNIX Hosts for Terminal Emulation

We've seen that the world of UNIX is the world of TCP/IP. That has been the case since the early 1980's. But easily or not, this is starting to change. As UNIX gets more of a foothold in traditional corporate environments, it finds NetWare waiting. The majority of the millions of corporate PCs connected to anything are connected to NetWare servers.

NetWare managers and users may not understand the IPX/SPX protocol stack, they just know that the NetWare shells, as they call them, take more memory than they want to give up. Even though NetWare takes less memory than the alternatives, any memory loss is too much.

Memory paranoiacs run screaming down the hall at the mention of adding TCP/IP stacks to network clients. That is why the gateways mentioned here have such appeal. Even more appealing, however, is making the UNIX machines talk IPX/SPX. Then the NetWare managers never need to modify a single client workstation or use another bit of memory.

The use of IPX/SPX to the UNIX host requires that host to somehow learn to speak IPX/SPX along with TCP/IP. There is no reason why UNIX hosts can't come out of the box speaking IPX/SPX, except for the tradition of using TCP/IP for all networking. Univel's UnixWare product is the first UNIX to ship configured with IPX/SPX, but Novell owned half of Univel at the time. Others are following; SCO started offering IPX/SPX as an option to complement its LAN Manager client software in late 1992.

By using only IPX/SPX, MCS UniLink Basic and Puzzle System's SoftNet Term provide all the advantages of the gateway products without the extra hardware or software on the server. Placing the IPX/SPX-to-TCP/IP conversion inside the UNIX host eliminates any possible performance drag on the server. It also halves the number of packets on the network per client keystroke. Each keystroke goes directly from the client to the UNIX host and back. With a gateway, a keystroke from the client goes to the gateway, then from the gateway to the UNIX host, then back to the gateway, before going back to the client. On busy networks with lots of terminal traffic, the extra load from gateways will add up.

Look for the UNIX hardware and software manufacturers themselves to offer IPX/SPX either standard or as a low-cost option before 1995. The purchase of USL (Unix System Laboratories) by Novell, making Novell the "owner" of UNIX, will help this transition. In addition, Novell has presented IPX/SPX to the UNIX standards committees as an alternative protocol to TCP/IP. Time will tell if the UNIX community can overcome traditional PC paranoia and act on this proposal in a timely manner. Or if Novell can make a strong case for IPX/SPX offering enough advantages to rank equal to TCP/IP.

UniLink from MCS

Primarily a custom communications programming shop, Micro Computer Systems, Inc. (MCS) also owns the patent on the EISA configuration utility used by most hardware vendors of EISA products. Long involved in strictly OEM business arrangements, MCS managed to produce the first IPX/SPX protocol stack for UNIX computers, named UniLink. This protocol bypasses the need for gateways completely, allowing the terminal emulation software to use IPX/SPX as the network transport between the PC client and the UNIX host.

Although it is now fashionable to use IPX/SPX as the total network transport, it wasn't so obvious when MCS released the product in 1988. It was ahead of even Novell, who first provided this option in the Portable NetWare NVT programs.

The programs of interest from MCS today are UniLink Basic and UniLink NetBIOS. The Basic product uses only IPX/SPX as a transport between client and host. The NetBIOS version uses that network programming interface and works with non-Novell networks.

The PC terminal emulation program is as much a programming demonstration as a product line for MCS. As a result, the PC side is spare, clean, and fast. It's an excellent demonstration while still being an excellent emulator.

USING UNILINK

The MCS product offers good performance for basic emulation without being complex to install and initialize. To make the connection to the host, from the command line, enter **LOGINPC** <*hostname*>. After the host connection is made, keystrokes are echoed back to the client PC immediately. You can press the Alt-F2 key combination to bring up the Already Connected window. From here, you can perform these functions:

- ▸ Switch between connections (up to four at one time may be open).

- ▸ Go to a DOS shell without disconnecting from your host session.

- ▸ Disconnect from a host session.

- ▸ Return to the Connect window, where another host session can be established.

- ▸ Go to a Setup window.

With the ability to support four host sessions at once, this program can be the primary client access tool for a serious UNIX person. The easy file-transfer options will be discussed later, but they are so simple the most UNIX-phobic DOS user can use them.

Terminal types supported include vt100, vt220, and Wyse60. The Wyse emulation is handy for those systems that support a PC-style keyboard, and not enough basic emulators include the Wyse. It's a nice touch from MCS.

INT14 support is coming, although the three basic emulations offered will be enough for many users. MCS is losing its unique window of opportunity for IPX/SPX emulators, and at least one other company already offers much the same program, including the INT14 redirector software.

For programming tools to link NetWare and UNIX transports, however, no one is in the same league with MCS.

RUNNING UNILINK UNDER WINDOWS

LOGINPC runs in a DOS session under Microsoft Windows. Having the IPX/SPX drivers up and running before starting Windows guarantees that LOGINPC will make connection when started in the DOS session.

As a general note, always start the networking protocols before starting Windows.

SoftNet Term from Puzzle Systems

I must admit a certain fondness and admiration for the Puzzle Systems, Inc., NetWare/UNIX product line. The first product I laid eyes on from this company was SoftNet Utilities for Sparc, a clever NetWare server emulator complete on one diskette. More on that later.

Fully integrated into whatever UNIX host windowing environment in use, SoftNet Term runs under SunOS Open Windows, HP Motif/VUE, and Silicon Graphics Motif/WorkSpace. The installation programs use the windowed environments, something many like products have not figured out. Unlike with MCS UniLink, the kernel does not require relinking. The product loads and is ready to support remote clients in less than six (yes, 6) minutes. Any administrator vaguely familiar with either NetWare or UNIX can make it through the installation procedures.

The program doesn't provide the NetWare client software. The IPX/SPX drivers and NetWare shells (NETX.COM, EMSNETX.EXE, or XMSNETX.EXE) must be available from a NetWare installation on the same network. Even the NetWare server clone must have a real NetWare server on the same network.

Presenting a major bargain, SoftNet Term Bronze (providing only INT14 support and a basic vt52 emulator) is now priced at $99 per five concurrent users. This means price is no longer a concern for NetWare to UNIX terminal emulation. Bean counters rejoice; integration no longer automatically means in debt.

The terminal emulator included is vt52, the lowest common denominator of the vt series of common denominators. Yes, the emulator works, and works quickly across the network to the UNIX host. No, you don't want to use a vt52 emulation for anything but the most basic functions.

There are three levels of SoftNet Term products. SoftNet Term Bronze, which has just been covered, is the lowest level of the product. Its function is to provide INT14 support for third-party emulators. SoftNet Term Silver includes Tiny Term emulation software from Century Software. SoftNet Term Gold includes either the full Term emulator from Century Software or Reflection 1 from Walker Richer & Quinn. Term has multiple DEC and ANSI terminal emulations and includes full scripting and file-handling capabilities. Reflection 1 specializes in HP emulations, and it includes as many or more bells and whistles as any other emulator product.

As shown in Figure 5.7, Reflection 2 for Windows from WRQ Inc. (the vt terminal version) works just fine over the INT14 emulation provided by SoftNet Term Bronze.

By using only IPX/SPX in the client station, the memory consumption of the PVT.EXE program is kept under 20K. Even the most frugal of TCP/IP transports takes about double that and requires much more administration.

F I G U R E 5.7

Settings screen for
Reflection 2 for Windows
over INT14

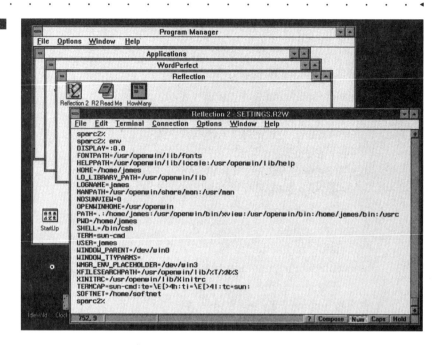

NVT in NetWare for UNIX

As discussed in Chapter 4, included with every NetWare for UNIX package is the NVT.EXE program, which is usually stored in the \PUBLIC subdirectory of the NetWare server section. The VT stands for *virtual terminal*, meaning that the terminal isn't real. This software provides the INT14 redirector for other terminal emulator products.

The NVT packet structure allows a maximum of 512 bytes of data. There are only four types of packets:

NVT PACKET TYPE	PACKET FUNCTION
NVT Client	Data from the NVT clients to the host; the host acknowledges receipt

NVT PACKET TYPE	PACKET FUNCTION
NVT Host	Data from the host to the client; the client acknowledges receipt
NVT Stop	Clients requesting the host to stop sending data
NVT Restart	Clients requesting the host to resume sending data

NVT isn't a complicated protocol, and there's no room for terminal emulation or any other bells and whistles. Some NetWare for UNIX vendors imply there is more terminal emulation provided by NVT than there really is. Third parties must provide those features.

Although you can send data between NVT clients and hosts, there are better ways to transfer files. Since NVT expects to run only on a NetWare for UNIX system, normal NetWare commands for copying files between the server and client are easier and faster than FTP. In the same manner, printer support is not as necessary as it is for some terminal emulators. All the NetWare printer utilities work perfectly well in NetWare for UNIX.

There is no reason to force the use of NVT in communicating with UNIX hosts acting as NetWare for UNIX servers. All the other NetWare client to UNIX products still work to the UNIX host box. Having NVT as part of the NetWare for UNIX package makes this integration much easier.

Several programs implement partial NetWare servers on UNIX hosts—a "stripped down" NetWare for UNIX if you will. SoftNet Term sprang from Puzzle Systems' earlier SoftNet Utilities product, which copied but did not license the functions of NetWare for UNIX.

Two other companies involved in a joint marketing arrangement have special terminal emulators within their server product, but they haven't released them separately as Puzzle Systems has. SPRY Incorporated sells SPRYSOFT NetWare

Client for UNIX, but focuses on the Sun market. Mini-Byte Software sells Net-Con, the basis for the SPRY product, but focuses on the SCO market. However, both of these programs are inexpensive enough to buy just for the terminal emulation feature.

PopTerm/NVT from RDS

One company involved from the beginning in the NetWare for UNIX arena is Rational Data Systems (RDS). Its product is a small but slick terminal emulator that does NVT one better. In fact, the system doesn't even load NetWare's NVT on the client; it provides its own inside the emulator.

RDS has been around since 1978 and has been delivering LAN-based emulations since 1985. RDS is a Novell-Authorized Porting House for NetWare for UNIX, as well as a founding member of the Portable NetWare Partners' Association.

Some of the NetWare for UNIX vendors relabel PopTerm/NVT as their own terminal emulator. Others just put information or a demo copy of the software in the box. One way or another, if terminal emulation to a NetWare for UNIX host is important, PopTerm/NVT will be looming on the horizon.

Over the years, RDS has improved the product to include quite a list of features:

- ► DOS and Windows versions
- ► vt52, vt102, and vt220 emulations
- ► Up to 10 concurrent sessions in a DOS product
- ► Small memory footprint (less than 80K DOS version)
- ► TSR can be loaded into upper memory
- ► No need for NetWare shell, just IPX drivers
- ► Prompts and messages in multiple languages
- ► Network ready (shared program files but individual session files)
- ► Text file logging and transmission

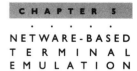

Figure 5.8 shows the PopTerm/NVT Connection Manager screen. Ready for selection is the Altos 4500 system running SCO UNIX and the Altos/SCO Portable NetWare version 3.01. The Control Panel (reached by pressing Alt-P) sets the terminal and session details, such as emulator type, screen size, the shape of the cursor, and the carriage return/line feed setting.

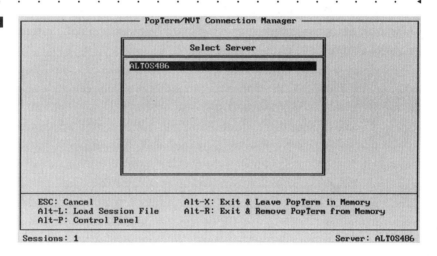

USING POPTERM/NVT

PopTerm/NVT performance is quick, the connections seem solid, the emulations work, and enough sessions can be open at once to confuse anyone. This is a program a full-time UNIX person could live with if forced to use a PC rather than a terminal. This might be a good program to run on some of the older PCs gathering dust in the closet.

It's not necessary to have the full complement of NetWare client programs running. Only the IPX/SPX drivers to connect the network interface card and the PC are needed. This not only lowers the RAM requirements on the client PC, but also avoids using one of the NetWare user sessions on the NetWare server née UNIX host.

The demo copies of PopTerm/NVT are full working copies except for a ten-minute time limit per active session. This is a good security device, because it's long enough to get a feel for the product without being able to get any real work done. RDS can unlock the demo copy with a serial number obtained by phone or fax.

RUNNING POPTERM/NVT UNDER WINDOWS

Taking the same competent, no-nonsense approach to Microsoft Windows as it does toward DOS, the new PopTerm/NVT for Windows version 2.0 installs quicker than any Windows application I've ever seen. It took less than 30 seconds to start the Setup program and connect to the Altos 4500 system running Altos/SCO Portable NetWare over SCO UNIX.

The keystrokes from the DOS version have traveled to the Windows implementation. The Alt-C key combination starts the Connection Manager, Alt-P calls the Settings screen, and Alt-D still disconnects.

Some Windows features include complete control over appearance, color, window size, and fonts. Macros are now included, and running under Windows allows cutting and pasting between the PopTerm screen and any other Windows application. Logging to a disk file or printer is supported as well.

The easy installation and flexible configuration make this product a good choice for regular UNIX access. Once the terminal connection is made to the UNIX host supporting the NetWare for UNIX application, any other UNIX host is reachable through Telnet or *rlogin* (remote login).

CHAPTER 6

Basic File Transfer between NetWare and UNIX

Even with terminal emulation, some files just wind up on the wrong system. They may have been on the right system last month, but someone may want to do something different this month. Chances are that whatever file you need isn't where you want it to be.

The UNIX world solved this problem years ago with FTP, the method used to transfer files to and from other systems. The protocol sits on top of TCP/IP and is one of the true standards; every UNIX system with TCP/IP supports FTP.

Not so important anymore is TFTP, for Trivial FTP. For the network transport, it sits atop UDP and will work on systems without a login defined for you. With TFTP, there is no interactive session with the remote host, and no user security validation. For security reasons alone, many systems no longer support TFTP.

FTP from NetWare Clients to UNIX Hosts

Every general-purpose TCP/IP emulation package for PCs includes FTP. The need for file transfer is universal, and a product would be ashamed to sit on the store shelves without FTP.

FTP is one of the delights in UNIX networking. If TCP/IP is up and working, FTP will work, almost without fail. The only caveat is that the username given when connecting to the remote system must have a password. If the user doesn't have a password and presses ↵ to bypass the password request (which works in NetWare), the connection will be refused by many systems.

FTP mechanisms can't be initiated from the NetWare server itself. The client programs to run FTP can be stored on the NetWare server, and the files being transferred can certainly be going to or from the NetWare server, but the client must execute the actual FTP program at the desktop.

FTP is fairly simple, and a few commands can do most of the work. The following are the most commonly used commands:

FTP COMMAND	SYNTAX	FUNCTION
ftp	ftp *hostname*	Establishes file transfer session to named host
ascii	ascii	Sets the type of file transfer to ASCII (text only)
binary	binary	Sets the type of file transfer for binary files
get	get *filename*	Copies remote file to local system
put	put *filename*	Copies local file to remote system
bye (or quit)	bye	Closes the FTP session

After you issue the *ftp* command, the prompt changes from the normal system prompt ($) to the FTP prompt (ftp>). If you want to see the other commands that are available, type **help** or a ? at the FTP prompt.

File Transfer with LAN WorkGroup

LAN WorkGroup (and the stand-alone program sold as LAN WorkPlace) has excellent file-transfer capabilities. Not only are the DOS utilities strong and complete, but the Windows versions are among the best in the business. Rapid Filer (called File Express in earlier LAN WorkPlace versions) is an outstanding file-transfer program that will have the most UNIX-phobic user blithely flinging files from PC to NetWare server to UNIX host without a second thought.

LAN WORKGROUP DOS PROGRAMS

The programs from LAN WorkGroup are essentially the same as those from LAN WorkPlace, which means that the product doesn't expect to be installed in a network environment. Although the network connection can't be taken for granted, the product runs well over the network.

As an example of the importance of file transfer, the largest chapter in the LAN WorkPlace for DOS *User's Guide* is the file-transfer chapter. The DOS utilities described are FTP, RCP, and TFTP.

Using LAN WorkGroup FTP

Once the TCP/IP program is loaded, you must settle a few details before flinging files about. First, you must either know the Internet IP address of the remote host or have that host listed where it's available to your workstation. That name must be in either the DNS (Domain Name System) name server on your network or the \NET\TCP\HOSTS file on the workstation.

The remote host must know and accept the IP address of your workstation. The login name and password must obviously be correct. Once this connection is made, the normal FTP prompt (ftp>) awaits your bidding.

Along with the basic FTP commands listed previously, LAN WorkGroup includes some handy additions:

LAN WORKGROUP FTP COMMAND	FUNCTION
DIR	Lists detailed contents of the remote directory
LDIR	Lists detailed contents of the local directory
CD	Changes the remote working directory

LAN WORKGROUP FTP COMMAND	FUNCTION
LCD	Changes the local working directory
APPEND	Appends a local file to a remote file
COPY	Copies files between systems; multiple option switches are available
MGET	Copies multiple remote files to a local workstation
MPUT	Copies multiple local files to a remote workstation
HASH	Toggles the printing of a # character for each block transferred
STATUS	Displays the current status of FTP

Options for copying entire directories with the COPY -R (Recursive) switch allow transfer of entire directory trees. Without this switch, only the files inside a directory will be copied, not the structure. This is a bit easier than the MGET and MPUT (Multiple PUT and GET) commands, and it's more familiar to the DOS and NetWare users.

LAN WorkGroup also allows limited script files, using the UNIX tradition of redirection of output and input (with the > and < symbols). The text file containing FTP commands and instructions is fed to the executable program as if the commands were being typed. The format is

FTP [-X] [-P] < script-file

The -X switch tells FTP to exit if any command in the script fails. The -P option lets FTP prompt the user for a password to further automate login procedures. Of course, the security team at your site might not like passwords sitting in ASCII text files, so check before using this option.

Using LAN WorkGroup RCP

RCP (Remote CoPy) is similar to FTP, but the host system must be running the RSH (Remote SHell) server, which is often referred to as RSHD (RSH Daemon). The remote host must have your name listed in the *.rhosts* (Remote HOSTS) file in the home directory of the user account. Your machine and user-name must be listed in the host's *host.equiv* (HOST EQUIValent) file. RCP determines your username from the DOS environment table. This information was set by the SET NAME command in the LANWG.BAT program during installation.

The simple command for sending a file with RCP is

RCP LOCAL_FILE *remote-host=file-destination.*

This command sends the named local file to the host, giving the file the specified name, or with the same name if a new name isn't included. To retrieve files from the host, reverse the order of the local file and remote file in the command:

RCP *remote-host=file-name local-file*

Different options allow the exclusion of file names with the extensions of .OBJ, .O, .LIB, .EXE, and .COM. You can copy directories recursively and access files from other user's accounts (when the proper permissions are set up). For example, to copy Evelyn's remote directory on the UNIX host *finance* to the \REPORTS directory on the local workstation, enter the following command:

RCP -R finance=/x/evelyn/reports/* \REPORTS

This command includes the -R switch for recursive copying. It gives the full path to Evelyn's directory, */x/evelyn/reports*, then specifies the entire contents with the * (UNIX doesn't need the *.* as does DOS).

Recursive copying allows workstations to back up to UNIX hosts and later restore those files. For example, Evelyn might use this command to dump her entire hard disk to the UNIX host:

RCP -R -B C:*.* finance=/x/evelyn/backup

The switches after the program name set recursive copying and treat all files as binary. ASCII files will transfer better as binary than binary files will transfer as ASCII. When in doubt, use binary (with this product, the -B switch).

Using LAN WorkGroup TFTP

TFTP is represented in LAN WorkGroup, although I would counsel against using it. The lack of password security on the connection is a bit too trusting. Another reason to avoid TFTP is that the remote system must already have a file with the same name. Not only that, the file must have universal (other) write permissions.

With all that said, if you still want to send a file named ACCOUNTS.TXT in the MARCH directory of your workstation to a UNIX host named *sales* using TFTP, here goes:

```
TFTP MARCH\ACCOUNTS.TXT sales=/x/march/accounts.txt
```

LAN WORKGROUP FOR WINDOWS PROGRAMS

Even though the label is officially LAN WorkGroup for DOS, the Windows programs are first-rate. If the LAN WorkGroup installation program finds Windows on the local hard disk, it transfers and configures the Windows-specific files.

When you open the LAN WorkGroup Group window, you see what looks like a ton of icons. Although only 24 icons appear, their bright Novell red color stands out. All the DOS utilities have icons in the group.

Using Rapid Filer

A single program that interfaces to several FTP utilities, Rapid Filer allows transferring files of any kind between any two systems that support FTP. It allows the user to copy, transfer, rename, and delete files and directories. You can transfer files in the following ways:

- ▸ Workstation to remote host
- ▸ Remote host to workstation

▸ Workstation file system to file system

▸ Remote host to remote host

For the first time, a UNIX-phobic user may transfer files between a Sun running SunOS and a DEC running VMS, without knowing a single UNIX, FTP, or VMS command. And your hand never needs to leave the mouse, because Novell has implemented drag-and-drop techniques for the procedures.

Figure 6.1 shows a Rapid Filer directory listing. In a liberal use of icons, seven different file types are represented: binary, text, executable, word processing, profile, spreadsheet, and directory. The program recognizes the file types by their extensions and configures the icons inside the LWP_GLBL.INI file in the \NET\HSTACC directory. Instructions for specifying more extensions are in the manual. Currently, you must edit that file manually, but a move is underway to provide a front-end editor. In any case, you won't need to access this file often. Installation does not require editing the file.

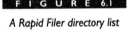

F I G U R E 6.1

A Rapid Filer directory list

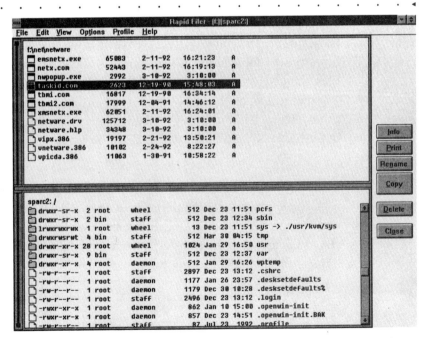

Clicking on the Rapid Filer icon brings up a split screen behind the Open a Remote File System dialog box, as shown in Figure 6.2. You can store profiles that automate entry of the host name, username, password, and initial directory. Rapid Filer provides seven operating system choices: DOS, OS/2, UNIX, NetWare, VMS, VM (Virtual Machine from IBM), and MVS (Multiple Virtual Storage from IBM). An Other option is included for good measure.

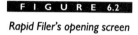

Rapid Filer's opening screen

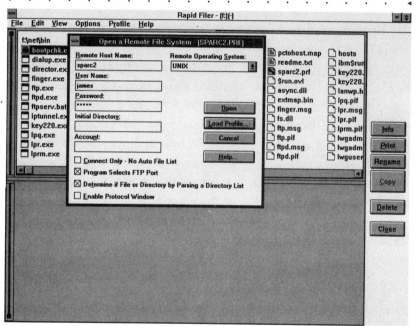

After profiles have been entered and the host connection established, names can be given to hard-code the session details so they're available to all users. It's a good idea to make these profiles Read-Only on the NetWare server. It's easy for users to click the wrong button and save something screwy over a carefully crafted connection configuration.

The Rapid Filer screen is straightforward. The top window in the split screen shows the local system's files. The typical Windows menu bar runs across the top of the screen. Six command buttons run down the right side of the window. These buttons offer quick ways to get file information or print, rename, copy, or delete a file or files. The last command button closes the connection.

All manner of FTP details can be configured within Rapid Filer. The pretty face doesn't mean there's less intelligence involved. The type of file (ASCII or binary) can be set in a window or be decided by the program at the proper time. You can select multiple files by holding down the Ctrl key while clicking the mouse, and then have an operation performed against the lot. File listings can be brief or detailed.

One of the program's handy functions is writing the file names to disk. Pick the files of interest (or select all files), and then choose the Copy File Names to File option on the Edit menu. Fill in the File Name field, then stand back.

Another time-saving tool is the Search for Files dialog box, shown in Figure 6.3, which is accessed through the Search option on the File menu. Rather than trying to remember the UNIX *find* command (as in *find / karl.3 -type f -print*), you can fill in the actual name (with wildcards if preferred) and click. You can specify the starting directory for the search, with the current remote directory shown in the Start Search At text box. This method doesn't have as much flexibility as the actual *find* command, but if all you need is to find a shy file, it works fine. Once the file is found, every instance is listed in the Search Results dialog box. Highlight the file you want and click the Go To button to make that directory the current directory.

Through Rapid Filer, you can create, delete, and rename directories, and even copy entire directory trees between any two systems. You can print text files from within Rapid Filer (as long as Windows printing has been set up). Most of the functions found in DOS file managers can be found here in Rapid Filer.

New UNIX administrators may want to use Rapid Filer for much of their housekeeping. It takes time for people to get comfortable using the UNIX command line, and this program offers one way to avoid that.

FIGURE 6.3

Searching for a file with
Rapid Filer

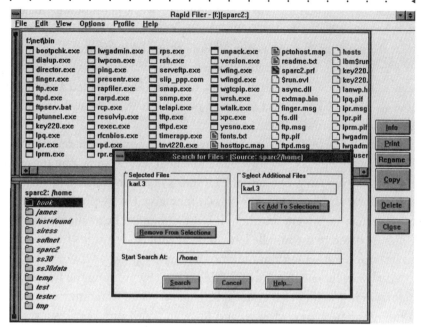

File Transfer with Novix from Firefox

With Novix, you can transfer files in two ways: by using its own FTP client or by using the optional LAN WorkPlace utilities, including Rapid Filer. Although the standard FTP client software is not Windows-based, it's easy to use. The Rapid Filer utility comes in the Novix/LAN WorkPlace for DOS optional package. Novix has modified its program to support the LAN WorkPlace APIs, and this is the first fruit from that labor.

Although FTP is a TCP/IP-based system, remember that Novix uses TCP/IP only between the UNIX host and the NetWare server acting as a gateway. Between the NetWare server and the client, only IPX/SPX is used. Does this cause a problem for FTP? Not at all. Novix has done the work necessary to make the transition between IPX/SPX and TCP/IP transparent to file-transfer operations. To the host, Novix clients are presented as any other FTP clients.

The configurations for group access to the various services offered by Novix continue in the FTP areas. Whether the program is loaded from the command line (NVFTP.EXE) or from the main Novix screen, only authorized users are allowed access to the FTP utilities.

The FTP Client Service screen shows server connection details across the top, including the Firefox gateway in use, the host server name, and the current working remote directory. The actual FTP status messages scroll in a small window on the bottom of the screen. The screen may give UNIX-phobics a bit more information than they want, but help is close at hand. The available function key options are listed in the middle left window, with descriptions that are clear enough to prompt the paranoid into taking the next step.

After you choose the Transfer File option (by pressing the F2 key), the middle right window comes to life. Both the *put* and *get* UNIX commands run from here, although they're labeled Send and Receive. With one keypress, you can choose between ASCII or binary files. The file name field can include wildcard characters, so *.* will send or receive an entire directory.

You can delete files just as easily. Directories can be changed, but there is no automated procedure. Pressing the F4 key brings up a field in which you can type the desired directory name. You can see full UNIX file information or just a basic list of file names.

There is an extra added attraction in the automation of file operations: a learning mode. When you turn on the learning mode before initiating a command line session, Novix will write pertinent information to an ASCII file. That file can then be fed to the command line program for future execution with the command:

NVFTP /i<*filename*>

The command uses the /i (for Input) option. You can use the learning mode and then play back this script from within a DOS batch file, and repetitive tasks are no longer a chore.

Taking this ease of use one step further, Firefox includes several utilities and batch files to control the timing of transfers. WAITFOR.COM, WAITSECS.EXE, FTPDELAY.BAT, and FTPWAIT.BAT allow control down to the second for repetitive transfers.

WAITFOR.COM suspends initiation of the process until a certain time of day. WAITSECS.EXE waits a given number of seconds between transfer operations. Use this utility to ensure that connections get made, leaving enough margin for busy networks or slow host systems. It's no fun to see an important transfer go down the tubes because a connection took three seconds too long.

FTPDELAY.BAT and FTPWAIT.BAT use the DOS facility to provide parameters to a batch file so variable information can be supplied upon execution. This way, you can provide a different list of files for transfer today than were transferred yesterday. An ASCII file containing the file list must be named on the command line:

FTPDELAY *<time> <filename>*

The FTPDELAY batch file will run at the specified time and read the *<filename>* for the list of files to be acted upon.

File Transfer with MCS UniLink

The lack of TCP/IP for a transport mechanism does not slow down the ability for MCS UniLink to transfer files. In fact, UniLink provides a nice method of file transfer, with options presented to the user in DOS-type windows. Scary (to UNIX-phobics) words like *FTP* and *protocols* are avoided. Even basic UNIX commands such as *pwd* and *ls* (Print Working Directory and LiSt files) are hidden behind function-key options. The screens for UniLink are less complex than those of Novix, so they're less confusing to UNIX neophytes.

After UniLink's Login/pc program has made connection to one or more UNIX hosts, file transfers are started from the Connect window, shown in Figure 6.4. Up to four host connections can be active at any one time, and files can be transferred to or from any of the active connections. To pick the host for the transfer, move the highlight bar to the desired host and press the F key to display the File Transfer Login window. If there is no current session to that host, UniLink will start one.

Since FTP opens a different connection than the Telnet terminal emulation session, a login name and password must be given when there is a session in progress. The login name can certainly be the same as the one for the active emulation session. The Transfer Filenames window appears after the user enters a name and password.

In as simple a representation of FTP as can be found anywhere, the window includes two fields: Host Filename and Local Filename. Fill in either blank, and choose the desired transfer direction. Instructions across the bottom of the window include

To Host=F4   From Host=F5   Dir=F6   Change Dir=F7   Esc

If you fill in the Local Filename field, pressing the F4 key sends that file to the current host directory. The file will be stored with the same name as on the local system. If files need to go the other way, give a Host Filename and press F5 to transfer the file from the host to the local machine, into the current directory unless another one is specified.

FIGURE 6.4

MCS UniLink's Connect window

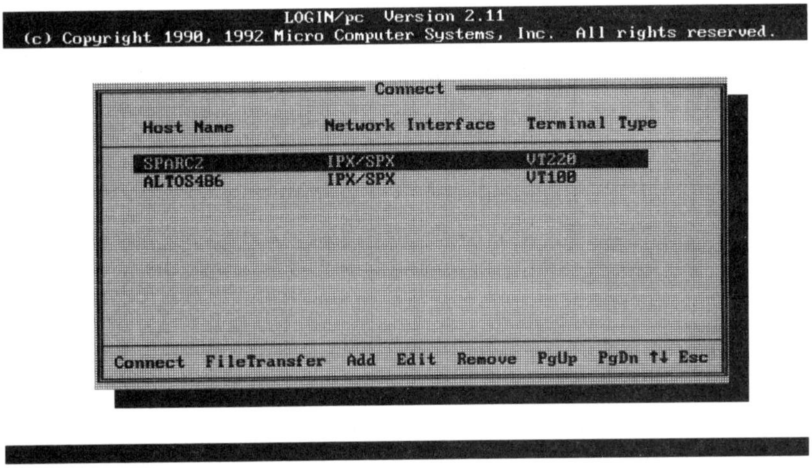

```
                              LOGIN/pc  Version 2.11
        (c) Copyright 1990, 1992 Micro Computer Systems, Inc.  All rights reserved.

                              ══════ Connect ══════
        Host Name          Network Interface    Terminal Type

        SPARC2             IPX/SPX              VT220
        ALTOS486           IPX/SPX              VT100




        Connect  FileTransfer  Add  Edit  Remove  PgUp  PgDn ↑↓ Esc
```

Two special conditions will change the procedure. If a file will overwrite a file of the same name on the target system, the Overwrite Filename window pops up. This window forces you to acknowledge that a possible error is in the making and offers a chance to change that name.

If a UNIX file with an invalid DOS name format is being transferred, another warning window pops up. The transfer will not proceed until a valid DOS name is given in the Local Filename field in the Transfer Filenames section. This is about the only limitation UNIX-phobic users may encounter that will be unusual for them. Most likely, the response will be "That name must be a mistake—you can't have that many letters in a file name." That's correct for DOS, of course, but we have expanded our horizons lately, haven't we?

The UniLink NetBIOS version provides the same FTP capabilities. If you need a simple file-transfer mechanism, the MCS product line deserves a look.

File Transfer with TCP/IP Gateway from Ipswitch

The TCP/IP Gateway from Ipswitch supports FTP in much the same manner as does Novix from Firefox. The protocol between the client and the gateway is redone into TCP/IP for connection to the UNIX host.

The Ipswitch product has a few extra features. It offers more than the basic number of commands—so many that only a UNIX person will ever use them all. Ipswitch even provides support for the *proxy* FTP commands, which allow connection to two different hosts concurrently. Once connected to both, files can be sent directly between the two hosts without the PC getting in the middle of the transfer.

The *net.ini* program, essentially a limited script processor, automates some tasks. A host can be connected and the user logged in automatically. Macros can also be executed from within this utility.

A minimal *rcp* program is included, as is TFTP. There is nothing out of the ordinary in either product.

File Transfer with NCM

As with the other gateways, NCM's file transfer makes the jump between NetWare (IPX/SPX) and UNIX (TCP/IP) in the gateway. There is a little more flash to the NCM product, since there is a bit of windowing for the UNIX-phobic.

In the naming convention department, NCM allows the downloading of a file from the UNIX host without checking on the DOS name restrictions. To keep DOS conformity, the product truncates the UNIX file name into a DOS file name format.

Along with using the ASCII windowing interface, you can run file-transfer procedures from the command line with the standard FTP commands. Exiting to DOS is allowed, so you can list current directories and the like. You can use wildcards in the file name options, but each file must be individually accepted. No recursive, noninteractive file transfers here.

The product also has a batch process to open, log in to the FTP server, perform a file transfer, and log out. This method uses all DOS batch commands, not a configuration file as in the Ipswitch product.

Although the interface is fairly friendly, many FTP and UNIX terms are presented. UNIX-phobics will find this system requires more FTP involvement than they will enjoy.

NVT Systems in NetWare for UNIX Products

The specifications for NVT do not include FTP options. The thinking behind that exclusion is simple: since the actual NetWare server sits on the UNIX host, all the files are available in different ways.

An easy way for a NetWare user to provide a file to a UNIX user is by using NetWare commands to place the file in a directory that the UNIX user can reach. The UNIX user can be given access to the files underneath the NetWare for UNIX directories, since the UNIX host controls the actual file system used. Once the file is placed (with DOS or NetWare commands) into a common directory, the UNIX user can then use UNIX commands to work with that file.

For example, suppose that a DOS WordPerfect file named CONTRACT.NOV was needed by a UNIX WordPerfect user. The DOS user might use this command to copy the file from the local PC to a NetWare drive on the NetWare for UNIX system:

```
COPY C:\WP51\CONTRACT.NOV F:\APPS\WP\CONTRACTS\CON-
TRACT.NOV
```

This example shows a typical deep directory structure that too many NetWare systems adopt. Personally, I prefer flatter structures, but this is a real-world example.

The UNIX person wishing to use that file under a UNIX version of Word-Perfect must give this command to start WordPerfect and open that file:

```
wp /usr/netware/sys/apps/wp/contracts/contract.nov
```

This command would open the WordPerfect application and load the *con-tract.nov* file. Lots of typing, right? An alternative would be to copy all the Net-Ware files to a common directory, and then copy all those files to a directory more accessible to the UNIX applications.

The example above could work just as well with a Macintosh with at least two of the NetWare for UNIX versions available. Both Connection NetWare for SPARC from ComputerVision and Altos/SCO Portable NetWare still support the Macintosh name space in NetWare for UNIX servers. The NetWare versions are equal to NetWare 3.01, while other NetWare for UNIX versions are comparable to NetWare 3.11. The code needed for multiple name space support was not included with the first release of NetWare for UNIX 3.11 code. Some NetWare for UNIX vendors may not include that Macintosh (and OS/2) name space support until NetWare for UNIX 4.0 is released.

THIRD-PARTY TERMINAL EMULATORS

All the stand-alone terminal emulators in competition with LAN WorkPlace from Novell come with file-transfer capabilities. NVT supports file transfer to the host. All file-transfer functions within the software will work when redirected over NVT just as well as when going through the serial port.

Existing emulators with scripts and other time-saving features should drop into the NVT environment with little change. The only real concern is where the UNIX host uses the particular serial port number for security purposes. Unless the software can be convinced to use a different port for security, the integration project may stall.

The important item to look for when investigating a third-party terminal-emulation package is its ability to use INT14, which is the most common method of redirecting the emulation software from the serial port to the network interface card. If the product's documentation doesn't say it provides INT14 support, then it doesn't. This capability is something manufacturers are proud of, and they'll list it on the label.

RDS POPTERM/NVT FOR WINDOWS

RDS PopTerm/NVT for Windows version 2.0, the most popular integrated NVT terminal application, includes limited file transfer. As shown in Figure 6.5, one of the options on the Terminal menu is Send File. This works with only ASCII files, and the file appears to the host as if it were typed.

For the return trip, use another Terminal menu option, File Echo (its hot-key combination is Alt-L). This option directs all characters from the host to a disk file as well as to the screen.

PopTerm/NVT isn't a heavy-duty file-transfer application, but it meets the minimum definitions for file-transfer capabilities. And it does come in a package that offers excellent, low-cost terminal emulation from both DOS and Windows for any NetWare for UNIX system.

FIGURE 6.5

*PopTerm/NVT's Terminal
menu*

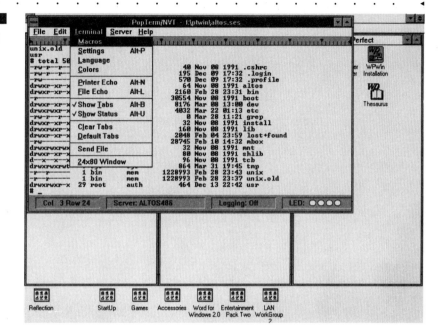

## CHAPTER 7

Advanced File Transfer from UNIX to NetWare

The UNIX world doesn't consider using FTP as both a client and a server from any single machine to be "advanced." That's what FTP does. Nothing special there.

In the world of PC LANs, however, NetWare is the only system that allows the PC file server to also act as an FTP server. Even Banyan, built on top of UNIX from the beginning and closely allied with SCO UNIX today, doesn't allow the type of UNIX to PC server file transfer that NetWare provides.

Part of the problem with network clients acting as FTP servers has been the limitations of DOS. With the growth of DOS and the primitive multitasking capabilities of Microsoft Windows, these restrictions are easing a bit.

NetWare servers couldn't act as FTP servers because they couldn't support multiple network protocols. The NetWare world was completely IPX/SPX until 1989. Until NetWare could handle both the protocols and the naming conventions of the UNIX world, there was no way to provide FTP service.

NetWare's FLeX/IP

True UNIX interaction involving a NetWare server first appeared in the form of TCP/IP support in version 3.11 of NetWare 386. TCP/IP was supported on the server, but only in an "encapsulation" mode. IPX/SPX packets were packaged inside TCP/IP packets, allowing them to travel through TCP/IP-only networks. For companies with TCP/IP-only backbones and WAN routers, this method worked.

Other companies complained, because they felt advertising TCP/IP without the ability to support FTP was misleading. After Novell released NetWare NFS Server, with support for FTP and NFS on the NetWare server, the companies then complained that they didn't want to pay for NFS when they only wanted TCP/IP. Some companies complain a lot, but Novell realized they had a good point. The FTP file transfer and print capabilities, a subset of the NFS Server software, became a product.

That's the history of FLeX/IP. It turns a NetWare operating system file server into a solid FTP server. It also provides full bidirectional printing. Many companies quit complaining and started rejoicing at the ability to share both files and printers between NetWare and UNIX.

NETWARE AS AN FTP SERVER WITH FLEX/IP

In use, there's little evidence that the FTP server is not a UNIX machine. The only clues are the server identification and that the NetWare permissions listed for files are in NetWare format rather than UNIX format. The commands for transferring files are the same as the UNIX commands, and the performance is as good as with most UNIX systems.

Figure 7.1 shows a session using PopTerm/NVT Windows to run FTP from the Altos486 machine to the NetFRAME file server. The username James is the same on both systems, with the same password. As the screen shows, the file *unix.old* was transferred from Altos486 to NetFRAME in less than six seconds.

The NetWare FTPSERV program performs reliably. Any FTP client can use the NetWare server as an FTP server. More than that, once the FTP client has access to one NetWare server, it has access to all NetWare servers.

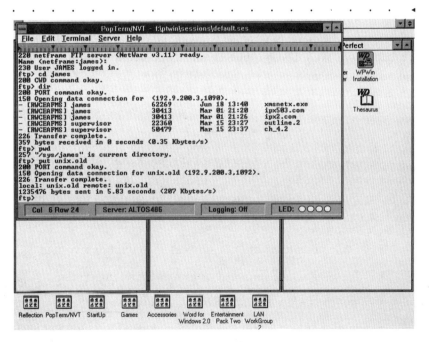

FIGURE 7.1

Transferring a file between an Altos486 and a NetWare file server

FTP ACCESS TO NON-FTP NETWARE SERVERS WITH FLEX/IP

After the FTP client to NetWare FTP server connection is made, the Novell folks allow a limited amount of interaction with other NetWare servers not configured for FTP. It's not standard and intuitive, but this is new ground we're blazing here.

To access a non-FTP server, you must reference the remote NetWare server with a long, cumbersome command string in every command. Yes, the typing will get a bit tedious, but this trick may come in handy one day.

The format for the server reference is

    command //server/volume/path

Let's take the famous hypothetical example: A UNIX client needs a Lotus 1-2-3 worksheet named BUDGET.WK1 or something equally bland. A DOS user on server ACCTNG_1 says that file is in the directory \LOTUS\BUDGETS. Once the UNIX client uses FTP to connect to ACCTNG_1, it finds that the file isn't there. Perhaps it's on ACCTNG_2, but ACCTNG_2 isn't an FTP server. You can use the following command to get a directory listing of the ACCTNG_2 directory in question:

    ls //acctng_2/sys/lotus/budgets

This command produces a listing of the \LOTUS\BUDGETS directory on the server named ACCTNG_2.

You can use the same command format to send and receive files. However, a few restrictions apply to accessing a non-FTP server:

- ▶ Anonymous users are not supported to remote servers.

- ▶ Files may not be renamed or moved between servers.

- ▶ Only the DOS name space is valid on remote volumes.

- ▶ Using the slash (/) for the root directory of the tilde (~) for the login directory works only on the local server.

Although this method is a bit cumbersome, with the right preparation and expectation level, it works fine. Some users consider that Novell has given them a site license for the price of FLeX/IP, since every NetWare server is now open to FTP clients. Once that first FTP connection is made, every other server is only a command away.

FTP from UNIX Hosts to NetWare Clients

A trend for the last few years has been to include some type of FTP server on DOS clients running TCP/IP client software. This inclusion is in recognition of the need for exactly the same types of NetWare-to-UNIX connections we are investigating here.

LAN WORKGROUP'S FTPD AND SERVING FTP PROGRAMS

LAN WorkGroup is a good example of a client TCP/IP package that will act as an FTP server. It offers both DOS and Windows versions and provides a wide spectrum of features. LAN WorkGroup is still the only TCP/IP client software that is server-based.

In LAN WorkGroup, each PC is administered from the server, but it has its own IP address. Once in FTP server mode on the PC, the FTP client need only type *telnet 192.9.200.2* (or whatever the actual address is) for connection.

FTP Server on DOS Clients

The DOS program FTPD.EXE (FTP Daemon), located in the \NET\BIN directory on the NetWare file server, will make a DOS-based PC an FTP server. The PC becomes a dedicated FTP server, which means that it can't be used for any other functions during this activity. One of the older PCs laying around can serve a useful purpose once again.

You wouldn't use this FTP server every day, but it may come in handy for special situations. The process is simple enough that a batch file can load the FTP server software quickly when needed.

Performance was very good in testing, no doubt reflecting the speed of a 386/40 PC with a fast 3Com EtherLink III network interface card dedicated to a single task. Between the home-built 386/40 PC and a SPARCstation 2 running across an empty network, transfer rates were outstanding. Using *get* to transfer a large binary file (1,235,476 bytes) took 6.4 seconds, with a throughput rate of 193K per second. Using *put* to transfer the same file took 5.7 seconds at a throughput of 217K per second. Both operations were initiated by the SPARCstation.

What this approach lacks is security. The entire DOS FTP server file system is available to any authorized FTP client. By extension, the files on any attached file servers will be available as well. You can set up basic password protection for these files by creating the DOS file named FTPDUSR.LOG. The format of the FTPDUSR.LOG (a very UNIX-type file) is

username [*:password*]

To help counteract the security hole it creates, the FTPD.EXE program stops as the FTP client closes the remote connection. In other words, this is a one-shot transfer system. If you want the FTPD.EXE program to continue, use the batch file named FTPSERV.BAT to loop through the program.

Actually, the one-shot approach makes sense in certain situations. With the FTPDUSR.LOG file providing some password protection and the program stopping after the connection is closed, the window of security vulnerability is small. Any intruders or accidental tourists discovering the server would have only a single chance at getting something they shouldn't. If you transfer files after regular work hours, the one-shot approach is more secure.

You can have the program write to disk a log file of all server activity. The log file option is one of only two command line options. The other option is to turn on *verbose* mode to write more information to the log file.

For example, the following command opens the FTP server software in verbose mode (with the -v option) and writes a log file to \NET\HSTACC\FTP.LOG, the default location:

```
FTPD -v -lftp.log
```

The resulting log file looks like this:

```
Connection from sparc2.nwdnsdomain.com on Thu Apr 15 11:22:18 1993
<--- 220 FTP server, Novell LAN WorkPlace v4.1 (NetWare & EXOS).
Starting FTP Protocol Processing
USER james
<--- 230 User james logged in.
PORT 192,9,200,1,4,96
<--- 200 PORT command okay.
LIST
<--- 150 Opening data connection for (192.9.200.1,1120).
<--- 226 Transfer complete.
PORT 192,9,200,1,4,97
<--- 200 PORT command okay.
STOR unix.old
<--- 150 Opening data connection for unix.old (192.9.200.1,1121).
<--- 226 Transfer complete.
QUIT
<--- 221 Goodbye.
User james logged out on Thu Apr 15 11:22:40 1993
```

The following is some of the screen activity from the SPARCstation2 (referred to as sparc2 in the log file), the FTP client. The listing picks up after the login and a directory listing. Although the file transfer numbers are too big for the *ftp* calculator to handle in whole numbers, the transfer rate was about 202.5K per second. The last line is the prompt for the SPARCstation2.

```
ftp> put unix.old
200 PORT command okay.
150 Opening data connection for unix.old (192.9.200.1,1121).
226 Transfer complete.
local: unix.old remote: unix.old
```

```
1235476 bytes sent in 6.1 seconds (2e+02 Kbytes/s)
ftp> bye
221 Goodbye.
sparc2%
```

FTP Server on Windows Clients

Using the FTP Server from a Windows-equipped LAN WorkGroup client eliminates the need to dedicate the machine as an FTP server. Although Windows is built on top of DOS, which is not multitasking, Microsoft has programmed a bit of multitasking into Windows. The results are that users can continue working while an FTP client is transferring files to or from their PCs.

Since each LAN WorkGroup client has a separate IP address, port configuration and identification aren't necessary. Starting the Windows FTPD version is as easy as clicking on the icon labeled Serving FTP (although FTPD can be run from within a DOS window under Windows). This displays the screen shown in Figure 7.2.

The performance of Serving FTP under Windows is considerably less than that of FTPD under DOS. This is the tradeoff for not needing to dedicate the FTP server. In testing, file-transfer operations were initiated by a SPARCstation 2 to a 386/40 homemade clone with an Etherlink III card, across an empty network, just as in the DOS-version test. Using the *get* command to transfer the same large (1,235,476 byte) binary file took 14 seconds, at a throughput rate of 88K. Using the *put* command, the operation took 42 seconds, at a throughput of 29K per second.

You can set up and control access restrictions by creating a file with a table of usernames and passwords. The file can have any name, and it will remain hidden from the directory listing. You fill out the restrictions table through the Restriction Setup window, accessed through the Options pull-down menu. The names and passwords in this table don't need to be consistent with those in any other security file. If you don't create a file with a restrictions table, any FTP client has full access to everything.

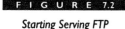

Starting Serving FTP

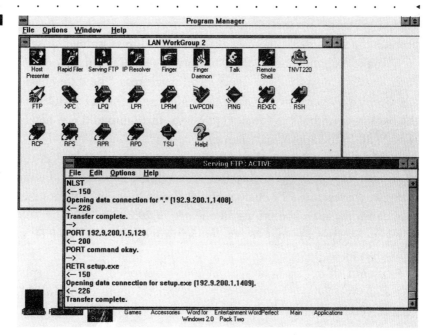

The Serving FTP program can also keep log files of the FTP server responses to clients. You can change the home directory for FTP clients from the Change Home Directory window, accessed through the Options menu. One handy option beeps when an FTP client logs in or out of the PC server. The log file closes when Serving FTP stops.

Another advantage of the program is the ability to support multiple connections at once. From one to fifteen users can be active to the Serving FTP station at one time (fifteen sounds wonderful, but not much work would get done on that system at that time, believe me).

CATIPULT'S INETD AND INETDW PROGRAMS

Catipult from Ipswitch offers a similar FTP server capability for both DOS and Windows users. Use the INETD program to make a DOS-based PC an FTP server.

The INETDW program is for Windows-based machines. Configuration and initiation of these programs are a bit more complicated because the Ipswitch product is a gateway, which uses the same IP address for every user.

To make a connection to the FTP server with Catipult, the FTP client must enter a unique port number along with the address. The different port numbers allow multiple clients to use the same IP address. If the \ETC\HOSTS file contains the name and address of the target system, the command can be given as *telnet sparc2* (fill in the appropriate name).

On the gateway machine itself, port numbers are assigned in the ETC\SERVICES file. To make the connection through the gateway to the individual PC acting as a server, the FTP client includes the address and port number. The client command might be something like *telnet 192.9.200.2 768*. The *768* is the port number, which must match exactly the number in the PC FTP server's configuration files.

Password files are configured and controlled by the entries in the ETC\PASSWD.TXT file on the server PC, or through the optional USERAUTH (USER AUTHorization) program.

Configuring Anonymous FTP on NetWare

One of the handy systems with FTP in the world of UNIX is "anonymous FTP." This is a friendly method of allowing other UNIX clients access to certain public information available on the system. No password is needed for anonymous FTP, although the protocol always asks for a password anyway. If a different password is needed, such as *guest*, that information will be given at login.

To enable Anonymous FTP access on the NetWare FTP server, you must create the NetWare user ANONYMOUS. This is done in SYSCON, just as for every other user. Don't give that user a password. It would be prudent to give ANONYMOUS file-access rights only to the directory and subdirectories that will be available to the FTP clients. Assign these rights in the File Access Rights areas of SYSCON, and through the GUESTDEF parameter in the FTPSERV.CFG file.

## CHAPTER 8

Sharing UNIX NFS File Systems via NFS Gateway

It's hard for PC people to understand both the performance and pervasiveness of NFS (Network File System) in the UNIX world. Every vendor supports NFS, and most networks of more than one UNIX system use NFS. Every UNIX program can run over NFS, generally without even knowing it's running across a network. Many machines in an NFS network act as both client and server at the same time, another strange concept for PC users. DOS peer-to-peer networks on a good day are a mere shadow of NFS.

Accessing File Systems with NFS

Sun Microsystems released NFS to the world in late 1984. NFS is based on RPC (Remote Procedure Call) technology, which allows a computer to use a remote file system just like a local file system. The XDR (eXternal Data Representation) routines support RPC code to help mask the differences between the local and remote file systems for the computer executing the programs. Between late 1984 and early 1986, sixteen different vendors using five different operating system platforms implemented NFS. In February 1986, all involved parties shared files over Ethernet at a Uniforum conference.

NFS was built to be independent of the operating system, and it uses RPC functions to provide a standard data file representation usable by any other NFS-equipped machine. The underlying transport protocol is UDP, running over IP. This stateless protocol does not require constant machine-to-machine activity to keep the link active. Each NFS procedure call contains all the necessary information to properly execute that request. Once a request is fulfilled, no more activity is required until the next time the machines need to interact.

The stateless nature of NFS makes crash recovery simple. If either the client or server crash or lose connection to the network, neither machine has any open files or indexes that must be rebuilt for recovery.

EXPORTING WITH NFS

Most UNIX operating systems require little to initiate NFS upon booting the system. If directories are listed in the *letc/exports* file when the machine is booted, those directories are *exported*, which means that they are advertised as available to NFS clients on the network. Exporting a file system under NFS is as difficult as issuing this command:

    /usr/local

This command allows any NFS client to mount the */usr/local* directory, and by extension all subdirectories, of this NFS server. This is often called "exporting to the world."

The following instruction gives everyone access to the */usr/bin* directory, but with only read-only rights:

    /usr/bin -ro

This instruction allows only machines named *hermes*, *zip*, and *tutorial* to have access to the file system on this host:

    /usr -access=hermes:zip:tutorial

You can see that it doesn't take a genius to share directories under NFS, especially if you don't get into tightly controlled security. The idea, after all, was to make sharing easy.

It's illegal to export both the parent directory and a subdirectory within the same file system. In other words, you can't export both */usr* and */usr/bin* in the examples above from the same system. However, there's nothing stopping a client from mounting a subdirectory of an exported directory. This allows a server to export */home* and clients to attach to the subdirectories where they belong. User Steve can mount */home/steve* while user David mounts */home/david*.

MOUNTING NFS SERVERS

The other side of the server exporting a file system is the client attaching and using that file system. The *mount* command is used both by a UNIX machine to mount its own file systems (like NetWare mounts SYS and other volumes when it starts up) and the remote, exported file systems.

The options for mounting a remote system are less involved than the options for exporting that system. It makes sense that security would be more a concern of the server than of the client. After all, the server is the one sharing information, and it should be allowed to decide what to share.

The command structure for mounting a remote NFS file system for SunOS is as follows:

mount -t nfs *servername:/remote-directory local-mount-point*

The first option, -t, specifies the type of file system. In this example it's NFS. Sometimes, this option can be left out, especially if the remote systems to be mounted are listed in the *etc/mnttab* (mount table) file.

The *servername:* is the machine name of the remote server to be attached. The *remote-directory* lists where on the remote file system the attachment will take place. The *local-mount-point* provides a location within the local file structure to start using that remote file system.

The commands for NFS are similar across UNIX platforms. The following command will take care of the remote mounting listed with our friend Steve (introduced in the preceding section) to a server named *hero*:

mount -t nfs hero:/home/steve /mnt/hero

This command would attach all the files in and under the directory named */home/steve* to Steve's machine starting at the directory */mnt/hero*. The */mnt* directory is standard in most UNIX systems when networking is installed. This is an easy place to make attachments, but there are no strict rules regarding the location.

The Novell NFS Family of Products

NFS Gateway is one of the members of the Novell NFS product family. Other members include NFS Server, FLeX/IP, and NFS Gateway. Before going into detail about the Gateway, let's review how it fits in with the rest of the family.

The first one to appear was NFS Server. By using this software, the NetWare server also becomes an NFS server, able to be used by UNIX clients in the network. UNIX clients attached to the NetWare NFS server don't see NetWare; they see a UNIX file system.

Included in NFS Server is a full print gateway, which allows NetWare clients to print to UNIX printers and UNIX clients to print to NetWare printers. Also included is an FTP server, which lets UNIX clients copy files to and from the NetWare server.

The next product released was FLeX/IP, which is a subset of NFS Server. It includes the print gateway and the FTP server. With FLeX/IP, UNIX and NetWare systems can print back and forth, and UNIX clients can transfer files to and from the NetWare server.

NFS Gateway is the latest NFS product from Novell. It works in the opposite direction: NetWare clients can use UNIX file systems in the same way that they use NetWare volumes. The UNIX systems working with NFS Gateway act as file servers to Novell clients.

How NFS Gateway Works

If NFS Gateway came from a third party, it would be hailed as the slickest new product of the year. Since it comes from Novell, some of the adulation is subdued. After all, we've already seen Novell provide a wealth of options for high-level connectivity between NetWare and UNIX.

With NFS Gateway, the NetWare file server acts as an NFS client to the UNIX-based NFS servers in the network. Just as our friend Steve can mount the file system on the server *hero*, so can your NetWare server.

Once this mount is accomplished, all the files in the remote file system are available to all NetWare clients of the NetWare server running the NFS Gateway software. All the files on the remote UNIX system appear as DOS files to the Net-Ware client. The UNIX file system appears as another volume on the file server. The NetWare client can't tell the difference between a volume that is on the remote UNIX host and one that is on a NetWare file server. Well, a few hardware-specific disk utilities, such as VREPAIR, DSPACE, SALVAGE, PURGE, CHDIR, and CHKVOL, won't function on the NFS volume. But this is to be expected, since these utilities require direct access to the hardware in order to perform their functions, and the hardware is not under the control of NetWare.

Figure 8.1 shows the VOLINFO results from a NetWare client attached to the NFS Gateway server. The SPARC2 volume is mounted on a SPARCstation2, and the ALTOS volume is mounted on an Altos 4500.

Benefits of Sharing via NFS Gateway

The immediate benefit of this type of file sharing is UNIX file availability to all NetWare clients. Any NetWare client of that server can see and use all the files in the UNIX file system, just as the user can access all other NetWare files.

This isn't a casual accomplishment. The amount of work that is required to make it happen is considerable. As much as anything, the performance of the NFS Gateway stands as a compliment to the power of NetWare NLMs as an application platform.

F I G U R E 8.1

The VOLINFO results from a NetWare client attached to the NFS Gateway server

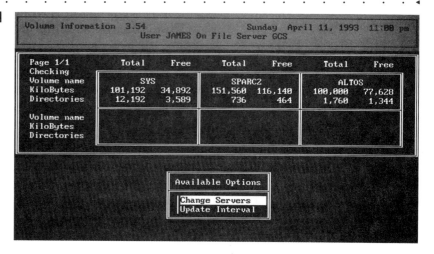

One important benefit of sharing NFS volumes in this way is that you don't need to change the clients. A typical network may have hundreds of clients but only a dozen servers. Every network administrator working today would rather reconfigure a server than configure all the clients of that server.

Another benefit of NFS Gateway is that it uses only the IPX/SPX protocols in the client. Many NetWare clients are still using physical media types that don't support TCP/IP well, such as Arcnet and Token Ring. TCP/IP support of these networks is possible, and in fact, growing quickly on Token Ring networks, but it's always more difficult to configure than TCP/IP on Ethernet.

For those NetWare clients with Ethernet that aren't using Novell's ODI drivers, adding TCP/IP is difficult. The ODI drivers are the updated NetWare client drivers that make support for multiple protocols possible over a single network interface card. Although Novell's intention is to have the IPXODI driver be the primary workstation interface shell, many users have yet to make that upgrade. NetWare 4.0 will force users to use ODI drivers.

The 640K limitation of DOS raises problems with a driver upgrade as well. The new drivers take more memory than the old standbys IPX.COM and NET3.COM, as does every new program iteration. Millions of NetWare users don't have the luxury of expanded or extended memory, and they must live within that 640K straightjacket a while longer. Using a solution that requires no additional programs for the client postpones the memory upgrade headache and expense.

NFS Gateway Security

NFS Gateway uses both NetWare and UNIX security. The user must have a login to the NetWare server and be mapped to the volume corresponding to the NFS file system. Since the UNIX file systems are mapped as distinct volumes on the NetWare server, there is little chance for a user to see an interesting directory name and start poking around.

To map a new drive to a volume under NetWare, the user must give the volume name within the MAP command itself. The only reference to this volume will be the listing of all volumes as the result of the VOLINFO command. In some networks where security is a concern, many of the Novell utilities such as VOLINFO are hidden from users. Descriptions of the security options for NFS Gateway are given in the installation instructions.

Figure 8.2 shows how a NetWare client maps a drive to the UNIX host through a NetWare volume.

In a typical NFS network, the exported file systems often have few restrictions on them. In fact, increased security and easier administration of that security are on the list of improvements for NFS according to many users. The attitude today is often, "Here's a file system, have fun." That's hard to reconcile with good security procedures.

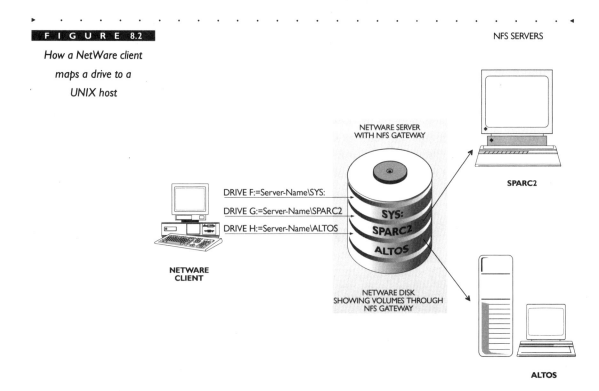

FIGURE 8.2

*How a NetWare client
maps a drive to a
UNIX host*

NFS SERVERS

NETWARE SERVER
WITH NFS GATEWAY

DRIVE F:=Server-Name\SYS:

DRIVE G:=Server-Name\SPARC2

DRIVE H:=Server-Name\ALTOS

SYS:

SPARC2

ALTOS

SPARC2

NETWARE
CLIENT

NETWARE DISK
SHOWING VOLUMES THROUGH
NFS GATEWAY

ALTOS

Among other NFS users, both clients and servers, this attitude works well. Everyone is of a like mind concerning the information available, and other UNIX users will know what should and shouldn't be messed with on a UNIX file system.

Among PC users with a newly installed NFS package for the PC, however, these assumptions don't hold. The PC user has not had years of NFS usage to hone that spirit of community. There is no understanding of what's what within a UNIX system. The proverbial bull in a china shop is a fitting analogy. The PC users will be in a new world, and they won't know the local customs. The "Ugly American" is reincarnated as the "Ugly New Client."

NFS Gateway controls the access of PC users to NFS hosts. You can decide which file systems are available and which aren't. You may want to give access to subdirectories of the official exported mount point on the NFS server, and keep UNIX-illiterate users away from system files. This is a good guard against the well-meaning but clumsy guest on the UNIX system.

Using NFS Gateway

To describe the use of NFS Gateway from a typical user's point of view is to describe the routine. The Gateway volumes are used exactly like any other Net-Ware volumes.

After the system is configured and the NFS servers are mounted, the NetWare client can use the servers without any extra effort. The VOLINFO utility in Net-Ware shows the NFS volumes alongside all the other volumes. FILER, the NetWare file maintenance utility, works on the NFS volumes. A series of old DOS directory utilities developed with no awareness of NetWare also worked on these volumes. It's certainly interesting to use a DOS text viewer on the */etc/hosts* file (and any other text files on the system).

Running Windows 3.1 as a NetWare client changed nothing. Since I mounted the root directory of one UNIX system, it took about five minutes for Windows File Manager to get a grip on over 600 directories holding thousands of files. Grip them it did, however, with no errors or discernible problems.

Using DOS WordPerfect 5.1, I launched the program from the PC client and started editing files on the Sparc2 created by WordPerfect for SunOS. The program needed to convert from 5.0 to 5.1 when the file was loaded, but it worked as it should. I had no problems loading or saving files under any application I tested with NFS Gateway.

CLIENT REQUIREMENTS

The requirements on the client are minimal. The client must have the following information:

- ▸ Name of the NetWare server running NFS Gateway
- ▸ An account on the Gateway server
- ▸ Password on that server
- ▸ Name of the Gateway volume accessing the remote file system
- ▸ Drive letter to map to the Gateway volume

These details may be included in batch files and login scripts on the NetWare side. If the NetWare administrator chooses to "hide" the existence of NFS Gateway, the users would never know. They would see only a drive letter mapped to a volume and not be aware that the volume exists on a non-NetWare server. Figure 8.3 shows a user attached to three different UNIX hosts at one time.

| **FIGURE 8.3**<br><br>*A listing of one NetWare client mapped through NFS Gateway to Altos, Sun, and Dell UNIX systems* | ```
F:\LOGIN>map

Drive  A:    maps to a local disk.
Drive  B:    maps to a local disk.
Drive  C:    maps to a local disk.
Drive  D:    maps to a local disk.
Drive  E:    maps to a local disk.
Drive  F: = GCS\SYS:    \LOGIN
Drive  R: = GCS\ALTOS:   \USR
Drive  S: = GCS\SPARC2:  \JAMES
Drive  T: = GCS\DELL:    \
         -----
SEARCH1:   = Z:. [GCS\SYS:    \PUBLIC]
SEARCH2:   = Y:. [GCS\SYS:    \SYSTEM]
SEARCH3:   = C:\DRDOS
``` |
```

NFS GATEWAY COMMANDS

Several client utility commands are included with NFS Gateway. The utilities work only from a DOS client on files residing on the Gateway volume. These commands allow the NetWare client to view and manipulate files on the attached NFS volume in a traditional UNIX manner:

COMMAND	FUNCTION
CHGRP	Allows a file's owner to change the group ownership of a UNIX file
CHMOD	Allows a file's owner to change the read, write, and execute permissions
CHOWN	Allows the supervisor with UNIX root access to change a file's owner
LS	Lists files in UNIX format, with standard UNIX switches

NFS Gateway also includes two files that help the translation of ASCII files between DOS and UNIX. The command DOS2UNIX converts DOS files to UNIX format. Its format is

DOS2UNIX *DOS-file > UNIX-file*

The command UNIX2DOS converts UNIX files to DOS format. Its format is

UNIX2DOS *UNIX-file > DOS-file*

NFS GATEWAY PERFORMANCE

Casual users will never know that they're using a UNIX drive and file system. All the advantages of NetWare file caching are applied to the NFS drive as well, so the performance compares favorably.

In early testing, the Novell PERFORM2 program gave a reading of just under 485K per second throughput on a BitWise NetWare server. Running through this server acting as the NFS gateway to the SPARCstation 2, the PERFORM2 throughput was 433K per second. Paying only a 15 percent penalty for all the translation going on is painless.

In a test of another product, SoftSolutions Document Management System, both the NetWare and UNIX versions were active. One client PC was able to attach to both databases on both systems through NetWare NFS Gateway. While the only "official" connection method is PC-NFS on the PC client, NFS Gateway allowed client access and full functionality. The UNIX database was queried just as easily and quickly as the NetWare database.

Figure 8.4 shows a NetWare client attached through NFS Gateway to the Altos system, with the root directory listing in the DOS window. The PopTerm/NVT window shows a UNIX listing of the same directory as seen by any UNIX client.

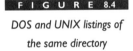

FIGURE 8.4

DOS and UNIX listings of the same directory

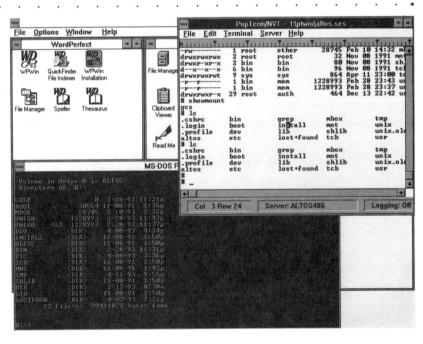

FILE LOCKING

As might be expected in a system allowing multiple-user access to the file system, NFS has a decent file-locking system in place. In typical UNIX style, the locking is advisory. The first user to access a file will have full access (if the user's permissions allow that, of course). A second user will be advised the file is in use but won't be forcibly locked out. The second user will be allowed to read and even write to that file (in most systems).

Once again, the UNIX community of users is given the benefit of the doubt in situations where bad things can happen. Intelligent and courteous users are expected to be using the systems. But don't make that mistake when introducing a new batch of DOS users into an existing NFS network. One of the better features of NetWare is its strong file locking and access controls. This tradition of user mistrust is carried over into NFS Gateway.

The product has locking problems, primarily because DOS and NetWare programs have no reason to look for and heed NFS advisory locks. A UNIX user and a DOS user both going for the same file at the same time will likely both be able to read and write to that file. Perhaps as DOS gets smarter in the ways of networking, this won't happen. Today, it will happen, so be ready for it.

NFS Gateway will properly interact with the lock daemons on the NFS server. The NFS Gateway Volume Information screen, shown in Figure 8.5, contains a field labeled Remote Lock Manager Required, with a Yes/No setting. If the setting is Yes, the NFS server's lock manager is used to manage lock control from the NFS server. This is in addition to the automatic file-lock control inside NFS Gateway.

If the Remote Lock Manager Required field is set to No, only the NetWare lock controls will be used. These are just as good on the NFS Gateway volume as on any other NetWare volume. File integrity problems between NetWare users will not be allowed by NetWare, whether on the local server disk or on the remote file system.

Although the DOS locking is secure with NFS Gateway, be careful with concurrent DOS and UNIX file activity until some testing is done. It's a lot to ask of DOS to respect NFS file locks.

Since file locking is dangerous, don't even think of asking about record-level locking between DOS and UNIX clients on NFS remote file systems.

▶ . . . . ◀

The NFS Gateway Volume
Information screen (where
NetWare client access
rights are set on the
mounted NFS file system)

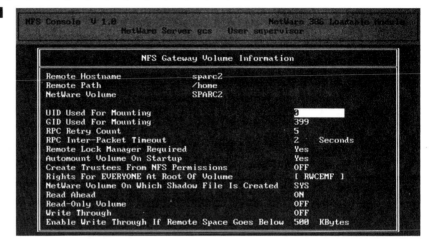

```
NFS Console  V 1.0                              NetWare 386 Loadable Module
                        NetWare Server gcs    User supervisor


                        NFS Gateway Volume Information

    Remote Hostname                          sparc2
    Remote Path                              /home
    NetWare Volume                           SPARC2

    UID Used For Mounting                     0
    GID Used For Mounting                     399
    RPC Retry Count                          5
    RPC Inter-Packet Timeout                 2        Seconds
    Remote Lock Manager Required             Yes
    Automount Volume On Startup              Yes
    Create Trustees From NFS Permissions     OFF
    Rights For EVERYONE At Root Of Volume    [ RWCEMF ]
    NetWare Volume On Which Shadow File Is Created   SYS
    Read Ahead                               ON
    Read-Only Volume                         OFF
    Write Through                            OFF
    Enable Write Through If Remote Space Goes Below  500   KBytes
```

▶ . . . . ◀

Maintaining NFS Gateway

Once the NFS Gateway system is installed and running, little ongoing maintenance is necessary. UNIX NFS servers stay active all the time, as do NetWare servers. After the link is activated, it will stay activated. Users will probably have the UNIX volume attached and mounted automatically through their login script or a batch file. A few will map a drive to the UNIX volume as needed, but those will be the power users. Normal users (if there is such a thing) like automatic scripts.

You perform NFS Gateway maintenance tasks through its NFSCON utility. The NFSCON program runs directly on the file server console. If the REMOTE.NLM and RSPX.NLM (Remote SPX) modules are executed on the server, any DOS workstation with proper access rights can run the RCON-SOLE.EXE program. This provides control of the server console while still keeping the server physically locked away from prying fingers.

MONITORING SERVER PERFORMANCE

Speed is important, and several areas help monitor and improve performance. Since server memory has a big bearing on performance, the Resource Usage display in the NFSCON utility is a good place to start looking for improvement areas. To access the Resource Usage window, go through the menu tree from NFS Gateway Administration Options, to NFS Gateway Statistics, to Resource Usage.

This window, shown in Figure 8.6, displays the actual amount of server memory and disk space used by NFS Gateway. The Minimum and Maximum Memory amounts are set in the Tunable Parameters window. The Memory in Use and Recommended Memory amounts are system figures, bound on the low side by the Minimum Memory setting. If the Memory in Use amount bumps against the Maximum Memory limit, it's time to head to the Tunable Parameters window and increase the memory allocation. Choose Tunable Parameters from the NFS Gateway Administration Options menu to see the window shown in Figure 8.7.

The last item in the Resource Usage window is Disk Space Used, which refers to the amount of space taken by the NFS Gateway shadow files. The shadow file keeps track of each file accessed by a NetWare user on the remote UNIX system.

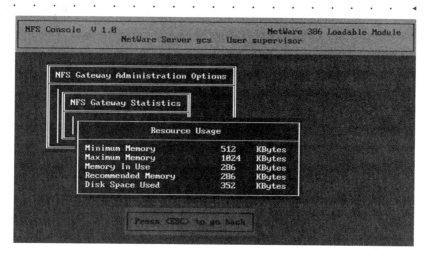

F I G U R E 8.6

NFSCON's Resource Usage display, showing how few resources are used by NFS Gateway

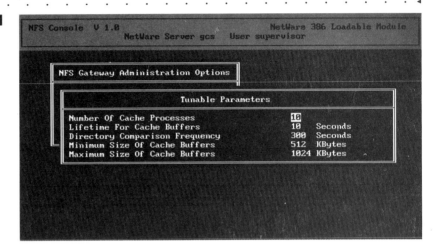

FIGURE 8.7

NFSCON's Tunable
Parameters window, listing
the values that can be
changed

Changes made through NetWare on the remote file system are noted immediately in the shadow file. Changes made to the UNIX file system by other NFS users may go unnoticed for a while. The Directory Comparison Frequency entry in the Tunable Parameters window lists the number of seconds between checks of the remote file system. The default is 300 seconds. If NetWare users are the primary users of that file system, this default time or longer is fine. Longer times will give slightly better performance. If the UNIX server has plenty of file activity through other NFS users, that 300-second delay should be shortened. Otherwise, the NFS server and the NetWare shadow file will get out of sync.

You can set the level of detail of error-tracking information through the Configure Error Logging Levels window (choose Configure Error Reporting from the NFSCON Main Menu, then select Configure Error Logging Levels). As shown in Figure 8.8, the error-reporting choices include None, Informational, Warning, Alert, and Debug. The default is Warning. It's a good idea to start with Informational and work up the alarm ladder. Get as much information as possible while the gateway is new, so plenty of examples will be available in case of problems. As the system stabilizes, move the warning severity on up to Alert, which gives essential notice about a critical problem or likely failure. Use Debug only for gathering detailed information for the Novell technical support staff.

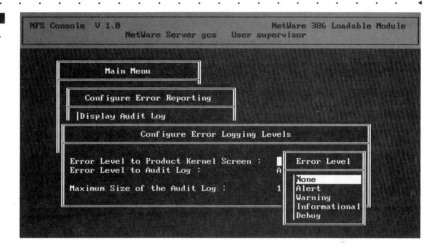

FIGURE 8.8

NFSCON's Configure Error
Logging Levels window

Error messages are displayed on the Product Kernel screen on the NetWare server console and written to the AUDIT.LOG file. You can see this file by choosing Display Audit Log (clever, huh?) from the Configure Error Reporting menu.

MAINTAINING SECURITY

UNIX in general is not known for super security, and NFS is not automatically better. Giving PC users some version of NFS client software and turning them loose can be trouble. They have a tendency to treat a remote file system as lackadaisically as they treat the DOS file system. Usually, NFS administrators will make it a point to edit their */etc/exports* file and exclude a few PCs.

While simplifying client access to remote UNIX file systems, NetWare NFS Gateway also increases security in two ways. First, the client must be configured within NetWare and have rights to the NFS Gateway volume. Second, the user must be listed either individually or in a group as having permission to access the UNIX NFS file system.

Not meeting either one of these requirements eliminates a NetWare client from using NFS Gateway. The management tasks to exclude an ungracious DOS/NetWare user are performed from the NetWare server. With a client-based NFS package, the client itself must be physically visited and changed. Most administrators dislike confrontation, and NFS Gateway allows complete control without confrontation.

MANAGING USERS

The mechanisms used to track user access rights go by various names, but *user database* is fairly descriptive. These are (for UNIX systems) most commonly NIS (Network Information Service) and DNS (Domain Name System). In order to successfully function within an NFS network, NFS Gateway must work with the existing name service in use, and it does so.

The concept of name services is a difficult one for NetWare-only administrators. It's only been within the last few years that every NetWare stand-alone server stopped being named FS1. Administrators got smart in naming their Novell servers, but NetWare administrators never consult with their UNIX counterparts before starting the name cycle. This may get sticky, since every machine in the same domain (read same network for this purpose) must have a unique name.

Ever hear the story about the first two automobiles in Kansas? Only two in the entire state, yet they ran into each other. There may be only one UNIX and one NetWare server in your company, but make sure they're not both named HQ1.

NIS and DNS

DNS is used as the naming system for the Internet. It controls a system of distributed naming databases all over the world. Domains are hierarchical (say that three times fast), and the names are separated by periods. When you see an Internet address, such as *someone@xyz.sscnet.ucla.edu*, that is a domain name at work.

NIS (and the new, improved NIS+) went by the name Yellow Pages until the phone company's lack of humor and goodwill forced a new name. The UNIX host files */etc/hosts*, */etc/passwd*, and */etc/group* make up the NIS for most UNIX systems.

See Appendix D for information about setting up name services in NFS Gateway.

The Novell Bindery

The Novell Bindery is the system file (actually files: two for early NetWare and three for NetWare 3.*x*) that tracks each user. Details about every user's privileges, file access rights, and security levels are kept in the Bindery.

NetWare 4.0 officially does away with the Bindery and introduces NetWare Directory Services (NDS). While the Bindery is concerned with the users and services of a single file server, NDS is a distributed and replicated database naming system. No single server holds the entire security information for that server's group of users. In fact, users won't know which server is technically their "home" server.

If you figured out this is strongly reminiscent of DNS, take a bow. Technically patterned after the emerging X.500 standard, NDS's approach sounds much like the domain and object orientation of DNS. If only these people could get together and make their abbreviations a bit more unique, this would all be less confusing.

After the UNIX users are gathered from the remote name services, they are matched with the NetWare users. This matching is just another step in the security procedures. Since the NetWare users will be guests in an NFS network, the administration of security for these new NFS guests must be strict.

Sharing NetWare Volumes via NetWare NFS

The first foray by Novell into the world of UNIX was with NetWare NFS Server. This product turns any NetWare 3.11 file server into a cost-effective NFS server that is able to match performance per dollar with any NFS system on the market. The lower cost of PC hardware gives a real advantage to using NetWare as both a file server and an NFS server. Even with the cost of the NetWare operating system and the NFS Server software, the all-Novell solution is much less expensive than any UNIX-based NFS server.

Since this was the first product of its kind, the Novell people took their share of abuse from UNIX fanatics that were affronted by Novell's audacity. Many people bought the product simply to break it and brag about breaking it. But NFS Server, even in its initial release, was strong enough to silence those detractors and convert quite a few.

Benefits of NetWare NFS Server

Some of the capabilities of the NetWare NFS Server include the following:

- ▸ Any NFS client can mount and use the NetWare disk.

- ▸ NetWare clients have full access to those NFS files (with proper access rights).

- ▸ The NFS server also acts as an FTP server (see the section about FLeX/IP in Chapter 7 for details on this feature).

- ▸ X Window terminals and vt220 terminals can control the NetWare server through XCONSOLE.

NFS Server includes other features, including printer support, which are detailed later in this book.

This product is more for the UNIX users trying to get to the NetWare files, although it can work both ways. Placing certain files in a central place can spark sharing between the different computing platforms.

One company uses this system for UNIX data file backup. All its accounting is done in Oracle on SCO UNIX systems. These files are copied every so often to a NetWare server running the NFS Server software. A tape backup is made of both the NetWare and SCO systems. If a file on the SCO system needs to be restored, the file can be transferred to the SCO system immediately if it's on the NetWare server. If not, it can be loaded to the NetWare server and then attached or transferred by one of the SCO systems. With this backup system, the company avoids the performance drag the SCO system would suffer during restoration operations.

Using NFS Server

If all goes well, the NetWare DOS and Macintosh clients may never know that a file is a UNIX file, placed there by an NFS client running UNIX. File formats are important, of course; a DOS or Macintosh user can't read an Oracle file into a Paradox database. However, that same user could read a WordPerfect for SPARC file with a DOS or Macintosh version of WordPerfect.

For those pesky ASCII files formatted differently in DOS and UNIX, Novell includes the DOS2UNIX and UNIX2DOS programs, which are described in Chapter 8. In this environment, DOS users won't be able to ruin UNIX system files (unless the UNIX administrators are dumb enough to park them on a NetWare server and leave them accessible).

From the UNIX client viewpoint, the NetWare NFS Server is just another NFS server. Novell suggests using the "soft" mounting, which sets the mount command to timeout if a mount is not successful. If you use a "hard" mounting, it may require some work to cancel a mount request to a server that's not responding properly. You should also be aware that mounting a NetWare server at the root directory invites disaster.

Using the *mount* command generally requires listing only the name and mount point of the remote server and the local mount point. If NFS is not specified, it will be assumed. For example, this is the command to mount the NetWare NFS Server (running on a NetFRAME, hence the name) from a SPARCstation:

```
mount -o soft netframe:/sys/james /mnt/netframe
```

Here is the actual */etc/fstab* (File System TABle) from the SPARCstation:

```
/dev/sd0a  /     4.2 rw 1 1
/dev/sd0g  /home 4.2 rw 1 3
/dev/sd1g  /usr  4.2 rw 1 2
/dev/fd0   /pcfs pcfs rw,noauto 0 0
netframe:/sys/james /mnt/netframe nfs soft,rw 0 0
```

The first four commands are for the local disk systems. The last command, looking suspiciously like the *mount* command, fills in the type (nfs) and describes a soft mount with read and write access (rw).

In both of these examples, the system will balk if the server NetWare server NETFRAME is not listed, with its TCP/IP address, in the */etc/hosts* file on the NFS client.

NFS Server Performance

NFS Server performance is quite respectable, and even outstanding in some areas. The NetWare system of file caching is as good as or better than most UNIX systems. Some file transactions between NFS clients and the NetWare NFS Server are handled directly from the NetWare file cache in RAM, so the speed is surprising. File transfers of over 1 MB a second have been seen regularly. Using a fast EISA (Extended Industry Standard Architecture) PC such as a 486/50 with plenty of fast RAM and a 32-bit EISA Ethernet interface card, such as the NE3200, will give excellent response.

More than a decade of optimizing speed on file reads and writes has given Novell a performance edge over all other PC LAN operating systems. With NFS Server, Novell extends that performance reputation into the UNIX world.

Maintaining NFS Server

After the NFS server software is installed and configured, little needs to be done to maintain it. The nature of NFS servers (and NetWare servers) is to stay up and available to clients at all times. Since NFS networks tend to be less changeable than PC and Macintosh networks, you won't need to update the client information often.

Administrators from the UNIX side will try to do administration the UNIX way: edit those text files! That will certainly work. The file structure in the Net-Ware server mirrors that of a typical UNIX host, so files are where the UNIX administrator expects them to be.

If there is a choice, however, Novell recommends using the NFSADMIN program at the server console (or with RCONSOLE, the remote utility) to perform basic administrative tasks. Changes made through NFSADMIN take effect immediately; changes made manually don't. The shortest delay is the SYNC_INTER-VAL set in the Tunable Parameter screen (default of 60 seconds). If changes are made to a client's permissions, they won't take effect until the client remounts the file system.

With the addition of XCONSOLE and the NFS support, a UNIX administrator can manage all the NFS particulars on a NetWare server. The files are available under NFS, and the NFSADMIN program can be run under X Windows, although in a text-only mode.

CHANGING FILE CHARACTERISTICS

You can modify files and directories to better support the NFS clients through the Change File Information option on NFSADMIN's main menu. This option brings up the Set File Information window. You must specify the individual file or directory name; there is no pick list here.

The UNIX permissions are given in either the octal format (777) or the symbolic format (rwx). The option of making any changes flow downhill through the subdirectories allows complete control over permissions at every level.

Trying to match the file permissions and access rights on a shared NetWare and UNIX volume may take a bit of experimenting. There is no right way to do it, but there are wrong ways. Files can be modified by NetWare users and ruined for UNIX NFS clients. Keep in mind that more access may be preferable to more problems.

Based on the control available, it's probably a good idea to give specific groups full access to the common NetWare/UNIX directories. It's easy to set up a different mount point for each different group if security is an issue. Within file areas serving one group, giving everyone full access will cause fewer headaches.

Figure 9.1 shows the Set File Information window with the DOS file OUTLINE.2 modified to be accessible to all UNIX clients. Figure 9.2 shows that same file from an NFS client, after the permissions and owner just set from the NetWare console have taken effect.

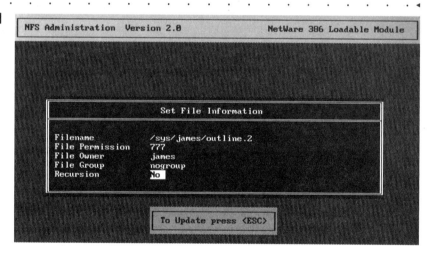

F I G U R E 9.1

Modifying UNIX file characteristics through the NFSADMIN program

BACKING UP AND RESTORING FILES

UNIX files that wind up on the NetWare server can be backed up by the UNIX client, but normally each server is responsible for its own files. Although you can do a UNIX backup that gets the NFS directories on the file server, don't count on the clients being that generous.

Many backup systems, including Novell's own NBACKUP, can't handle the extra attributes NetWare adds to files. They will back up and restore DOS files on the server, but the special NetWare attributes will be lost.

FIGURE 9.2

The modified file on an

NFS client

```
-rwxrwxrwx 1 root            132 Mar 29 04:02 net.bat
-rwxrwxrwx 1 root             40 Apr 12 10:39 nfs.testing
-rwxrwxrwx 1 james         22360 Mar 15 15:27 outline.2
-rwxrwxrwx 1 root             29 Mar  3 13:46 roll.bat
-rwxrwxrwx 1 root             41 Apr 12 10:59 testing
-rwxrwxrwx 1 root        1231537 Apr  2 04:07 unix.old
-rwxrwxrwx 1 root        1231537 Apr 12 11:14 unix.test
-rwxrwxrwx 1 root        1231537 Apr 12 11:28 unix2
-rwxrwxrwx 1 root          62269 Jun 18  1992 xmsnetx.exe
sparc2#
sparc2#
sparc2#
sparc2#
sparc2#
sparc2#
sparc2# pwd
/mnt/netframe
sparc2#
sparc2# ls -al o*
-rwxrwxrwx 1 james         22360 Mar 15 15:27 outline.2
sparc2#
sparc2#
sparc2#
sparc2#
 Sessions: 1                                        Server: ALTOS486
```

When NetWare attributes are a problem, you can be sure an entirely different file structure will be a problem as well. Dealing with NetWare attributes doesn't guarantee that different name spaces, such as those for Apple or NFS, will be handled properly by the tape backup hardware and software. Check the fine print to make sure, but the important question will be whether the tape system supports Macintosh files. If the answer is yes, it will support NFS files as well. Get one name space, get'em all.

If a UNIX backup system is used on the NFS server's UNIX files, the NetWare attributes on those files won't be retained. When the files are restored, NetWare attributes, such as inherited rights masks, trustee rights, and archive times and dates, will be missing. When these files are restored, the NetWare security controls also will be missing, so be careful.

NFS Server Security

NetWare administrators need to be aware of an important fact: NFS clients don't log in to the NetWare server. There is no control, monitoring, or management of those NFS clients. In fact, there is no way of knowing how many NFS clients have mounted the server except through one NFSADMIN screen. Typing USERLIST on a NetWare client will not help.

If security is a concern for the NFS server portion of the NetWare server, allow only those NFS clients that also have a NetWare login to use the system. Don't allow access by groups, only by individuals.

For those individuals, use the normal means within NFSADMIN to create user accounts. The special password that NFSADMIN assigns to the NFS clients won't allow access to the NetWare server portion of the system. For access there, those users must be assigned a NetWare password with the SYSCON utility. The NFS password can be modified or replaced to match.

Let me repeat the most important point: there is no real NFS security once the NetWare server's file system has been mounted. The UNIX NFS client is most likely a host to one or more other users, users who have no direct connection to NetWare security. Any client of the NFS client may have access to the NetWare server. If security is a real concern for you, be careful when authorizing clients. NFS security is much more trusting than NetWare; don't count on NFS help in protecting your system.

CHAPTER 10

Sharing Volumes
via NetWare for UNIX

Since both NetWare clients and UNIX users are resident on the same hardware in a NetWare for UNIX system, file interaction should be a piece of cake. It's better than most other file sharing, but the cake must be made from scratch rather than a mix.

NetWare for UNIX Controls

Because the files in a NetWare for UNIX system are all stored in a UNIX format on the disk, they are under the control of the UNIX operating system. The NetWare clients save those files in DOS, Macintosh, or OS/2 format, and the users are under the control of the NetWare operating system. Those users see the files in the format they expect, not in UNIX format. Matching the access rights of the NetWare client and the permissions on the UNIX files takes some administration.

The utility that controls the interaction between NetWare and the UNIX host operating system is *sconsole*. Individual NetWare users, printers, and access rights are controlled by the regular NetWare utilities. The primary NetWare utility used is SYSCON, which controls users' security and access rights.

Setting Up Hybrid Users

Hybrid users are UNIX users who can access files they saved previously as NetWare clients under the control of the NetWare for UNIX operating system. The *hybrid* utility, executed from the command line or within *sconsole*, connects the NetWare clients to their host *uid* and *gid* numbers. If this connection is not made, only *root* and the members of the UNIX root group can access those files.

EXECUTING *HYBRID* FROM THE COMMAND LINE

As you may remember from the chapter about Portable NetWare or NetWare for UNIX (Chapter 4), the command line version of the *hybrid* utility is

    hybrid -b NW*username* HOST*username*

The -b is for bind. You can use different names for the NetWare username and the host username.

To delete an existing hybrid user, use the same format, but with the -u option to unbind instead of the -b option to bind:

hybrid -u NW*username* HOST *username*

USING *SCONSOLE* TO CONFIGURE HYBRID USERS

Figure 10.1 shows *sconsole*'s Hybrid User menu, which contains the options for setting up and managing hybrid users. To access this menu, choose Administration from the main *sconsole* menu, and then select Hybrid User Configuration.

▶ . . . . ◀

F I G U R E   10.1

The sconsole Hybrid
User menu

```
SCONSOLE II V1.1                              Thu Apr 15 16:05:40 1993
                   User root on File Server ALTOS486
_____

                          HYBRID USER MENU
                    1.  List Hybrid Users
                    2.  Add Hybrid User
                    3.  Delete Hybrid User
                    4.  Hybrid User Parameters
                    r.  Return to Previous Menu
                    e.  Exit from SCONSOLE
                    ?.  Help

            Request:


_____



Sessions: 1                                        Server: ALTOS486
```

This should alert clever readers that there is no joint administration of NetWare and UNIX users, even when they are all running on the same system. The creation of NetWare users has no effect on the UNIX side of the host system. Similarly, the creation of UNIX users has no effect on the NetWare side of the system.

MATCHING HYBRID USERS

Before hybrid users can be matched, they must exist. The *sconsole* utility does not create users in either UNIX or NetWare. The NetWare for UNIX documentation includes more worksheets to avoid, one of which helps match the NetWare and UNIX users. The good news is that the usernames don't need to match. Figure 10.2 shows the screen to add hybrid users, filled in with two new users, who have been configured in NetWare and in UNIX.

▶ · ◀

FIGURE 10.2

Connecting a NetWare and a UNIX user to add a hybrid user

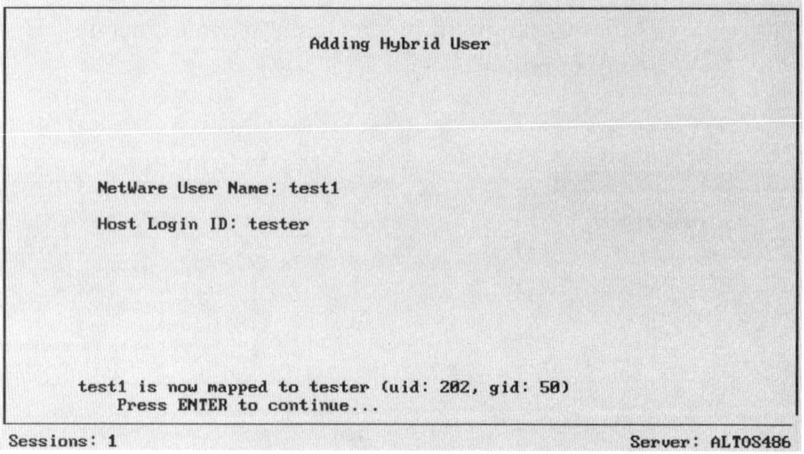

```
                              Adding Hybrid User



        NetWare User Name: test1

        Host Login ID: tester






        test1 is now mapped to tester (uid: 202, gid: 50)
           Press ENTER to continue...
Sessions: 1                                              Server: ALTOS486
```

As you can see, there's not much to this hybrid user business. There are no pick lists for usernames on either system, so that worksheet would be handy, had you filled it in.

The Hybrid User Parameters option on the Hybrid User menu sets the default hybrid user *uid* and *gid* (user and group ID) numbers. The default is zero for both, giving little authority to the created hybrid user. The changes you make to the hybrid user parameters affect any new hybrid users you create.

Giving NetWare Clients Access to UNIX Files

The location of the NetWare file structure in the UNIX system is away from the beaten path. Typically, UNIX files of group interest are no more than three levels deeper than the */usr* directory.

Figures 10.3 and 10.4 show the same directory on the UNIX host. The UNIX *root* user sees one directory (*/usr/netware/sys/access*) that the DOS user can't see. The DOS user sees this as the SYS (root) directory, while the UNIX user sees it as three levels deep from root. The NetWare user will never be able to see higher than the SYS directory because the UNIX-to-NetWare translation doesn't start before that directory.

F I G U R E   10.3

The UNIX directory listing of the NetWare SYS volume

```
# pwd
/
# cd /usr/netware/sys
# l
total 62
drwx------    2 pnw      pnw          4352 Apr 07 15:44 access
drwx------    7 pnw      pnw          5328 Dec 11 18:12 arev
drwx------    3 pnw      pnw          2384 Dec 11 18:42 arev10
drwx------    7 pnw      pnw          1936 Dec 11 18:45 arev30
drwx------    2 pnw      pnw          1696 Apr 12 23:49 book
drwx------    5 pnw      pnw           272 Dec 13 23:08 ir2
drw-r--r--    3 pnw      pnw           128 Apr 08 16:27 login
drwxrwxrwx    6 pnw      pnw            96 Dec 12 02:14 mail
-rw-------    1 root     other        2606 Dec 16 00:06 mbox1
drwx------    3 james    group          48 Dec 15 10:06 pc
drwx------   41 pnw      pnw           736 Mar 24 00:07 port
drw-r--r--    5 pnw      pnw          2144 Apr 08 16:27 public
drwxrwxrwx   12 pnw      pnw           864 Apr 08 16:27 system
drwx------    2 pnw      pnw           368 Feb 18 13:35 test
# pwd
/usr/netware/sys
#
 Sessions: 1                                          Server: ALTOS486
```

Placing UNIX files for individual users this deep into the NetWare server area is awkward. It's better to use a directory closer to the normal UNIX workspace as an exchange point.

FIGURE 10.4

The NetWare user listing
of the NetWare SYS
directory

```
G:\> dir

Volume in drive G is SYS
Volume Serial Number is C904-7CD9
Directory of G:\

MBOX1              2606 12-16-92   12:06a
MAIL       <DIR>        12-09-92    5:32p
LOGIN      <DIR>        12-09-92    5:32p
PUBLIC     <DIR>        12-09-92    5:32p
SYSTEM     <DIR>        12-09-92    5:32p
IR2        <DIR>        12-11-92   12:59p
TEST       <DIR>        12-11-92    6:02p
AREV       <DIR>        12-11-92    6:05p
AREV10     <DIR>        12-11-92    6:40p
AREV30     <DIR>        12-11-92    6:43p
BOOK       <DIR>        12-12-92   12:39a
PORT       <DIR>        12-12-92   12:31p
PC         <DIR>        12-15-92    9:50a
        13 file(s)          2606 bytes
                       113901568 bytes free

G:\>
G:\>
```

Although most administrators feel the need to supply every single user with
cross-platform access, that's generally overkill. When pressed, those same administrators will admit many of those users have no business with as much access as they have. With this in mind, it's simple to designate a few users on both
platforms as "cross-platform gurus." These people will be responsible for placing
and retrieving files from their counterparts on the other system.

Both power users and computer-phobics running a prewritten batch file can
easily perform this transfer function. After all, the whole idea is for people to use
the system they like and still have access to everything they need.

The administrator of the UNIX group will need to enforce DOS naming conventions on the UNIX files that will be transferred. Yes, each NetWare for UNIX
system performs name translation between UNIX and DOS, but truncated and
mutated file names lead to errors. Try to slightly deflate the egos of the UNIX
crew, so they don't use file name flexibility as more ammunition in the UNIX versus DOS war. All UNIX files that DOS users will access should be named in DOS
format.

Giving UNIX Clients Access to NetWare Files

On the other side of the coin, UNIX users should have little trouble getting to the NetWare files. Naming conventions are not a problem going in this direction, so the DOS users needn't worry about the files they leave for the UNIX folks.

The only concern will be the file permissions within the NetWare file structure. The hybrid user setup is important here. The purpose of creating a hybrid user is to allow the UNIX user access to those files owned by the NetWare user. Once MARILYN the NetWare user logs into the UNIX host as *marilyn* the UNIX person, she should have full access. If she's a hybrid user, she'll have that access.

Printing from NetWare to UNIX

As a preface to the discussion of integrating NetWare and UNIX printing, presented in this and the next chapter, let me say something: print less. Paper is an old technology. Information that's on paper is difficult to share, difficult to integrate with other information, difficult to secure, and expensive to maintain.

The goal of computing at one time was grandly stated as the way to "eliminate paper" and make the "paperless office" a reality everywhere. Now the copy machine has replaced the water cooler as an office gathering spot, and fax machines are ubiquitous. Even worse, they were originally labeled *telecopiers*, and designed to send paper long distances. Both examples just illustrate how paper-dependent business is today. Want to see a company grind to a halt? Turn off the copier.

Spare me the examples of the few document imaging and EDI (Electronic Data Interchange, a method of accounting between businesses over e-mail) success stories. I know they exist, and I'm sure there's a study showing exactly how many trees are saved by various e-mail systems in use today. These are but twigs saved from a forest fire.

Businesses cannot make a leap in productivity by using computers until paper is no longer the end result of every computer application. Various studies try to prove white-collar productivity is actually going down as more computers are implemented. They obviously don't count paper production as an improvement, since most offices are buried under a blizzard of paper. Do you think this suggests that mere paper creation does not qualify as productivity?

Look at printer sharing as a short-term benefit from better NetWare to UNIX integration. Focus on the long-term benefits of freely available information between different computer systems. Perhaps the easier it is to share information on the network, the less reason there will be to print that information.

Why Print from NetWare to UNIX?

UNIX printers often have two printers that NetWare systems don't: high-speed line printers and high-quality PostScript printers. There's nothing stopping NetWare administrators from buying line printers and high-end PostScript printers.

It has just been the trend to use dot-matrix printers and smaller laser printers on the network.

Many PC users had their own printer (usually a dot-matrix printer) before they connected to the network. Even today, the majority of PC outlets offer "packages," where the computer comes with a dot-matrix printer and software. This personal printer trend keeps the occasional long print job that one user produces from inconveniencing anyone else on the network. If all the various small printers around can handle the load, it's tough to shake loose the budget for a high-speed line printer to share.

Somewhat the same problem has occurred with laser printers. HP in particular has done such a good job selling inexpensive laser printers to everyone with a PC, it's hard to justify big bucks for a shared laser printer.

And when the company does feel the need for a shared laser printer, HP and competitors such as Compaq and IBM offer strong but affordable options. Shared printers with a print speed of around 20 pages a minute are easy to find and won't bust the budget.

All that being true, the true number crunchers still yearn for hundreds of pages of output. Perhaps a 2-foot stack of paper is some accountant method of establishing dominance within the tribe. Whatever the reason, a printer that gulps paper by the box and rattles the walls is a line printer, and it's likely to be found as a UNIX system printer.

UNIX PostScript printers often provide four to ten times the number of pages per minute of desktop laser printers, and four to five times the resolution. When an entire technical manual must be printed, with graphics, charts, and schematics, the NetWare users will eye the Imagen UNIX laser (or equivalent) longingly.

How to Cheat with Cross-Platform Printing

Before we get to the elegant methods of sharing printers, let's look at the low end. Just how cheaply can you share NetWare and UNIX system printers? How about less than a hundred bucks?

Several companies I've worked with faced a common dilemma: one expensive ($10,000) and fast (600 lines per minute) printer, but two computer systems. The NetWare users and the UNIX users both wanted a fast printer, but neither group had the money for a second one at $10,000 a pop.

Fortunately, there's a cheap solution to this problem: a gadget called *an intelligent serial printer switch box*, available from your local computer store. This contraption has four serial inputs (there are eight-port versions available) and one serial output, and it operates by intercepting the computer's higher voltage signal to the computer.

When a computer system wants to print, it raises the voltage on a pin in the printer cable. The printer then signals, with voltage changes on other pins, whether it's able to accept a print job or if it's busy. If the printer is busy, the system holds the job, waiting for the printer to become available.

The switch box scans each of the incoming serial lines for that higher voltage signal. When the signal arrives, the scanning stops, and the box's interior circuits connect the system to the printer. The system that needs a printer is fooled into thinking it has its own, dedicated printer.

If a second computer wants to print, the switch box sends a busy signal, just like a printer does. Since the computer is not smart enough (yet) to remember if it sent a print job that might still be printing, it waits patiently until the printer is ready. When the first system finishes, the switch box begins scanning, immediately latching onto the waiting system.

Figure 11.1 shows the least complicated cross-platform printing possible. Look, Ma, no protocols.

ADDING A BUFFER

Recently, one of these systems developed a problem, or rather the working situation changed (change is too often called a problem). A new UNIX system was installed, and the printing control wasn't as quick as the old system. The system would ask for the printer, then wait two or three seconds before printing. By that time, the switch box had moved on, sometimes starting a print job from the other system. The new UNIX system, still thinking it had control of the printer, started up as well. Printing was a mess.

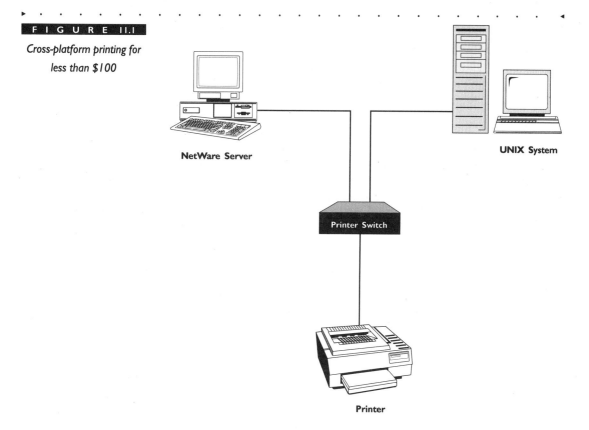

FIGURE 11.1

Cross-platform printing for less than $100

To end this problem without spending big dollars, the company placed a print buffer between the new UNIX system and the switch box. When the new system needed to print, the buffer captured the print job, then did the handshaking with the switch box itself. The new UNIX system is happy, the switch box is happy, and most important, the customer is happy.

ADDING DISTANCE WITH A PRINT SERVER

The obvious shortcoming of the intelligent switch box method is the necessity of placing both systems within serial cable distance of the switch box and printer. Is there a way to cheat, you ask, if the systems in question are spread all across a network? Yes, but it costs more.

UNIX printers have been directly connected to the network cable rather than the host system for quite a while. This allows for much higher throughput, since Ethernet runs quite a bit faster than both serial and parallel printer cables. Starting in about 1988, print servers have become available for NetWare printers as well.

As an example of cross-platform hardware/software, at least two types of print servers now support both NetWare and UNIX protocols and print jobs. Lantronix has released EPS1, with support for TCP/IP, NetWare, DEC's LAT (Local Area Transport), and AppleTalk. Axis Communications has a similar product, the AX-5, which handles both TCP/IP and NetWare, along with expanded PostScript printer feedback support. Check your favorite print server suppliers; they may well have models that do the same thing. Soon, some of the NetWare print servers may include TCP/IP support.

Multiple protocol print servers on the network appear to all systems as an available printer, much like an upgraded switch box. They are more intelligent, and they can provide high throughput and buffering. Look for these and similar products in the range of $500 to $1000, which is still cheaper than another printer. Figure 11.2 shows how these multiprotocol print servers work in a network.

Printing to UNIX Printers with NFS Server and FLeX/IP

NetWare's NFS Server and FLeX/IP have the same printing system. About the only differences between the two are the names of the administration programs (NFSADMIN and PLPDCFG for NFS Server and FLEXCON for FLeX/IP), and the startup files on the server (NFSSTART.NCF and FLXSTART.NCF, respectively). And in the FLeX/IP manual, printing is described in Chapter 6 rather than in Chapter 4 as for NFS Server. I think the high quality of reader involved here can keep up with these differences.

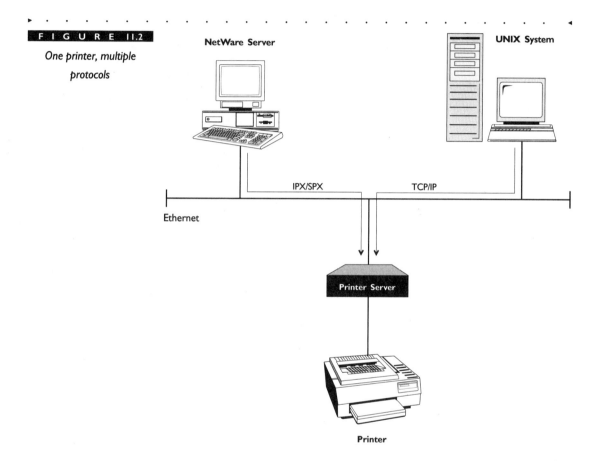

FIGURE 11.2

One printer, multiple protocols

Figure 11.3 shows the path of print jobs from the NetWare queues to the UNIX host print queues. Any NetWare queue can be routed to the UNIX host; no special queue software is needed. The only thing special about this print queue is that it was defined when installing NFS Gateway (see Appendix D for installation details).

▶ · ◀

FIGURE 11.3

*Print job route from a
NetWare queue to a UNIX
host queue*

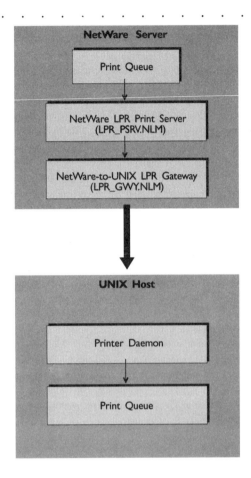

NFS SERVER AND FLEX/IP REQUIREMENTS FOR PRINTING

The UNIX hosts that control the printers to be shared must have the NFS Server's name and IP address in the *etc/hosts* file. Also, an entry needs to be made in the *etc/hosts.lpd* file or equivalent on the target system.

If the UNIX system requires more configuration or a different setup to accept remote printing, such as IBM's AIX using SMIT (System Maintenance Interface Tool), set that up as well. Unfortunately, Novell doesn't provide as much information about UNIX systems in the NFS Server manual as it does in the NFS

Gateway manual (maybe with the next revision, the NFS Server manual will be upgraded to be as good as the one for NFS Gateway).

When things don't work right—and they rarely do the first time when NetWare printing is concerned—check the printer configuration defined in the queue aimed at the UNIX host. As shown in Figure 11.4, the printer must be listed as Remote Other/Unknown to work properly in this situation.

The programs to modify the printer configuration are the same as those for installing the software. Try to modify things as seldom as possible, since every modification means another round of testing. If you've never before dealt with NetWare printers and their DOS users, you may be in for a shock. With a thousand variables capable of destroying printer settings at 100 paces, you might agree with me about using e-mail in place of more printers before long.

NFS SERVER AND FLEX/IP PRINTING COMMANDS

As far as the NetWare client is concerned, printing happens with the same commands as before. If a batch file or the login script sets up the CAPTURE (print output capture from the client's application) configuration, that CAPTURE command can aim at a UNIX printer just as easily as it can aim at a NetWare system printer. The NPRINT command, for printing existing files rather than capturing application output, works the same way.

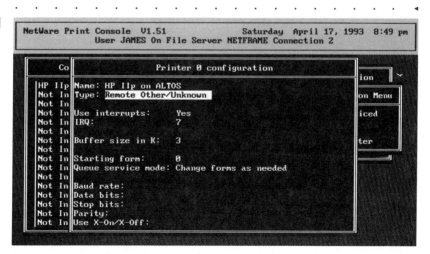

F I G U R E 11.4

NetWare to UNIX printer configuration

```
NetWare Print Console  V1.51              Saturday  April 17, 1993  8:49 pm
              User JAMES On File Server NETFRAME Connection 2

          Co |              Printer 0 configuration           |           ion  
     HP IIp |Name: HP IIp on ALTOS                            |
     Not In |Type: Remote Other/Unknown                       |           on Menu
     Not In |                                                 |
     Not In |Use interrupts:       Yes                        |           iced
     Not In |IRQ:                  7                           |
     Not In |                                                 |
     Not In |Buffer size in K:     3                           |           ter
     Not In |                                                 |
     Not In |Starting form:        0                           |
     Not In |Queue service mode: Change forms as needed        |
     Not In |                                                 |
     Not In |Baud rate:                                        |
     Not In |Data bits:                                        |
     Not In |Stop bits:                                        |
     Not In |Parity:                                           |
     Not In |Use X-On/X-Off:                                   |
```

If the user is going to direct printing to the UNIX printer only occasionally, the command used would be similar to

CAPTURE Q=ALTOS_Q1 NB NAM=NW_USER

This command starts the CAPTURE command, redirecting print output from the printer port on the PC to the network. Q=ALTOS_Q1 aims at the queue set up to route to the Altos486 UNIX system used in previous examples. NB stands for No Banner, which is optional but common with NetWare users.

The last command, NAM=NW_USER, gives the print output a particular name, different from the default (the NetWare login name). Some UNIX systems, especially IBM's AIX, must have the name of the print job owner listed in the system or they won't allow printing. If the NetWare user submits the job without specifiying the name, as is common with normal NetWare use, the AIX system will see it as the name SUPERVISOR, as in the NetWare SUPERVISOR. If this user (lowercase name *supervisor*) isn't listed in SMIT, the print job goes to the Great Print Job Burial Ground in the Sky, a very crowded place. Well, it actually goes to the */usr/spool/qdaemon* directory, but the *lpq* (Line Printer Queue) command will not show these jobs.

Save yourself some grief and put these commands in a batch file or menu pick list. Nothing aggravates NetWare users more than not getting their printouts faster than they can run to the printer. They will swear they never did a thing wrong. Nothing aggravates a NetWare administrator as much as fighting the print monster and users being consumed by that monster.

NetWare NFS Gateway to UNIX Printers

This is a trick section: there is no printing through NetWare NFS Gateway. Don't blame Novell for leaving out printing, just remember the philosophy behind the NFS Gateway product.

The goal of NFS Gateway is to make UNIX file systems appear as NetWare volumes. These file systems are supposed to be indistinguishable from regular NetWare volumes existing physically on the NetWare file server. That goal has been reached, since NFS Gateway works amazingly well. If you missed Chapter 8, go back and see exactly how well it works.

Since NFS Gateway is unidirectional (NetWare to UNIX only), bidirectional printing would be difficult or impossible to implement. Both NetWare NFS Server and FLeX/IP include printing support, so there's no reason to support printing in NFS Gateway. One NetWare server can support all three of these products at once, so adding printing will not require adding a server.

For those readers fooled by the table of contents into believing I found some magic way to print through NFS Gateway, my apologies.

Printing to UNIX Printers with NetWare for UNIX

With NetWare for UNIX client to host printing, the printers for the NetWare server are actually the printers for the UNIX host. In fact, even though a printer may be physically attached to the host system, NetWare treats that printer like a remote printer. Why? Because to NetWare, it is a remote printer. Remember, all the hardware and other system resources, such as hard disks and memory, are under control of the UNIX host. To NetWare, all system resources are remote.

The print job route from a NetWare client through the NetWare print utilities into the UNIX host is shown in Figure 11.5. It's less convoluted than might actually be expected. This is a testament to how well Novell engineers developed the print modules inside NetWare for UNIX.

Print jobs can be sent to any other NetWare print service, beyond the UNIX host system. Any RPRINTER (Remote PRINTER) system that a Native NetWare client can use, the NetWare for UNIX client can use as well. These include RPRINTER programs running on PC clients or other UNIX host systems.

FIGURE 11.5

The printing process in
NetWare for UNIX

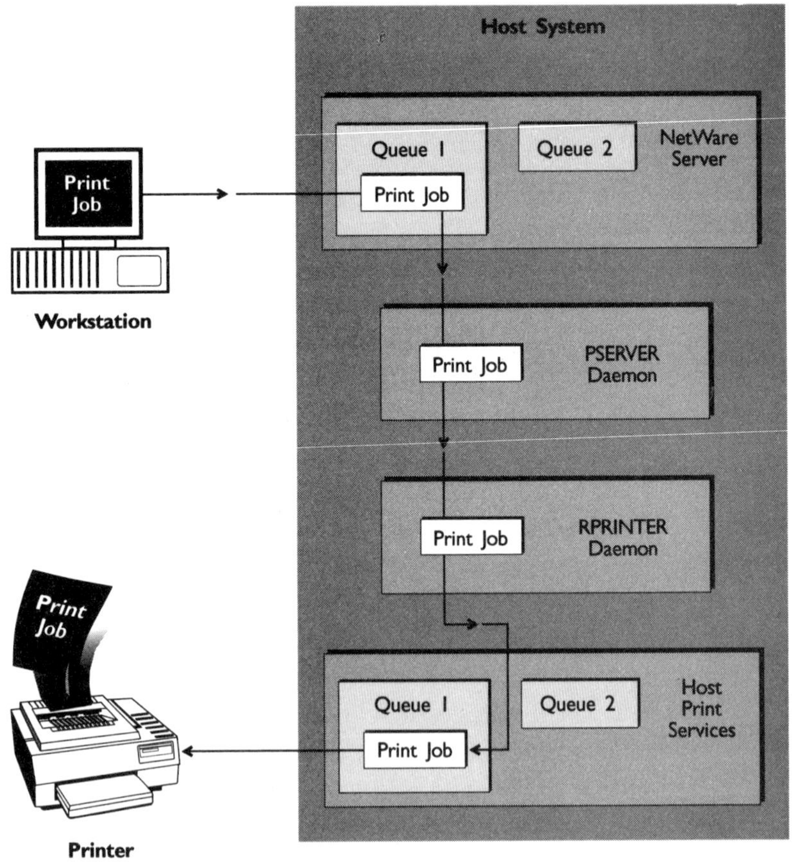

The configuration is not complicated, but it must be done in the right order. The worksheets in the manual listing the NetWare printer and queue names, along with the UNIX printer and queue names, would help here. Too bad you didn't fill them out.

Under NetWare, the SUPERVISOR must take the following actions:

▶ Execute PCONSOLE (Printer CONSOLE).

▶ Select Print Queue Information.

> ▸ Press the Insert key.

> ▸ Type the name of the new printer queue, save, and exit.

Under UNIX, the system *root* user must take these steps:

> ▸ Create a UNIX printer with *lpadmin*, *sysadm*, or *sysadmsh*.

> ▸ Run */usr/netware/bin/sconsole* (may be in */usr/pnw/bin*).

> ▸ Select Administration, then Printer Configuration, then Add Printer to System.

> ▸ Enter the name of the printer (same as the one created in the first UNIX step).

> ▸ Press Escape, then select Print Queue Configuration.

> ▸ Select the printer queue created in PCONSOLE.

> ▸ Select Printer, then Print Queue Configuration.

> ▸ Select the newly named printer and print queues.

> ▸ Exit *sconsole*.

Although both of these administrative programs do similar things, they don't look much alike or behave the same way. We've been through three different administrative systems to hook up one lousy printer, and the work didn't cover all the NetWare-specific setup needed in PRINTCON (PRINTer CONfiguration) and PRINTDEF (PRINTer DEFinition). Figure 11.6 shows the main printer configuration screen inside *sconsole*.

All griping aside, once these steps have been performed in the proper order, things will print, believe it or not. Make one queue per printer on the NetWare side, so there's less confusion for printer type and printing language. Nothing fouls up a printer faster than getting PostScript when it expects HPCL (Hewlett-Packard Control Language) or vice versa. The majority of printer problems are caused by applications not resetting the printer to the state in which they found it.

*The print services screen
from the Altos NetWare
for SCO Systems product*

```
SCONSOLE II V1.1                                 Sat Apr 17 22:26:58 1993
                      User root on File Server ALTOS486


                      PRINT SERVICES CONFIGURATION MENU
                         1.  Printer Configuration
                         2.  Print Queue Configuration
                         3.  Printer and Print Queue Assignments
                         4.  Scheduling Parameters
                         r.  Return to Previous Menu
                         e.  Exit from SCONSOLE
                         ?.  Help

                 Request:




Sessions: 1                                                Server: ALTOS486
```

To help with that, go into NetWare's PRINTDEF utility to the Edit Print Devices function. If you configure nothing else, pick the Re-Initialize option. This at least gives the printer a fighting chance to get strange codes flushed out now and then.

If the NetWare client is using the same printer all the time, put that CAPTURE command in the login script. Otherwise, help the user out with menu commands or batch files.

You might have noticed that your NetWare clients can print to a UNIX system printer without a single UNIX command. If the users don't know they are using NetWare for UNIX instead of Native NetWare, the printing systems won't tip them off.

Printing from LAN WorkGroup to a UNIX Host

The goal of LAN WorkGroup is to make users look and feel like typical NetWare users, even though they're playing with UNIX. Because of this, the support for NetWare to UNIX printing is a bit on the spare side, without extra queues available to one side or the other. The product includes some command line programs, as well as a configuration file on the NetWare server to help eliminate the need to type some of the command options.

The two groups of print utilities are the "L Group" (LPR, LPQ, and LPRM) and the "R Group" (RPR, RPS, and RPD). The L Group of utilities have more options but require the remote host to run *lpd* and have the workstation defined in the */etc/hosts.lpd* file. The R Group doesn't require the host to have a listing of the workstation, but the value of the variable DOS SET NAME will be presented as the username. Here's a summary of these utilities:

COMMAND	DEFINITION	FUNCTION
LPR	Line PRinter	Sends a file to the named printer
LPQ	Line Printer Queue	Checks the status of the named queue
LPRM	Line Printer ReMove	Removes print jobs from the queue
RPR	Remote PRinter	Sends a file to the named printer
RPS	Remote Printer Status	Checks the status of the named queue
RPD	Remote Printer Delete	Removes print jobs from the remote queue

The configuration files \NET\SAMPLE\GPRINT.CFG and \NET\SAMPLE\PRINT.CFG set up the parameters for the command line choices. If all is configured, the only command needed to print is

LPR *FILENAME*

You can use DOS wildcards in the file name, and several files may be listed for printing at one time.

None of the TCP/IP options examined here can redirect NetWare print queues to a UNIX host. If you need that feature, look toward the NetWare for UNIX products or get a print server that supports both systems.

Printing through TCP/IP Gateways to UNIX Hosts

Two of the TCP/IP gateway products discussed in this book have some form of Net-Ware to UNIX printing support, although they have better support for UNIX to NetWare printing. The best we can get in this direction is the ability to spool some jobs with a UNIX command line program, similar to LAN WorkGroup.

PRINTING FROM NOVIX TO UNIX PRINTERS

A variety of command line options is available with the Novix print command, but all the details can be configured in the Host Sessions and Services screen. The host must be listed with the name LPD and defined with an Access Type of Host Printer. This is another example of the strong security of Novix. If a host isn't defined, it's not reachable—for printing or anything else.

The command used to send an existing file to the host printer is

NVLPR /h*HOSTNAME* /f*PRINTFILE*

If only one host printer is defined, the name of the host may be dispensed with. The host must be configured to accept remote print in this form. The name and address of the NetWare server where Novix is running must be included in the /etc/hosts and /etc/hosts.lpd files.

PRINTING TO A UNIX HOST WITH CATIPULT

Similar to the Novix command line options, the printer definition for Catipult is set in the CATIPULT.CFG file for each user. It includes a space for both PRINTER and PRINTSERVER. The host named in PRINTSERVER must be listed by address, and it must also be running *lpd*. If these variables are set, the command line is as easy as

LPR *FILENAME*

Any UNIX host printer may be addressed with command line switches, but the LPR command expects to find an *lpd* server on the host. Catipult also includes the companion commands LPQ and LPRM. LPQ reports on the status of the printer queue, and LPRM allows removal of print jobs from that queue.

Printing from UNIX to NetWare

Many feel printing from UNIX to NetWare is extremely worthwhile. The UNIX world has seen the explosion of high-quality yet inexpensive laser printers, color printers, and plotters in the world of DOS, Macintosh, and NetWare. Many UNIX users are frankly jealous. Adding insult to injury, DOS and Macintosh programs now produce some outstanding printed materials. Desktop publishing is just one area, but it's the most visible. The presentation quality of spreadsheets, database tables, and word processed documents illustrates the flexibility and power of desktop printing. The output often also illustrates the triumph of layout over logic, but that's a different problem.

As in the previous chapter, the focus here is on the NFS Server program rather than the FLeX/IP subset product. All the ways to "cheat" (with switch boxes or print servers) when setting up printers work just as well on this side of the fence as they do when printing from NetWare to UNIX. All the reasons to avoid printing when possible hold true no matter which system's printers are being used.

Advances in NetWare Printing

One reason that printing runs so well from UNIX to NetWare is the work Novell has done the last few years. The ability to route printing from one Net-Ware server to another kicked into high gear when Novell rewrote the print routines as separate NLMs in NetWare 3.0. The capabilities had been available under NetWare 286 with VAPs, but the better performance, memory control, and use of server resources in NetWare 386 made life much simpler.

With NetWare 386 NLMs, more types of programs can be written. Add TCP/IP support (starting with NetWare 3.11) into the mix, and suddenly we have a PLPD.NLM that is the equivalent of a UNIX *lpd* but runs on a NetWare server. From there, routing the UNIX print jobs to a predefined NetWare print queue finishes the sequence. Just another example of how far Novell has been going to better support UNIX. Figure 12.1 is a diagram that shows how easy this is (or at least is supposed to be).

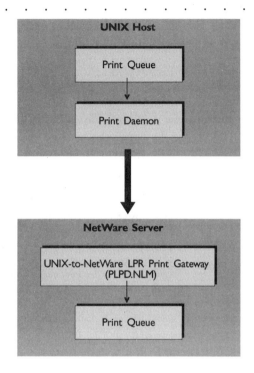

How print jobs travel from remote queues to NetWare queues

UNIX to NetWare Printing through FLeX/IP and NFS Server

As explained in Chapter 11, the printing system of NetWare NFS Server and FLeX/IP work the same way. The only differences are the names of the administration programs and the startup files on the server.

PRINTING REQUIREMENTS

In order to print from UNIX to NetWare with FLeX/IP and NFS Server, the UNIX host must aim the print job at the NetWare with the gateway installed, and the NetWare queue must be open to remote print jobs. The UNIX host must have

the name and IP address of the NetWare server exporting the print queues in the
/etc/hosts file as well as in the */etc/hosts.lpd* file. These entries are in addition to
the entry in the */etc/printcap* file, which should look something like this:

```
ap0 | Engineering LaserWriter Plus :\
  :lp=:rm=netframe:rp=UNIX_Q:sd=/usr/spool/ap0:mx=0:
```

The commands in this entry work as follows:

ap0	Specifies the name of the NetWare printer, which is a LaserWriter Plus
lp	Specifies the output device; for a remote printer, this must be left blank
rm	Specifies the name of the NetWare NFS host where the print server (PLPD.NLM) is running
rp	Specifies the NetWare print queue name
sd	Specifies the UNIX spool directory for jobs that are sent to this printer
mx	Disables the 1 MB limitation on the size of the print jobs

Setting up */etc/printcap* files is not for the faint of heart. It's not something Net-
Ware administrators can do on their own, and many UNIX administrators avoid
it whenever possible.

When configured, the UNIX *lpr*, *lpq*, and *lprm* utilities will be routed to the
appropriate NetWare queue. Many of the L Group flags and switches, such as -c,
-d, -g, -m, -n, *-num fon*, -t, and -v, are not supported. The -p and -f flags that emulate the UNIX *pr* and *fpr* (Fortran filter) are supported, along with the -J flag for
the job name.

The table of NFS users allowed into the NetWare system was built when the
software was installed. That setup is important for printing as well. If some UNIX
users who aren't listed in the PLPD.NLM program want to print to the NetWare
printers, add them now.

The default setting for all print jobs submitted to the NetWare queues from the PLPD program is to add a form feed at the end. If you dislike wasting that paper, change the setting in PCONSOLE in the Job Description menu. Setting the Suppress Form Feed field to Yes will eliminate the ending form feed.

SCO AND IBM RS/6000 PRINTING

SCO users have a special section in the manual, because many SCO systems do not support *lpr*. Add the following entry in the configuration file */usr/spool/lp/remote*:

```
netwarelp:rsh nfs1 lpr -Pnwlp
```

After you add this line, printing with the command *lpr -dnetwarelp file-name* will work.

If you don't like this approach, or you have other systems that don't support *lpr*, the only alternative is to route print jobs through other NFS clients that do support *lpr*. The recommended method is to use *rsh* (Remote SHell) for the copy and then to execute *lpr* remotely. Seems convoluted, doesn't it. How about e-mail? Document imaging looking better?

Printing from IBM RS/6000s can be strenuous as well. AIX has no */etc/printcap* file, so everything must be done in the administrative program, SMIT. The critical configuration is to add a remote print queue and give it the name of the NetWare print queue being exported by PLPDCFG.NLM. Trick here: the name can't be longer that seven characters. The Name of Queue field needs that information, and the Destination Host field needs the name of the NetWare server. This name must be in the *hosts* file as well, and there's no place to add it through SMIT. If it's not in there before starting all this printer setup, remember to add it. The Name of Device to Add field is for a device name required by AIX, but it has no effect in the UNIX to NetWare print service setup. Don't ask me, ask IBM. This name also has a limit of seven characters.

Once all this is done, start up the *lpd* subsystem from the command line, then go back into SMIT to check the status. Don't you wish menu systems did everything (or nothing)? Going in and out of the menu system makes no sense.

UNIX to NetWare Printing with NetWare for UNIX

This is another trick section (like the NetWare NFS Gateway to UNIX Printers section in the previous chapter): there is no UNIX to NetWare printing from within NetWare for UNIX. Why? The NetWare printers are the UNIX printers, remember? The NetWare system is under control of the UNIX host. All system resources are controlled by UNIX.

Aha, you say, what about using NetWare for UNIX to get to a different Net-Ware server and its printers? Has Novell left that out?

Well, yes and no. The UNIX-only clients have no access through the NetWare print system in the NetWare for UNIX computer, so they have no access to any remote NetWare servers either. However, if the UNIX users are also NetWare users, they do have that access. One NetWare client can be attached to several different NetWare servers (maximum of 8 in NetWare 386, 50 in NetWare 4.0). NetWare for UNIX clients can attach and use print services from another Net-Ware server in the network. Since they are hybrid users, they have access to files on both the UNIX and NetWare portions of the host system.

Printing from a UNIX Host to LAN WorkGroup

This section is a bit of a hybrid, since the section title implies that a UNIX host can initiate printing through LAN WorkGroup. That's not the case. LAN Work-Group users can initiate the printing of UNIX files, however, and they do it so easily it deserves mention.

You can print a UNIX text file through LAN WorkGroup in two ways. One is through RapidFiler, where files can be picked and clicked and sent to the printer of choice. The second is by routing terminal emulation sessions through the printer.

The printer of choice in both these cases is the one configured for the workstation at the time, through Microsoft Windows. By configuring an available network printer within Windows, any UNIX host file can be spooled and printed to that printer. The printer setup is strictly between the workstation and Windows; the UNIX host doesn't get involved here at all. Figure 12.2 shows an example of how to route printing through the workstation to the printer of choice.

F I G U R E   12.2

Printing from RapidFiler

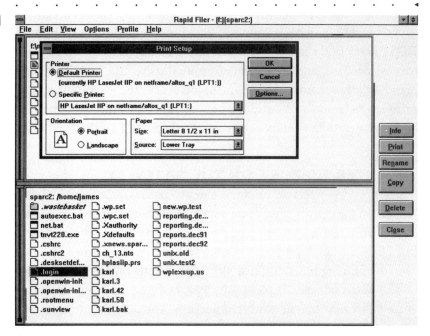

In this illustration, the printer chosen is physically attached to the Altos486 UNIX system. Using the NetWare NFS Server print gateway described earlier, the NetFRAME file server is exporting the print queue to the Altos486 host. That's a long way to go to print a SPARCstation2 *.login* file, but it makes for a good example.

Printing from a UNIX Host to Novix

The only TCP/IP gateway that supports UNIX host printing, Novix from Firefox, takes advantage of its tight integration with the NetWare server. Novix provides two ways to support host printing.

WORKSTATION AS PRINT SERVER

The workstation can actually become a print server itself. The NVLPD.EXE program works as a background TSR and spools UNIX print jobs out through the DOS PRINT.COM facility. The jobs spool in the workstation in whatever directory is specified, and they can be rerouted using the NetWare CAPTURE command. In other words, once the print job gets to the workstation, it's just another print job as far as the PC and the network are concerned. The print job may also be forwarded to the Novix server software running on the NetWare server.

PRINTER SUPPORT ON THE GATEWAY

The printer support on the Novix gateway itself is more flexible. The program will "listen" on the network and route data from host-established connections to the file server's print queues. Once there, the standard NetWare printing process is in control. No workstation programs need to be running; Novix gateways on routers perform the printing functions, just like those directly on NetWare servers.

The UNIX host sends print jobs by specifying the Novix gateway IP address and a *telnet* port for the print connection. The default port number is 515, but any port number can be configured. The configuration screen is shown in Figure 12.3.

As you might expect, you need to provide information about the NetWare queue name. But after seeing some of the other systems, this looks simple. Of course, you must still set up the NetWare printer and queue properly.

Novix can support two types of UNIX host printout: "raw" data, where all received characters are sent to the printer, and the LPD form, used mainly with BSD UNIX and often copied by other UNIX systems. LPD format includes a system of

FIGURE 12.3

Configuring Novix to
support UNIX host printing

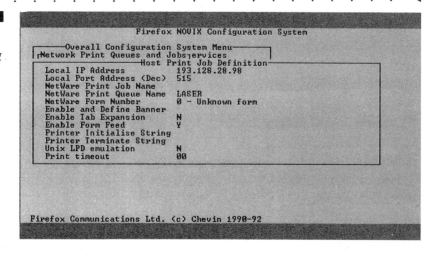

```
                      Firefox NOVIX Configuration System
          ─Overall Configuration System Menu─
         ┌Network Print Queues and Jobs┐ervices
                        ─────Host Print Job Definition─
          Local IP Address           193.128.28.98
          Local Port Address <Dec>    515
          NetWare Print Job Name
          NetWare Print Queue Name    LASER
          NetWare Form Number         0 - Unknown form
          Enable and Define Banner
          Enable Tab Expansion        N
          Enable Form Feed            Y
          Printer Initialise String
          Printer Terminate String
          Unix LPD emulation          N
          Print timeout               00



     Firefox Communications Ltd. <c> Chevin 1990-92
```

handshake messages between the server and client and involves the transmission of a control file as well as the data file that contains the information to be printed. The expectation is that any print setup from a UNIX host to a printer attached to a terminal server will work with Novix.

Print jobs are spooled in the \TCPGWAY during the passing of data to Novix from the UNIX host. These temporary spool files should disappear when passed on to the NetWare print system. If they don't, the name format is $T, so they should be easy to find. If you see'em, kill'em.

Shared Application Services

So, now that we've got all these connections between NetWare and UNIX, what do we do with them?

Strange but true, people today expect their computers to do some sort of productive work. Whether we agree that the e-mail football pool is productive work or not, something of value should be happening on these silicon sorcerers we call computers.

Cross-Platform Application Development

Cross-platform applications are at the beginning of what will be a long, long run. It's only been a few years since the earliest PC to Macintosh applications became available, and there aren't more than a double handful of those yet. As difficult as writing Macintosh and PC applications is, writing UNIX and NetWare applications involves a thousand more variables. Top-notch networking applications for even one platform are rare, and to bypass all the thousands of potential roadblocks when combining two or more different operating systems takes an enormous amount of work.

Just because the task is tough doesn't mean that people aren't successful in developing cross-platform applications. Over the last several years, various APIs have been published by various groups and committees to ease the workload. Some are built upon the technology that supports NFS, and some are built on newer and (possibly) better techniques.

Various groups with various plans are competing to be the cross-platform saviours. All the major UNIX providers are "open" and "interoperable," as are committees like the OSF (Open Software Foundation) with DCE (Distributed Computing Environment). Whether one group's definition of "open" agrees with another group's definition has been the subject of much debate. Frankly, some vendors' claims of openness bring to mind the story of a pig's ear and a silk purse.

The standards derived from multiple companies making products work together in response to customer demand have the best chance of long-term success. The official standards groups can help focus attention on areas of conflict and make sure all groups get heard. Unfortunately, these committees can't force users to switch to the anointed standard. Customers have minds of their own and prefer to get working systems for their dollars. So the marketplace will help establish standards for quite a while.

The best result of all the corporate PR about standards is that vendors have now been on record for more standardization for several years. Even companies with the most proprietary product lines are embarrassed to keep saying "standards are coming…next year." Nothing motivates a vendor like the twin cattle prods of public ridicule and competitor improvements.

Perhaps soon, all this network plumbing will be finished and applications will flow as cool water from a faucet. Perhaps soon, client-server will mean any client and any server. Today, however, we're still priming that pump. The water is beginning to flow, but no one will confuse this dribble with a river.

In the past year, I have made an effort to find good examples of cross-platform applications. The good news is that most of them are very good. The bad news is that there are so few.

Electronic Mail

Many companies find that any expense in integrating NetWare and UNIX is paid for simply by having a single e-mail system across the entire company. E-mail never succeeds unless top management is committed. Having two or three different mail systems isn't committed. Would it make sense to have two different phone systems, keeping marketing from talking to accounting? Of course not, but too many e-mail systems are like that.

E-MAIL PROGRAMS WITH GATEWAYS

Once again, the UNIX world and the Internet have preceded the PC world in solving communication problems. SMTP allows messages to travel above any reliable protocol (TCP/IP on the Internet). The sequence of message delivery, receipt, acknowledgment, and reply is detailed, with delivery exceptions covered. Forwarding? Routing? Multidomain addressing? All situations are covered. Studies have shown about half the total Internet traffic is e-mail. Figure 13.1 shows the official SMTP mail route diagram.

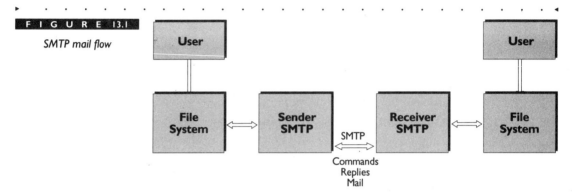

FIGURE 13.1

SMTP mail flow

Since DOS and NetWare don't have such a system, e-mail gateways are used. There are two different types of gateways to consider. One is between the same program on two different systems (PC to UNIX, for instance), and the other is between two different e-mail programs (cc:Mail to WordPerfect Office, for example).

Novell is helping to set guidelines and standards for developers to follow. The NGM (NetWare Global Messaging) specification offers advancements over the current MHS (Message Handling Service). These are not e-mail programs; they provide transport methods and translations for e-mail packages between different systems. Novell has also released SMF (Standard Message Format) specifications. These define how an application should interface to the various Novell messaging services.

The problems to be solved with NetWare e-mail packages operating with different systems are similar to those that SMTP solved already. We need ways to handle the different addressing schemes (From:, To:, and so on), as well as exception handling. MHS particularly helps in this pursuit, and it's the standard for many NetWare customers. If enough MHS gateways are on enough different e-mail products, information can get wherever it needs to go.

The connection of the same program running on unlike platforms requires less software hassle, since the address fields all match up. If vendors use a different format on their Macintosh e-mail than on their PC e-mail, they deserve to suffer serious problems. Many of the UNIX e-mail vendors are starting to offer NetWare versions, and the NetWare e-mail providers are repaying the favor by releasing UNIX versions.

Assuming the address, routing, and message fields do match up properly, the trick is to provide transport between the two systems. Remote connections usually include async dial-up lines or a value-added network (VAN) between the two gateways (often called *mail boxes* or *mail hubs* or *connection servers* or *post offices* or *mail gateways* and on and on). The major e-mail providers, such as MCI Mail, AT&T EasyLink, and CompuServe, are well-known systems that also act as VANs. They provide their own e-mail software or just the transport for other software products.

Between Network A and Network B, there must be several things. The two gateways are normally separate from the mail servers, so there will be four total boxes (two on each side). Between the two gateways will be either an async line, a VAN, a TCP/IP connection, a direct cable connection, or a third-party translation program. Figure 13.2 shows the circuitous route traversed just to bet on Monday Night Football.

The most popular third-party translation program for mail systems is from SoftSwitch. This company made its reputation with mainframe-based e-mail translations, but it released a UNIX version of its software in 1992. The fact that a company can be successful just doing e-mail translations is both good and bad. Good because some companies are serious enough about e-mail to pay for better connectivity, but bad because it's necessary.

The direct connection shown in Figure 13.2 seems like a bad joke, but it isn't. Even advanced e-mail vendors are behind the curve on the integration techniques now available between NetWare and UNIX. Several companies apologetically state that there still must be two gateways between two different networks, even when the transport protocol barrier has been beaten. Oh well.

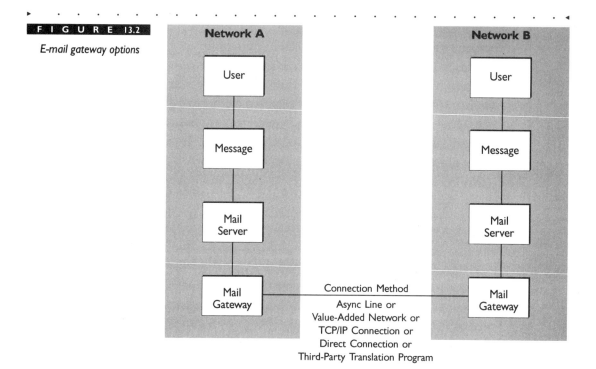

FIGURE 13.2

E-mail gateway options

E-MAIL WITH X.400 AND X.500

One of the harder jobs being done in the standards world is setting up worldwide directory services and addressing schemes. That's the area where X.400 and X.500 are fighting to develop standards and workable products. X.400 e-mail addresses look like:

/g=John /s=Doe /p=amalgamated /a=telemail /c=us

The goal of X.400 was to be the standard for all addressing, but it has yet to work out that way. The cost and complexity of existing systems has kept X.400 as a translation mechanism between disparate systems. That fits with what we're doing here, doesn't it? No matter how awkward the address, if it can be written down once into a directory for the e-mail front-end in use, it will do the job.

While many people consider X.500 just a bigger X.400, that's not the case. X.500 is an emerging directory service standard that will pay big dividends sometime in the next three years. How big? The directory services in NetWare 4.0 are patterned on X.500. If and when the standards get set solidly enough for each vendor to make products that will work together, X.500 will help the cross-platform applications market. The elusive goal is to make computer directory services as easy to use as a telephone.

Right now, the worlds of NetWare and UNIX have completely different addressing schemes. Novell had been criticized by many because it lacked a true distributed directory. Banyan Systems, with its StreetTalk, had been anointed as the system for PC LAN directory services. StreetTalk is an excellent product, but the low market share of Banyan has kept the spread of the product minimal.

In NetWare 4.0, Novell uses X.500 as a basis for its own NetWare Directory Services (NDS). This is an admittedly early implementation of X.500, based on standards that are still vague and prone to be interpreted differently by each vendor. However, when more systems use X.500, the addressing scheme of NetWare will be the same as the addressing scheme of all other distributed systems. That could be handy.

Word Processing: WordPerfect and WordPerfect Office

Developers of the most popular word processor ever, the WordPerfect Corporation actually started by making products for Data General computers. While most companies work hard to port from DOS to UNIX, WordPerfect ported from UNIX to DOS years before it became fashionable.

COMMON FILE FORMATS

One of the best decisions made by WordPerfect was to keep the file format the same for all platforms. A file written on a Macintosh can be transferred to a PC and work perfectly well. A file written on a SPARCstation2 can be used by an OS/2 user. Any file, from anywhere, can be used by any other system running WordPerfect.

The WordPerfect application itself must be written for each platform. A Microsoft Windows version of the WordPerfect program won't run on any system except a PC running Windows. The Macintosh application will not run on an SCO system. Application binary compatibility is different than cross-platform file compatibility and will take many years before it works properly.

Even before networking and DOS to UNIX connectivity, this common file format was handy. Even SneakerNet works fine for swapping a few files around, and with WordPerfect, those files would work on all involved systems.

With the advent of networking and the integration of NetWare and UNIX, SneakerNet is dead. In its place can be systemwide document management and control. With the ability of every user on every platform to have access to data files on all other platforms, programs such as WordPerfect can be implemented on every desktop. Then each desktop user would have access to the same information as every other user. What an idea, shared information!

PRACTICAL EXAMPLES

For the WordPerfect user, many of the techniques described here will give immediate benefit. Don't have enough printers for the UNIX group, but lots of HP LaserJets around? Use either NetWare FLeX/IP or NFS Server to provide a print gateway between UNIX and NetWare. Have a fancy but underutilized PostScript printer on the UNIX side of the house, but none for the PC users? Those same print gateways work both ways.

Need to get copies of contract files from the legal department using NetWare to the manufacturing group running UNIX? You can transfer files with one of the several options discussed, or make the NetWare server an NFS server as well. Perhaps put NetWare for UNIX on one of the UNIX systems in engineering. On the low end, start an FTP Server session in a Windows PC running LAN WorkPlace.

While WordPerfect Office still needs connection servers and gateways between all the different systems, its developer was the first company to offer a complete scheduling and e-mail package that communicated across platforms. That lead is still strong, as it's being challenged by companies doing either scheduling or e-mail, but not both. More software vendors are starting to follow WordPerfect's example of file compatibility across platforms. Perhaps soon that feature will be normal rather than noteworthy.

Databases: SQL and Otherwise

One of the best applications for UNIX systems has always been databases. The advantages of large memory segments for caching and shared program work space, coupled with the fact that all the data can be cached in the same memory work space, gave UNIX the lead in database performance early on. That lead, fueled now by multiprocessor systems, keeps getting larger and larger.

A larger lead over what, you ask? PCs, especially those PCs on a network. As the performance of PCs has gone up, the amount of data in databases has gone up even faster. Graphical front-ends and multimedia data threaten to clog networks, slowing PC networks even more.

This is where client-server, in all its hype and glory, comes in. Allowing the PC (or your desktop system of choice) to handle the presentation of information, while a UNIX system crunches the data into information, takes advantage of the strengths of both platforms. This is where SQL (Structured Query Language) databases fit best in the world.

When Novell added support for TCP/IP in NetWare version 3.11, the database companies threw the development of NLM products into high gear. Before version 3.11, the NLM databases could communicate only with NetWare clients over IPX/SPX. After version 3.11, they could also communicate with existing UNIX databases running over TCP/IP. Software developers with strong installed bases in the UNIX world positively drooled over the large numbers of NetWare users that suddenly could potentially buy their products.

ORACLE SERVER FOR NETWARE

The biggest name in UNIX databases is Oracle. It won the NLM database race, being the first to actually market an NLM version of a UNIX database. The first version still required Oracle's SQL*Net product to reach TCP/IP databases. By the time Oracle Server for NetWare version 1.1 shipped in early 1992, NetWare version 3.11 had TCP/IP well under control. With this product, Oracle NLM-based systems can be a full partner in a TCP/IP database network.

Taking advantage of the flexibility of NLMs, Oracle implemented Novell's DFS (Direct File System) features. This allows the normal read and write disk caches to be bypassed, improving upon NetWare's already outstanding file service performance.

Since more than 70 different SQL front-end products work with Oracle Server for NetWare (and other Oracle databases), few SQL customers should feel left out. Figure 13.3 shows Oracle's illustration of support for multiple clients over IPX/SPX and a host connection over TCP/IP.

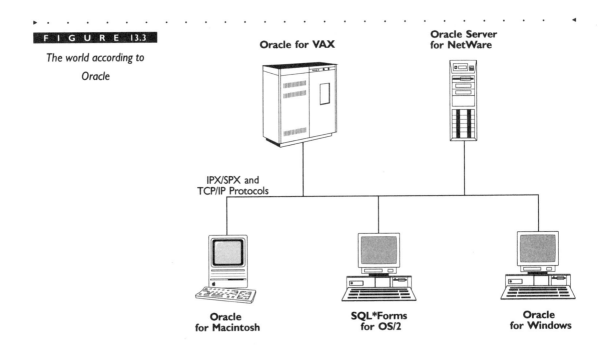

FIGURE 13.3

The world according to Oracle

Oracle for VAX

Oracle Server for NetWare

IPX/SPX and TCP/IP Protocols

Oracle for Macintosh

SQL*Forms for OS/2

Oracle for Windows

Source: Oracle

One of the extra features of using an NLM approach is automatic login to the Oracle database, verified by the NetWare Bindery. Multiple languages are supported, which will make it easy to export to other countries with NetWare 4.0's language module. Soon users in every country will know the joys of rebuilding garbled data files.

GUPTA SQLBASE NLM

A self-professed "PC-centric" company, Gupta rolled the dice with Microsoft Windows early on. Strongly allied with Windows and NetWare, Gupta has also expanded its reach into traditional UNIX SQL territory.

The first "foreign" database Gupta developed links to was Oracle, in the middle of 1990. In 1991, Gupta developed a graphical front-end for the Novell Btrieve program. Btrieve is a server-based (VAP and now NLM) product from Novell that supports only character-based applications. Gupta now supports links to most of the major UNIX databases.

With Windows and OS/2 as preferred clients, Gupta will be in the NetWare camp for quite a while. As the company expands, connections to existing databases will be crucial. Working as an NLM on a NetWare server gives Gupta easy access to the world of TCP/IP.

SYBASE SQL SERVER FOR NETWARE

Another strong UNIX database company similar to Oracle, Sybase released its NetWare product in the middle of 1992. Over 100 PC-based tools and applications are available for use with SQL Server for NetWare. Many of the more popular PC applications and databases have connections for Sybase built in.

Sybase has a strong reputation, especially in the Sun market. The NLM SQL Server for NetWare can communicate, through the TCP/IP supplied by Novell, with all of those UNIX databases.

NETWARE SQL AND BTRIEVE

Btrieve is a key-indexed record management system first introduced in 1983. Many application developers use Btrieve, unbeknownst to many application customers.

If you run accounting applications on NetWare, you probably use Btrieve. If not accounting software, then certainly Novell's LANalyzer, Communications Services Manager, or the Network Management System. If not these, then many of the contact manager, scheduling, or project management software packages.

Since Novell purchased Btrieve in early 1987, it has included support for the product in NetWare 2.*x*, 3.*x* and 4.*x*. The first actual client-server application on a PC LAN, Btrieve gained much more respect from developers than from end users.

Adding a pretty face onto Btrieve is the job of NetWare SQL. This product provides direct relational access to Btrieve-based data. Any SQL front-end, including those built into spreadsheets, query tools, and report writers, can work with NetWare SQL.

With the new integration products available, the path is clear for UNIX-based products to take advantage of NetWare SQL. This ability to retrieve data, no matter which system holds that data, is the key to distributed computing.

X Windows Client-Server Applications

Novell opened the door slightly to X Windows support with the XCONSOLE NLM included with the NFS Server and FLeX/IP software. For the first time, a non-NetWare client could manage the NetWare file server.

Today, this makes a NetWare server manageable by an SNMP management station. All management stations have the ability to *telnet* into the SNMP device being monitored. This feature is used for configuration, since most vendors don't yet trust or support SET commands (no security). Now the NetWare SNMP NLM can be configured in the same manner.

Since many network administrators are controlling a wide variety of equipment today, special PCs for managing NetWare servers are a luxury for some. The ability to completely manage a NetWare server through the RCONSOLE utility helps logistically. The fact that RCONSOLE can now be run from any X Windows or vt100 style terminal helps even more.

For those of you not familiar with NetWare utilities, RCONSOLE controls file server system information, but has no control over users or files. Although

RCONSOLE users can install new products and manage all the various NLMs on the server, they cannot get their hands on anything else. This helps soothe the security conscious, because data, passwords, and all file and printer access privileges are separate from the authorities of the RCONSOLE operator. This is strictly *telnet* support of server management.

Big deal, you say. Supporting *telnet* is old hat in the UNIX world. True. However, it's brand new in the PC networking neighborhood. Novell has quietly included what many feel is just the tip of an interoperable iceberg with X Windows support. The ability to support TCP/IP and X Window terminals today portends even more UNIX to NetWare interaction in the future.

Other Office Automation Products

The river of cross-platform products is swelling, and the dam is starting to leak. This is affirmation of the "if we connect it, they will come" nature of software. Provide transport layers between dissimilar systems, and the software developer's job is much easier. The developers of Lotus' Notes supposedly spent 60 percent of their time making connections between platforms, since there weren't any trustworthy transports when they started. When this type of barrier to software development is broken, companies without the resources of Lotus will be able to bring products to market. This might not thrill the people at places like Lotus, Microsoft, and WordPerfect, but it makes users ecstatic.

Some software companies are already bravely crossing flimsy rope bridges across yawning chasms of differing protocols. WordPerfect has set the standard for file compatibility across platforms. SoftSolutions, makers of a document management system closely allied with WordPerfect and Novell, has crossed that rope bridge as well.

SOFTSOLUTIONS

Once a product that supported only WordPerfect and NetWare, SoftSolutions version 3.0 now works on all PC LAN systems and most UNIX platforms. One single document database can concurrently support DOS, Windows, UNIX, and

OpenVMS clients, with Macintosh client support on the way. If you prefer, multiple databases on multiple platforms can be searched by a single client. The order of remote database search can be prioritized, and WAN links are supported between servers on different platforms. Figure 13.4 is SoftSolutions' example of its system.

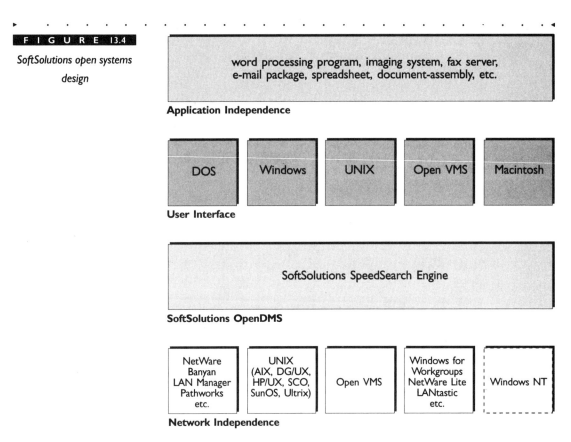

FIGURE 13.4

SoftSolutions open systems design

The SoftSolutions Server Enhancement Modules (SEM) are NLMs that provide the client-server horsepower for their Novell network customers. Since any client can query any database (if it has a connection), protocol pathways are important.

The solution in the past for PC clients accessing UNIX databases was to use PC/NFS from Sun. Although this certainly works, adding NFS to each PC can be expensive in both dollars and RAM. In testing, I was able to concurrently access both the Sun and NetWare database engines from a single DOS client using only IPX/SPX on the PC. Although SoftSolutions had no way of knowing its product would work through the beta version of NetWare NFS Gateway, it did. Figure 13.5 shows the database profile screen.

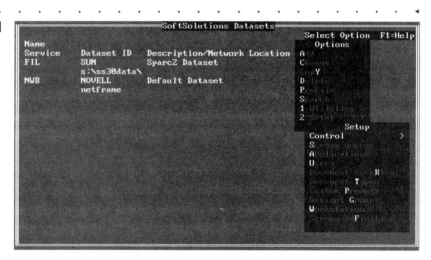

F I G U R E 13.5

Concurrent access to multiple dataset platforms

The NetFRAME dataset is on the default NetWare server, and it's the default dataset. The Sparc2 dataset is on a SPARCstation2 running SunOS. It's reached through NFS Gateway on a second Novell file server.

CLOCKWISE

ClockWise version 2.0 is a UNIX scheduling program that now has a NetWare version for DOS clients. In an example of breaking barriers between the two worlds, the marketing literature states "Interoperates with our UNIX version on a LAN running PC/NFS, Portable NetWare, or equivalent."

The program uses a single scheduling database that runs on either NetWare or UNIX. Clients from both operating systems can use this database, much like the SoftSolutions approach. The trick is to get PCs to UNIX, or UNIX to a NetWare server.

Experience suggests that the same NetWare NFS Gateway that worked with SoftSolutions will work with ClockWise. The mention of Portable NetWare (NetWare for UNIX) in the ClockWise literature suggests another way of connecting client and server. That file-sharing capability between UNIX and NetWare running on the same host system described in Chapter 10 just became a bit more important.

Boycott for Better Connections

SoftSolutions is an excellent product, but is no longer the only document management software that can work in this type of mixed environment. ClockWise is at the front of the pack for schedulers, but that lead may not last too long. If your favorite software doesn't work across platforms, complain. The software (and hardware) providers won't know how important connectivity is if we don't tell them.

How can we tell the vendors we want better connections? Don't be shortsighted in purchasing. Even if you might run a single environment today, you realize that will change (or you wouldn't be reading this book). Don't settle for single-platform products, because they will be outdated when things change, as you know they will. Whether it's choreographed or whether it's chaos, change will come.

Try to put the roadblocks as far down the road as possible. By this, I mean choose the network foundation today that will get you the farthest tomorrow. Stick with standards, such as can be found, in every area of your computing environment. But remember that standards for standards sake alone don't make sense, and that some standards have little real-world support. The marketplace makes standards as well, and at least the standards made by market share usually help sway the committees. The reverse is not alway true. The OSI protocol is having little luck replacing TCP/IP, even though that's what the committee planned.

Above all, don't be shy when dealing with vendors. Demand better connections.

Novell and USL: What Happens Next?

When Novell acquired USL (Unix Software Laboratories) in the spring of 1993, all the "Crown Jewels" of Unix were included. Which parts of Unix might Novell appropriate for NetWare in this vast technology transfer? What positive (and negative) consequences might be in the future?

New Technology

Official word about future technology benefits is nonexistent. The complex nature of NetWare precludes any immediate upgrades. The development of Net-Ware 4.0 was too far along to include any substantial changes, no matter what Novell might have gained from USL.

Another reason for little immediate action by Novell is the fact that all of USL's technology has been known and available to NetWare developers since the summer of 1991. That was when USL was spun off from AT&T, and Novell surprised many UNIX watchers by becoming one of the original equity investors. As such, the Novell folks were in a position to see what was available in the technology arena and to license the pieces that were interesting to them. At the time, Novell executives said that the company had an active interest in UNIX since the early details of SVR4, several years before the spin-off of USL. So we might expect that there are no secret treasure chests of technology that Novell will have access to above and beyond what every other licensee is authorized to use.

No substantive information is available, and there will be none until probably mid-1994. Novell has been concerned about the impact of the purchase on UNIX licensees and loyalists. The Novell executives have handled this well, as evidenced by the lack of hysteria among the computer community. Novell has portrayed this acquisition as positive for all involved parties. Popular opinion seems to regard the acquisition as positive as well.

A good question to ask now seems to be: What will NetWare gain from UNIX? You can also ask: Will UNIX gain anything from NetWare?

Off the record, long-term NetWare third-party developers and Novell executives have mentioned several areas of UNIX technology as particularly helpful to Novell. These included programming interfaces in the code (APIs), multiprocessor support, and process scheduling changes.

Programming Wars

New APIs in UNIX can be modeled after existing and proposed NetWare APIs without compromising existing applications. By adding these hooks in the software for developers, the technical challenges of porting UNIX applications to NetWare will be lessened. Database companies that make both NetWare and UNIX versions, such as Oracle and Sybase, will benefit immediately. While the same compiled code will never run (well, probably never in the next few years) on both systems, the amount of product code that will need to be changed should decrease from as much as 50 percent to as little as 5 percent.

This API coordination is one important battle in the war to lure developers. Microsoft, the avowed enemy of Novell and more recently the UNIX world as Windows NT hits the streets, has so far won the PR battle for common code across multiple platforms. The number of Windows APIs is still numerous, with more differences between them than anyone at Microsoft will admit, but they all say "Windows" somewhere in the name. That kind of consistency looks good, and sometimes it's better to look good than to run good. If programmers are swayed by the hype and don't discover until later how wide the disparity is between some API sets, they have only themselves to blame.

Software publishers in the commercial market have the most to gain from consistent APIs. They also have the biggest stick to use against the operating system vendors, since applications often drive upgrades and operating system changes. I would guess that the resistance to Windows of many WordPerfect users was stronger before the WordPerfect for Windows version was released than it was after. Although WordPerfect alone might not be able to make a big difference, add those users with the users of Lotus 1-2-3, Paradox, Harvard Graphics, and so on, and a trend emerges.

To digress just a bit more, Microsoft defends its Windows applications products by pointing out that few big software companies started writing Windows applications when Windows was released. That's true for two important reasons that sometimes get left out of this discussion. First, Windows was fairly awful at the beginning. Only in version 3.1, the fifth major iteration of the product, is Windows stable enough (usually) to trust as the primary operating system for important applications.

Second, IBM and Microsoft both were telling the big developers to get ahead of the curve on OS/2. If you want to be a computing force in the 1990's, they told developers, you better ante up on OS/2 starting now. Even the largest software companies have limited resources, and few could commit large development teams to both Windows and OS/2. WordPerfect, as an example, bought the OS/2 story hook, line, and sinker. This is probably the reason for its late Windows version introduction.

The tale of WordPerfect for Windows shows how technoid details that end users never see have enormous impact on the computer business. The story that developers want to hear from Novell is that UNIX will continue on, only stronger. Tying software development to APIs that work on both NetWare and UNIX can only make the developers even happier. If the company is traditionally UNIX oriented, the NetWare option gives it millions of potential new customers. If the company is NetWare oriented, the power of UNIX servers in the client-server arena suddenly improves its product performance tenfold with little effort on the company's part. Both sides win.

NetWare has long been a fan of the RPC (Remote Procedure Call) method for distributed computing. NetWare 386 added support for Streams, giving more UNIX flavor to NetWare NLM programs. Aligning these functions between NetWare and UNIX would again help developers to provide a NetWare version of UNIX programs. Even those developers not interested in making applications for a second platform benefit. Interprogram communication is going to be more important tomorrow than today, and the more options developers have, the better the results should be.

The Novell–HyperDesk Connection

Novell bought 20 percent of HyperDesk in early 1993, gaining access to all of that company's products. The most important of those products is Distributed Object Management System (DOMS). Perhaps you noticed the object-orientation of NetWare 4.0? That's just the beginning, folks.

OOPS is no longer an admission of a mistake; it stands for Object Oriented Programming System. *Programming objects* are self-sufficient code modules that are reusable. They're popular with the New Age programmers. Cynics point out that structured programming had all the benefits of OOPS without the pretentiousness, but what's a good idea without buzzwords?

DOMS is part of a new breed of object-oriented software labeled "middleware" because it works in between dissimilar systems. In this case, it goes between unfriendly application layers and their supporting layers. The OMG (Object Management Group) has set some standards for this area, and HyperDesk is the first company to produce DOMS products. Novell is the first large PC company (if you can still call Novell a PC-centric company, something once claimed proudly) to get into this area.

This arrangement gives developers an alternative to Microsoft's WOSA (Windows Open Services Architecture). In typical Microsoft fashion, WOSA serves the world of Windows and Windows NT, but pretty much stops there. All the distributed pieces of the Microsoft programming puzzle for developers lean much too heavily on Windows.

With Novell getting into the act, perhaps with NOSA (Network Open Services Architecture, the name suggested by Nina Lytton of the *Open Systems Advisor Newsletter*), developers have an option to WOSA. It will be simple for Novell to set common APIs for NetWare and UnixWare since it controls both of them. It will be much more difficult for Novell to force USL and the UNIX source code licensees in that direction.

But another angle is that the UNIX licensees are pushing themselves in the direction of object-oriented technology. HyperDesk's ORB (Object Request Broker) provides a means for Novell to offer all NetWare's file, print, naming, directory, and other services to developers through a uniform API. That same ORB technology is being implemented by UNIX heavyweights (Sun, HP, and DEC) through support of the CORBA (Common ORB Architecture) specifications from the OMG. Had enough MLAs (Multi-Letter Acronyms)?

Developers will someday, if this continues in the best possible direction, be able to write one program and compile it for all the different operating systems. Do you have a great utility that scans text for words that came to English from Portugese? With this system, you write the text-scanning routines once, and the files from various operating systems will be reached through the File Scan object. The savings in programmer time will get you your yacht down payment faster than previously possible.

The Pull of NetWare

Let me mention two quick examples of the tide pulling in the direction of NetWare, both from our friends at Sun. First of all, Sun officials admitted when they unveiled NetWare SunLink that customers demanded the ability to connect NetWare and SunOS more fervently than they demanded any other product. Now, PR people are prone to make statements such as these no matter what limited value the released product may actually have. However, NetWare SunLink is the only product in the SunLink family, or in all of Sun for that matter, where the SunLink name comes second. It's not SunLink NetWare, it's NetWare SunLink. My guess is that placing NetWare first was not an accident.

The recent upgrade of Sun's SoftPC product, the software that emulates a PC operating system inside SunOS and Solaris, also typifies this Novell pull. The most requested improvement in the product was the ability for that virtual PC to be able to connect to a NetWare file server.

Some other companies placing Novell protocols inside a UNIX system of one kind or another have already been discussed. It's easy to see the trend here of NetWare support soon being a regular feature of all UNIX systems and customer requests. Novell doesn't need to force UNIX buyers to support NetWare; the NetWare customers are forcing the issue themselves. Between the two, a focused customer base can sway a vendor much faster than can Novell.

Process Scheduling

NetWare and UNIX use different process scheduling schemes. UNIX is based on an equal time, equal share process. NetWare uses a weighted priority scheme to enhance certain functions' performance.

In NetWare, the oldest continuing process rises up the priority ladder to get more system attention. This provides the extra speed necessary to finish file activities and keep client job requests moving quickly in the system.

The NetWare system is in contrast to the UNIX method of preemptive multitasking, where certain processes can always interrupt and get service when necessary. NetWare is nonpreemptive, and therefore less suited for applications requiring guaranteed response times.

One developer of a NetWare for UNIX product mentioned privately that perhaps Novell should teach UNIX how to handle multiple processes in the way that NetWare handles them.

What Can UNIX Learn from NetWare?

This brings up an area many observers have become excited about: Novell teaching UNIX how to succeed in the market. After all, NetWare has become by far the dominant LAN operating system, even after repeated attempts by giants Microsoft and IBM to control that market. If you can say nothing good about Novell, you still must grudgingly admit that it controls the LAN market. Novell must know how to get customers and keep them happy.

That "getting and keeping" knowledge will be important for UNIX in the next few years. The traditional UNIX customer will not stray from UNIX unless Novell completely messes it up. Even then, the investment in training, hardware, and most important, software will provide enormous inertia to stay put.

The "getting" part is for UNIX on the desktop. Only the most fanatic UNIX-oid can make a claim for raw, character-based UNIX as the operating system of choice for the corporate desktop. The majority of the world realizes that graphical interfaces and ease of use are the tickets for enlarging the market share of UNIX.

Novell has done well at making Corporate America comfortable. Even in the beginning of the corporate push by Novell, when networks were listed as "office equipment" to avoid getting the MIS group involved, NetWare made users like the operating system. The MIS groups that once tried to thwart Novell are now integrating NetWare into the corporate network, running more critical applications every day.

How Will Novell Influence UNIX?

How Novell will influence UNIX is the big question, of course. UNIX fans and developers have worried for quite a while about the future of UNIX. AT&T, where UNIX was developed, never pushed and marketed UNIX with the committment that UNIX deserves. In fact, even worthless and derivative operating systems had considerably more marketing support than did UNIX.

The spin-off of USL verified the accusations that AT&T was unable to properly sell UNIX because of government restrictions. AT&T was dismembered by the Consent Decree in 1984, and the computer division was officially separated from government oversight. The miserable marketing done by AT&T after 1984 can't be blamed on the government; AT&T management must shoulder that responsibility. The creation of USL was a belated attempt to provide UNIX the marketing and management necessary to compete in the red-hot wars of computer operating systems.

Remember, all this happened during the creation of OS/2, developed by IBM and Microsoft because DOS couldn't keep up with the demands of the users. Customers wanted a GUI, they wanted multitasking, they wanted networking, they wanted larger memory segments available for programs, and they wanted robust development platforms. I contend that if AT&T and USL were doing their jobs, UNIX would have filled that gap and we would be five years farther down the road today, rather than at the beginning of the commercialization of UNIX by Novell.

UNIXWARE: THE FACE OF UNIX UNDER NOVELL?

The early guideposts for the future of UNIX may (or may not) be seen in the new UnixWare product from Univel. Univel is the company created jointly by Novell and USL (before the buyout) to help commercialize a specific vision of what UNIX SVR4.2 should be. That specific vision was to make a commercially successful product to be sold by NetWare dealers primarily for NetWare installations.

Novell executives are well aware of the extra burden the purchase of USL has placed on them. While it's appropriate to release one UNIX version among many with a blatant NetWare bias, it's not appropriate to push that bias into the official source code of UNIX.

But since this is all we have to go on, let's take our best shot at figuring out what UNIX might become under Novell.

The feature list of UnixWare is impressive, and it reflects the "serve the customer" aspect Novell brought to UNIX. Features of UnixWare, some standard and some optional, include the following:

- ▸ The ability to run programs written for SVR4, SCO, X, DOS, and Microsoft Windows

- ▸ Support for fairly typical PC hardware platforms

- ▸ The ability to use NetWare server services

- ▸ The ability to communicate with traditional UNIX systems with TCP/IP and NFS

- ▸ The ability to load systems from UnixWare or NetWare servers across the network

- ▸ A long heritage as a multitasking, multithreaded operating system

The NetWare interaction gathered the most press. Never before had a UNIX system started out aimed at NetWare users. The biggest target market of Unix-Ware seemed to be those NetWare customers getting into UNIX, not the traditional UNIX world.

UnixWare offers both a Personal Edition and Application Server. This seems to be a logical breakdown, given that Novell bought Digital Research for its desktop DOS expertise and already knows plenty about being a server system. It also reflects the way the UNIX desktop market is going.

The Personal Edition, able to support two concurrent users but realistically meant to serve only one power user as a multitasking desktop system, initially shipped without TCP/IP support. Univel officials constantly denied that the Personal Edition was meant to compete with Windows, OS/2, or Windows NT.

I think that attitude was a mistake. Originally $495 without TCP/IP or Windows support, the Personal Edition was later offered for half that price. It would have been a better idea to offer TCP/IP, NFS, and Windows support initially at the $500 mark and gone into the market with courage and purpose. Not only would the company have avoided the backtracking soon after release, but it would have set the price and benchmark for Windows NT months before Microsoft was ready to roll out product.

The Application Server comes complete with everything a PC-based UNIX operating system should. Besides TCP/IP and NFS, NVT also ships with the system. This allows any NetWare client, as well as typical UNIX systems, to become clients to the Application Server.

Following the trend set by Sun with Solaris, the C compiler doesn't ship with either system. This puts probably the final nail in the coffin of the "traditional" UNIX system, in which many of the applications are developed by the system administrator and users. The rise of shrink-wrapped UNIX applications is upon us, and there are several binary-compatibility specifications available so application developers can write one program that runs on any Intel microprocessor-based UNIX host.

UNIXWARE AND NETWARE FOR UNIX

One question for many people concerning the Application Server was the use of that platform to support NetWare for UNIX. Since Novell controls both Unix-Ware and NetWare, isn't that a natural next step?

Well, yes and no. The Univel executives have always said that NetWare for UNIX was something of interest. This may be just politeness, but more likely it's smart marketing. Certainly UnixWare salespeople want a shot at NetWare installations, as does every other NetWare for UNIX vendor. But is this a priority? I doubt it.

UnixWare already includes the ability to share files and printers with NetWare clients. NVT is provided, so those legacy character-based UNIX applications are accessible to NetWare clients as well. These are two big advantages of NetWare for UNIX, and UnixWare already has them.

Is this a tempting platform for developers once common APIs are available between UNIX and NetWare? Certainly. This pairing will be less complicated than most others for initial development of a mixed-operating system application. But that's still several years away, unfortunately.

NetWare has little to gain by dumping the Runtime operating system in favor of UnixWare. Some people believe this is coming soon, but I doubt it. Novell engineers are proud of their performance and won't willingly give up that lead. Porting all of NetWare to a UnixWare Application Server environment will take that peformance lead away. For that reason before all others, don't look for it to happen anytime soon.

THE MARKETING OF THE NEW UNIX

NetWare dealers have first crack at selling UnixWare, but they must show UNIX proficiency to be authorized. UNIX resellers of SCO, Sun, or other brands must show some level of NetWare proficiency before they are authorized to sell UnixWare. Novell has developed the strongest and largest operating system reseller channel in the computer business to sell NetWare. Whether that success will be repeated with UnixWare, and UNIX in general, remains to be seen.

Marketing has been the weak point of UNIX from the beginning. Cynics might say that DOS has marketing but no engineering, while UNIX has strong engineering and no marketing. Novell has been cursed at times for having more dealers than can adequately support the customers, but the success and penetration of NetWare can't be faulted. While NetWare has some weak points, it's getting better every version and has always been the leader of the market.

How will Novell carry this plan of dealer saturation into the UNIX market? Where UNIX in the past was limited to OEMs and those few dealers able to write vertical market applications, Novell will open things up. It won't get 11,000 dealers as it has with NetWare, but the dealer base will expand tremendously. Look for more hardware and networking dealers to sell UnixWare every day, and the overlap of strong UNIX and NetWare resellers to be 90 percent by the end of 1994.

This does not say Novell will sell the USL Crown Jewels, the UNIX source code, to anyone besides official licensees. Univel will continue to carry Novell's particular vision of UNIX to market under the UnixWare name. The revenue stream of licensees to large companies (Sun, IBM, SCO, DEC, HP, and everyone else you care to name) must continue. Major changes in that market are far in the future.

Even though the source code must remain separate from the crassly commercial concerns, it's just good business for Novell to better integrate APIs from NetWare and UNIX. Novell may well be clever enough to get the source code licensees to ask for those common APIs, to better integrate NetWare and UNIX based on customer requests.

Novell executives have long shown the ability to get along with every company while competing with those same companies. This is in the world of DOS, where the spirit of sharing and community is as common as winning lottery tickets. The UNIX world will soon realize that Novell is tough to beat, but profitable to accommodate.

NetWare/IP: More Integration Coming Soon

One of the oft-reported but not yet official programs at Novell is NetWare/IP. This is the project porting all the NetWare client utilities from IPX/SPX to TCP/IP.

The NetWare server can certainly speak TCP/IP with the best of them, as we have seen in numerous examples. The missing part has been the ability to speak TCP/IP to NetWare clients. That's what NetWare/IP is all about.

This is not as simple as porting a few NetWare utilities to UNIX. All the NetWare utilities are tightly bound into NCP (NetWare Core Protocol) and rely on IPX specific functions in many cases. Separating some of these utilities from IPX is a tough job, one that has lasted for several years (according to rumors).

Success will be accomplished, however. UnixWare has some of the work already shipping, since the utilities are executed as UNIX utilities, not DOS. File and print services are available to the UnixWare client running UNIX programs, even if the transport mechanism is still IPX/SPX today. At least the Novell engineers and programmers have released a live product that includes NetWare utilities running on a UNIX platform.

UNIX hosts already make contact with the NetWare server, the UNIX naming convention is supported, and NetWare servers will work with UNIX name servers.

Most of the puzzle pieces are in place. NetWare/IP is a logical next step, just as NetWare NFS Gateway was a logical next step from NetWare NFS Server.

Novell has been methodically nailing down all corners of the UNIX tent. Every area of interaction has been identified and systematically dealt with. From printing to file service to terminal emulation to FTP to NFS to NetWare for UNIX, every bet is covered. Areas not yet represented by products, such as NetWare/IP, are in the gunsights, you can be sure.

Coming Attractions

Watch the papers for details on the new IPX/SPX protocols. Novell has been working to make its protocols perform better over WAN links. Burst mode protocol is the first step in that area, and more improvements are coming.

The development of a new NetWare "Internet," or global network of distributed IPX-based networks, is well underway. Much has been made of the conflicts within the Internet community concerning commercial use, growing popularity, and a limited number of total IP addresses available.

IPX/SPX was based on XNS (Xerox Network Services) protocol. The numbering scheme used allows well over four billion total addresses to be connected. Compare that to the Internet IP limit of just over two million, and the potential for NetWare to support a worldwide scheme becomes apparent.

Why would this happen? What will Novell gain from this? Not much in direct dollars, since each network will be responsible for its own hardware, software, and connection costs on the network. But this would certainly slam-dunk those PC LAN competitors that gripe about NetWare's inability to work in a wide, distributed environment, wouldn't it?

Remember also that the world is looking for an alternative to SNA. As applications migrate from the mainframe to PCs, the ability to provide that application to widely dispersed users is vitally important. What better way to prove that ability than a global NetWare-net?

New Hardware Options

The most obvious benefit for Novell from a horsepower standpoint is multi-processor support, codified in USL's SVR4.2, which was released last year. With the multiprocessor support built into the kernel, this code headstart could help Novell shorten the time to market. Judging from Novell's history and operating system philosophies, however, this is unlikely.

Novell has always slanted performance heavily toward file service for the Net-Ware clients. Novell is extremely protective of its products' performance advantages over LAN Manager and Banyan VINES, and will not easily forfeit 10 percent or more of their performance for the overhead required in current multiprocessor technology. Since file and print services are not CPU bound, symmetrical multiprocessing will have little advantage.

Asymmetrical multiprocessing is a different matter. More than five years ago, Novell released a disk coprocessor board to speed disk activity. This was before SCSI (Small Computer Systems Interface) drivers allowed the throughput they do today. The company has some experience with a master-slave processor arrangement.

Novell officials privately mentioned that multiprocessor support, when and if added to NetWare, will be in the form of an NLM. The NLM arrangement—loading a background process after the main server kernel program, and working under the control of the operating system, as does the UNIX daemon—is asymmetrical. An NLM is best suited to a master-slave processor pairing, as with the earlier disk coprocessor board.

The Philosophical Fit

More than any other PC company, Novell understands the sense of community and shared interests that has long been a UNIX tradition. Ray Noorda coined the term "coopetition" and still maintains that a rising tide raises all boats. This idea fits well with the UNIX spirit of community and shared search for better systems that made UNIX a success.

For those last diehards that still object to Novell "owning" UNIX, I have one question: What other company with the resources to make it in today's market (something USL was too small to do according to some analysts) would better advance the cause of distributed computing and UNIX than Novell?

Is Novell trustworthy? It has long avoided making applications that run over its own network. Specifications for e-mail and management, yes, but applications, no. Btrieve, the only program that could be called an application, exists more to serve other applications by providing fast record retrieval at the server than as an end-user product. Both Btrieve and the new SQL product have minimal market presence with end users. The other NetWare NLMs look more like operating system extensions than applications, and Novell has made it easy for competitors to challenge every one of those products.

Can you imagine Microsoft taking over UNIX? How about IBM, HP, or DEC? (the snake-oil description of UNIX by a DEC founder still rankles many UNIX fans). Sun? AT&T again? Government committee?

Each of the companies mentioned has strong application and/or hardware lines in the market. I doubt HP could take over UNIX and convince DEC that everything is still fair, open, and equitable. I doubt any hardware vendor could resist the temptation to tweak some low-level functions to "slightly" improve performance of UNIX on their particular hardware platform. Microsoft has always been accused of tweaking DOS to better support its own applications, so Microsoft couldn't make anyone feel comfortable.

Novell turns out to be the best choice for a variety of reasons. The most compelling reason, however, is the concentrated effort Novell has put forth the last few years to better serve the UNIX community along with its own NetWare customers.

This is a new generation for computer operating systems, asked to do more every day. UNIX is 20 years old, and is ready to step out into the larger world of corporate workhorse. Think not of Novell "owning" UNIX, rather that Novell accepts guardianship of UNIX.

Of all the companies that could direct the spread of UNIX, the best choice is Novell.

Recommended Reading

A ton of books have been written about NetWare, and nearly as many about UNIX. The books listed here are the ones I consulted during the research and writing phase of this book. I can't grade the quality of every NetWare and UNIX book on the market, but I can say these proved to be the most useful to me. Take these references as a starting point. They are organized not by quality but by authors' last name.

Books on UNIX

Comer, Douglas
Internetworking with TCP/IP
Prentice Hall, 1988
Englewood Cliffs, NJ

Enck, John
A Manager's Guide to Multivendor Networks
Professional Press Books, 1991
Horsham, PA

Feibus, Andrew
UNIX, Quick!
Professional Press Books, 1991
Horsham, PA

Frisch, Aleen
Essential System Administration
O'Reilly & Associates, Inc.
Sebastopol, CA

Heslop, Brent; Angell, David
Mastering SunOS
SYBEX, 1990
Alameda, CA

Heslop, Brent; Angell, David
Mastering Solaris 2
SYBEX, 1993
Alameda, CA

Kehoe, Brendan
Zen and the Art of the Internet
Prentice Hall, 1993
Englewood Cliffs, NJ

Kelly-Bootle, Stan
Understanding UNIX
SYBEX, 1992
Alameda, CA

Kitalong, Karla; Lee, Steven; Marzin, Paul
Inside Solaris: SunOS and OpenWindows
New Riders Publishing, 1992
Carmel, IN

Lynch, Daniel; Rose, Marshall (Editors)
Internet System Handbook
Addison-Wesley Publishing Company Inc., 1993
Reading, MA

Norton, Peter; Hahn, Harley
Peter Norton's Guide to UNIX
Bantam Computer Books, 1991
New York, NY

Topham, Douglas
A DOS User's Guide to UNIX
Simon and Schuster, 1990
New York, NY

Books on NetWare

Currid, Cheryl; Gillett, Craig
Mastering Novell NetWare
SYBEX, 1990
Alameda, CA

McCann, John; Ruef, Adam; Guengerich, Steven
NetWare Supervisor's Guide
M&T Publishing, Inc., 1989
Redwood City, CA

Miller, Mark
LAN Protocol Handbook
M&T Publishing, Inc., 1990
Redwood City, CA

Product Sources

This appendix lists the products mentioned in the book along with their sources. It also identifies the equipment used to test the NetWare-to-UNIX products and includes the addresses of the companies that offer this equipment.

Products for Integrating UNIX and NetWare Networks

The products are grouped somewhat arbitrarily but as logically as possible:

- ► TCP/IP software on the NetWare client

- ► TCP/IP gateways

- ► TCP Gateway 386

- ► NetWare on UNIX hosts

- ► NetWare on VMS hosts

- ► IPX/SPX on UNIX hosts for terminal emulation

- ► IPX/SPX on VMS hosts for terminal emulation

- ► Cross-platform products

- ► NetWare for UNIX program partners

Many companies provide a wide variety of products, but I've tried not to let them overwhelm the companies with only one applicable product.

TCP/IP SOFTWARE ON THE NETWARE CLIENT

LAN WorkGroup
Novell, Inc.
122 East 1700 South
Provo, UT 84606
801-429-7000
800-453-1267

All major PC TCP/IP packages will coexist with NetWare in the PC or Macintosh client. The advantage to LAN WorkGroup is that it is manageable from a central location: the NetWare file server.

TCP/IP GATEWAYS

Catipult
Ipswitch, Inc.
580 Main Street
Reading, MA 01867
617-942-0621
Internet: *support@ipswitch.com*

TCP GATEWAY 386

This category includes TCP Gateway 386 and other assorted versions of this product.

NCM (Networking and Communications Management, Inc.)
6803 Whittier Avenue, Suite 100
McLean, VA 22101
703-847-0040

Novix
Firefox Communications
P.O. Box 8165
Kirkland, WA 98034-0165
206-827-9066

PowerFUSION (NetBIOS only)
Performance Technology
800 Lincoln Center
7800 IH 10 West
San Antonio, TX 78230
512-349-2000

NETWARE ON UNIX HOSTS

This category includes products for NetWare on UNIX hosts; they are not full NetWare for UNIX.

NetCon
Mini-Byte Software
1154 St. Georges Avenue
Avanel, NJ 07001
908-855-9660

SoftNet Utilities
Puzzle Systems Corporation
16360 Monterey Road, Suite 250
Morgan Hill, CA 95037
408-779-9909
Internet: *jal@puzzle.com*

SprySoft
Spry, Inc.
1319 Dexter Avenue North
Seattle, WA 98109
206-286-1722
Internet: *sales@spry.com*

NETWARE ON VMS HOSTS

This category includes products for the VMS version of NetWare for UNIX. The Leverage for NetWare product is the successor to the early NetWare for VMS product sold by Novell.

Leverage for NetWare
InterConnections, Inc. (an Emulex Company)
14711 N.E. 29th Place
Bellevue, WA 98007
206-881-5773

MultiWare
TGV, Inc.
603 Mission Street
Santa Cruz, CA 95060
408-427-4366

IPX/SPX ON UNIX HOSTS FOR TERMINAL EMULATION

PopTerm/NVT
RDS (Rational Data Systems, Inc.)
1050 Northgate Drive
San Rafael, CA 94903
415-499-3354
Internet: *melissa@rds.com*

SCO IPX/SPX
SCO
400 Encinal Street
Santa Cruz, CA 95061-1900
408-425-7222
Internet: *infor@sco.com*

UniLink
MCS (Micro Computer Systems, Inc.)
2300 Valley View Lane, Suite 800
Irving, TX 75062
214-659-1514

IPX/SPX ON VMS HOSTS FOR TERMINAL EMULATION

TES (Terminal Emulation Services) NetWare and WinTerm for Windows
InterConnections, Inc. (an Emulex Company)
14711 N.E. 29th Place
Bellevue, WA 98007
206-881-5773

CROSS-PLATFORM PRODUCTS

Axis AX-5
Axis Communications
99 Rosewood Drive, Suite 170
Danvers, MA 01923
508-777-7957
Internet: *info@axisinc.com*

ClockWise Scheduling Software
PhaseII Software Corporation
444 Washington Street
Woburn, MA 01801
617-937-0256

EPS1
LanTronix
26072 Merit Circle, Suite 113
Laguna Hills, CA 92653
714-367-0500
Internet: *sales@lantronix.com*

Legato NetWorker Tape Backup Systems
Legato Systems, Inc.
260 Sheridan Avenue
Palo Alto, CA 94306
415-329-7880

Optical Drives: CD-ROM, WORM, Read/Writable, Jukeboxes
Micro Design International, Inc.
6985 University Boulevard
Winter Park, FL 32792
407-677-8333

SoftSolutions Document Management System
SoftSolutions Technology Corporation
Parkview Plaza
635 South State Street
Orem, UT 84058
801-226-6000

WordPerfect Word Processor
WordPerfect Office
WordPerfect Corporation
1555 N. Technology Way
Orem, UT 84057
801-222-5300

NETWARE FOR UNIX PROGRAM PARTNERS

This category includes companies that provide full NetWare server implementations on a UNIX host. This list contains all the official NetWare for UNIX licensees. Most of these companies have products available, although some do not offer those products directly to end users or in the United States. The location given is for the contact point for NetWare for UNIX, which may or may not be a sales location. It's easier to get information about products from a local sales office.

Altos
San Jose, CA

AT&T/NCR
Lincroftk, NJ

ComputerVision Services
Framingham, MA

Data General
Westbro, MA

Digital Equipment Corporation
Littleton, MA

Dolphin Server Tech
Oslo, Norway

Feith Systems and Software
Fort Washington, PA

Hewlett Packard
Cupertino, CA

Hitachi Software Engineering Company
Yokohama 231, Japan

IBM Corporation
Armonk, NY

ICL Corporation
Bracknell Berkshire England

Innovus
Hamilton, Ontario

Intergraph Corporation
Huntsvill, AL

MIPS/Silicon Graphics
Sunnyvale, CA

Pyramid Technology Corporation
San Jose, CA

Rational Data Systems
San Rafael, CA

Sequent
Beaverton, OR

Stratus Computer
Marlboro, MA

SunConnect (A Sun Microsystems Company)
Billerica, MA

Texas Instruments
Dallas, TX

Unisys Corporation
Mission Viejo, CA

Wang Laboratories, Inc.
Lowell, MA

Network Equipment

The following equipment was used for testing the NetWare-to-UNIX connections discussed in this book.

COMPUTERS

NetFRAME NF100 NetWare File Server is one of the earliest of the "superservers." The NetFRAME line includes high-performance file servers, ranging from 386/25 models (like the one used for this book) up to systems with multiple 486 processors. The memory and IO systems of NetFRAME are specifically designed for NetWare support, and its performance under load consistently ranks well above that of standard PCs used as NetWare servers. Add the fault-tolerant design, the huge amount of RAM supported, and the custom remote control management, and the reasons for the NetFRAME's large base of corporate installations becomes obvious.

NetFRAME Systems, Incorporated.
1545 Barber Lane
Milpitas, CA 95035
408-944-0600

Sun SPARCstation 2, listed as *sparc2* in the book, came with a huge (19-inch) color monitor, 32 MB of RAM, a CD-ROM, and a 400 MB disk. More than anything else, this system points out what PC-based GUIs should strive to be. The

OpenLook interface and SunOS operating system is another example of UNIX's maturity and experience compared with DOS.

Sun Microsystems, Inc.
2550 Garcia Avenue
Mountain Valley, CA 94043
415-960-1300

The parts of both *altos486*, the UNIX system, and ALTOS486, the NetWare file server, were played by an Altos 4500. This 486, EISA-based unit with 32 MB of RAM, a 400 MB hard disk, and a complete SCO/Altos UNIX operating system, may have been the single most used server in the lab.

Acer America - Altos
2641 Orchard Parkway
San Jose, CA 95134
408-432-6200

File Server GCS lives on half of the 200 MB disk of the 386/33 portable BitWise computer. Equipped with 8 MB of RAM, 3.5 and 5.25 floppy disk drives, and a full complement of serial and parallel ports, the system does primary duty as a portable file server. When booted under DOS, the system becomes a portable network analyzer for on-site troubleshooting.

BitWise Designs, Inc.
Building 50, Rotterdam Industrial Park
Schenectady, NY 12306
518-359-9741

UNINTERRUPTIBLE POWER SUPPLIES (UPS)
Two uninterruptible power supplies (UPS) were used in the lab: MinuteMan 425 and 1250 from Para Systems. Numerous Texas spring thunderstorms proved no problem for these systems.

Para Systems, Inc.
1455 LeMay Drive
Carrollton, TX 75007
214-446-7363

NETWORK INTERFACE CARDS

A variety of network interface cards from Thomas Conrad, 3Com, and SMC/Western Digital were used. Models from Thomas Conrad include the TC5043-T 10Base-T interface cards, along with the TC5055 8-port 10Base-T concentrator. 3Com provided several EtherLink II and EtherLink III cards. Standard Microsystems Corporation sent two Elite16-T 10Base-T cards, compatible with the Western Digital network drivers required by some systems.

Thomas-Conrad
1908-R Kramer Lane
Austin, TX 78758
512-836-1935

3Com Corporation
5400 Bayfront Plaza
Santa Clara, CA 95052-8145
408-764-5000

Standard Microsystems Corporation
80 Arkay Drive
Hauppauge, NY 11788
516-273-3100

KEYBOARD

This book was typed on a Trak101 trackball keyboard from KeyTronic. This keyboard incorporates a Microsoft-mouse compatible trackball in the spot usually sporting the four cursor keys in the inverted-T pattern. When not acting as a mouse, the trackball controls the cursor movement faster than the built-in keypress repeat ever will. If your desk has too little room and/or too much stuff, this system works great. Keytronic managed to keep the keyboard the same size, even though it includes the trackball and three different mouse button configurations.

KeyTronic
P.O. Box 14687
Spokane, WA 99214-0687
509-928-8000

Getting Upgrades, Patches, and Information

The two main sources of information about NetWare and UNIX are NetWire for Novell and the Internet for UNIX (as well as anything else you might be interested in).

Accessing the Internet

The Internet is the worldwide community of primarily UNIX and TCP/IP users, vendors, customers, and researchers. Most of the network advances in the last 15 years have been the direct result of the Internet community. PC LAN users don't know this, and they usually have odd ideas of what the Internet is and what it does. If that's the case for you, read on. Daniel Dern, author of *The Internet Guide for New Users* (McGraw-Hill, 1993; ISBN 0-07-16511-4) and editor of *Internet World*, has been kind enough to supply Internet neophytes with ways to become connected. You can reach him through e-mail:

ddern@world.std.com

or through *Internet World*:

Meckler Corporation
11 Ferry Lane West
Westport, CT 06880
800-MEKKLER

He wishes you luck.

INTERNET ACCESS RATES

Access to the Internet today is available to any and all, including commercial organizations and individual end users. The current access rates are as follows:

- ▸ $1 per hour or $20 per month (plus applicable phone costs)
- ▸ Dial-up TCP/IP connections at $5 to 10 per hour

▸ Full-time, leased-line connections for several hundred to several thousand dollars per month (factors include organization size and connection speed)

You can also access Internet information indirectly via e-mail from other networks, UUCP service, or through CD-ROMs, books, and periodicals.

DIAL-UP ACCESS

The PDIAL (Public Dial-up Internet Access List), maintained by Peter Kaminski, lists U.S. organizations offering dial-up terminal and IP access to the Internet. You can get the list by sending e-mail to:

info-deli-server@netcom.com

with SEND PDIAL in the message subject or body. This is probably the most succinct place to start.

INTERNIC INFORMATION SERVICES

For information about the PDIAL and other groups offering Internet access for individuals and organizations, as well as how to evaluate and select an appropriate service provider, contact the InterNIC Information Services' Referral Desk. The address is:

General Atomics/InterNIC
P.O. Box 85608
San Diego, CA 92186-9784

You can also phone or fax:

Voice Response: 800-444-4345 ("phone tree")
Referral Desk: 619-455-4600 (Monday–Friday, 5:00 A.M.–7 :00 P.M., PDT)
Fax: 619-455-3900

Another alternative is to contact the company through e-mail, either to be handled by the referral desk staff:

info@internic.net

or through the automatic mail server:

mailserv@is.internic.net

Send a message to this address with SEND HELP in the message body for full information.

If you currently have Internet access (or know someone who does), the InterNIC's on-line information can be accessed in a number of ways, including the following:

- ▸ Gopher server at *gopher.internic.net*

- ▸ Anonymous-FTP server: *is.internic.net* (see directory *infosource*)

- ▸ WAIS server: *internic-infosource* (selected from list of WAIS servers)

- ▸ Telnet server (to local Gopher client): Telnet to *is.internic.net*; for gopher, login as *gopher*

USENET NEWSGROUPS

For UNIX and Novell information, the best place to start is the Usenet Newsgroups. If you are not familiar with the Usenet in general, start by reading the Periodic Postings messages in the *news.announce.newusers* Newsgroup.

Good Newsgroups include *comp.sys.novell*, *comp.unix.**, *comp.protocols.**, and *comp.os.**. To help select and make use of these Newsgroups, you should start by reading the FAQ (Frequently-Asked Questions and answers) documents available in *news.answers*.

These postings are also available by e-mail: send a message to:

mail-server@pit-manager.mit.edu

with the following in the message body:

send usenet/news.answers/news-newusers-intro help

Getting NetWare Information

In addition to the information available on NetWire, Novell's electronic information service, Novell offers plenty of technical help through its databases, Novell Research Program publications, and educational programs.

The following descriptions of resources are from the *Novell Buyer's Guide* (October 1992), which is available in either paper or electronic form. Contact your local Novell office or reseller for a copy.

NETWIRE INFORMATION SERVICE

NetWire provides easy access to timely information for all NetWare users. NetWire allows users to access information and technical support 24 hours a day, at a reasonable cost. Users can submit questions to a Novell technician or system operator (sysop), a carefully selected, knowledgeable NetWare user. Users can also download files and technical information dealing with product modifications and enhancements.

Sharing information with (and questioning) a pool of more than 70,000 NetWare users is invaluable. Novell is constantly striving to enhance NetWire to better meet the service needs of the NetWare user community.

Accessing NetWire

You can access NetWire through the CompuServe Information Service. It requires a modem, a communications program, and a workstation. If you are already a member of CompuServe, simply type **GO NOVELL** at the ! prompt.

CompuServe is offering a free introductory membership to explore NetWire. The membership includes $15 (U.S.) of usage credit and step-by-step instructions. For information, contact:

> CompuServe, Inc.
> Representative #200
> 800-848-8199 (U.S. and Canada)
> 614-457-0802 (International)

NetWire Information Sources

NetWare users can access the following information by selecting the appropriate menu on NetWire:

- ▶ **Message boards:** These allow users to get fast, expert responses to NetWare questions by submitting queries to a select group of NetWare technicians and specialists. Virtually all responses are sent out within 24 hours.

- ▶ **Library of files:** NetWire users can access product enhancements, patches, fixes, shell drivers, utilities, technical bulletins, IMSP bulletins, STP bulletins, and FYIs. These files are available from a long-term storage and retrieval location.

- ▶ **IBM file finder:** This online, comprehensive, keyword-searchable database contains file descriptions designed to provide quick and easy reference to the files on NetWire. Users can search by topic, file submission date, forum name, file type, file extension, file name, or submitter's identification.

- ▶ **Novell press releases:** These provide the latest product news.

- ▶ **Novell product list:** This list provides access to a complete, up-to-date list of all Novell networking and communications products.

- ▶ **Calendar of events:** This calendar lists when and where education courses, conferences, seminars, and trade shows will take place.

NOVELL RESEARCH PROGRAM

Novell Research is a program through which Novell publishes technical information about designing, implementing, and managing NetWare-based systems. Novell Research publications are written by Novell consultants and engineers, with the help of outside industry experts when necessary. The information contained in these publications is based on laboratory research and actual field experience of the authors. The publications cover topics in these main areas:

- Network design and optimization strategies

- Network management tactics

- NetWare internals and theory of operations

- Novell product implementation guidelines

- Integration solutions for third-party products

- NetWare programming techniques

This information is designed to benefit Novell's technical audience, consisting of systems engineers, support engineers, consultants, programmers, network supervisors, and information systems personnel.

Publications produced by Novell Research include the following:

- **NetWare Application Notes (AppNotes)**: Issues are published monthly by Novell. Each issue contains several articles that address different aspects of working with NetWare, including design, implementation, development, and optimization. The material is based on technical research performed by Novell personnel.

- **Novell Research Reports**: These reports are in-depth treatments of key technical issues, such as network backup and security. They represent the results of technical research performed by Novell personnel.

- **Novell Cooperative Research Reports**: These reports are the results of research performed by third-party industry experts. Cooperative research projects are planned for topics of general interest for which Novell cannot produce strategic research without outside assistance.

Subscription Information

NetWare Application Notes are available directly from Novell by subscription only. As of January 1, 1992, the one-year subscription rate for all domestic and international orders is $95. Subscribers also receive copies of selected Novell Research Reports and Novell Cooperative Research Reports as they become available.

Back issues of NetWare Application Notes are available for $15 each. Costs for back issues of Novell Research Reports and Novell Cooperative Research Reports vary. Contact the order desk for more information at:

> Novell Research Order Desk
> 800-453-1267, extension: 5380
> Fax: 801-429-5511

From outside the U.S. or Canada, orders should be sent by fax to: 408-929-6203. All orders must be prepaid.

NETWORK SUPPORT ENCYCLOPEDIA

The Network Support Encyclopedia (NSE) is an electronic information base containing comprehensive network technical information needed to install a network or to maintain and troubleshoot an existing system.

Using the text-retrieval software bundled with the encyclopedia, users can search through custom menus, browse through manuals and technical bulletins, download files and patches, and do string searches using Boolean logic.

NSE collects technical information from Novell and third parties into a single source, giving users easy access to all the network information they need.

NOVELL STANDARD VOLUME

The Novell Standard Volume, which replaces Novell's Technical Information Database (TIDB), includes Novell Technotes, Novell Labs (IMSP) hardware and software test bulletins, product documentation, a library listing of all files available on NetWire, and additional product information, such as product specification sheets, Novell press releases, and the NetWare Buyer's Guide.

The Novell Standard Volume is available on CD-ROM (updated up to 12 times per year) or diskette (updated quarterly).

NOVELL PROFESSIONAL VOLUME

The Novell Professional Volume contains all the information in the Novell Standard Volume plus downloadable NetWare patches, fixes, drivers, enhancements, troubleshooting decision trees, NetWare Application Notes, and additional manuals.

The Novell Professional Volume is available on CD-ROM and is updated up to 12 times per year. It offers the following advantages:

▸ Provides a single source of network technical information

▸ Makes it easy to retrieve needed information

▸ Helps users install and maintain their networks

▸ Regular updates keep information current and useful

▸ Helps users keep their NetWare operating system up-to-date

NOVELL AUTHORIZED EDUCATION CENTER (NAEC) PROGRAM

Novell Authorized Education Centers (NAECs) are educational partners with Novell and provide the channel through which Novell leverages its training expertise. Organizations that meet Novell's stringent education standards are authorized to teach Novell-developed courses using Novell Certified NetWare Instructors (CNIs).

Through the NAEC program, distributors, resellers, OEMs, consultants, and independent training organizations enter into an educational alliance with Novell Education to teach knowledge and skills vital to the use, maintenance, and sales of Novell products. The NAEC program is essential in supporting Novell's certification and authorization programs. Novell works hand in hand with NAECs to maintain the reputation behind the logo.

For more information about the NAEC program or to locate the NAEC nearest you, call:

> Novell Authorized Education Centers
> 800-233-EDUC (U.S. and Canada)
> 801-429-5508 (International)

You can also contact the nearest Novell office for NAEC program information.

CERTIFIED NETWARE INSTRUCTOR PROGRAM

The CNIs that provide training through NAECs must go through an intensive instructor training program, which qualifies them to teach authorized Novell courses. CNIs may specialize in one or more of the following areas:

- ► NetWare
- ► Communications Services
- ► Network Management
- ► Development
- ► TCP/IP and UNIX Connectivity

Periodic update training keeps CNIs current with the latest information about Novell products and course developments. With this continual training, CNIs gain increased knowledge and maintain sharp network training skills. For more information, call:

> Novell Authorized Education Centers
> 800-233-EDUC (U.S. and Canada)
> 801-429-5508 (International)

NOVELL TECHNOLOGY INSTITUTE AFFILIATE PROGRAM

The Novell Technology Institute (NTI) Affiliate program is designed to provide NetWare education to institutions of higher education. The program provides the training and materials needed to teach students about the latest network computing technology. NTI Affiliates offer students the quality NetWare training demanded in the industry by having CNIs on the staff.

Through the NTI Affiliate program, qualified organizations enter into an alliance with Novell education to teach knowledge and skills vital to the use and maintenance of Novell products. Novell works with NTI Affiliates to maintain the highest quality of Novell-authorized education. Organizations that meet Novell's stringent education standards are authorized to teach Novell-developed courses using CNIs. For information, call:

> Novell Authorized Education Centers
> 800-233-EDUC (U.S. and Canada)
> 801-429-5508 (International)

CERTIFIED NETWARE ENGINEER PROGRAM

The Certified NetWare Engineer (CNE) program helps service technicians provide quality support for NetWare networks by ensuring that they have received extensive training and met Novell's strict certification requirements. Once those requirements are met, Novell stands behind its CNEs with technical support and information.

Technicians who work for qualified Novell resellers or independent service organizations, self-employed technicians, or NetWare customers can become CNEs. CNE candidates must have a thorough working knowledge of DOS and microcomputers before participating in the program.

After thorough training pursuant to certification, CNEs receive priority access to Novell's support staff for help in resolving complex network system problems.

For more information on how to become a CNE, call:

> Novell
>
> 800-NETWARE (U.S. only)

Product Installation

This appendix describes the installation procedures for the products covered in the book:

- ► LAN WorkGroup from Novell
- ► Novix from Firefox
- ► Catipult from Ipswitch
- ► NetWare TCP/IP Gateway 386
- ► UniLink Basic and NetBios from Micro Computer Systems
- ► SoftNet Term from Puzzle Systems
- ► PopTerm/NVT from Rational Data Systems
- ► FLeX/IP from Novell
- ► NFS Gateway from Novell
- ► NFS Server from Novell

LAN WorkGroup Installation

Although LAN WorkGroup is developed and marketed by Novell, the first thought was to keep regular old BOOTP and just port it to the NetWare file server. Luckily, someone reminded Novell that configuring BOOTP servers is not a job for a typical NetWare administrator. The shipping version includes an installation and configuration system much like NFS Gateway. All files needing text entry have a nice NetWare-style front-end. For the first time, someone that can barely spell UNIX can install and configure a BOOTP server.

The NetWare INSTALL utility is run on the server (or remotely with RCONSOLE) to start the installation. A handy method to use when loading several diskettes worth of software is to copy them all to the server. The manual suggests this, but be sure and use XCOPY rather than COPY as the manual directs. Each floppy disk has multiple subdirectories, and the COPY command misses them. NetWare's NCOPY command, with the /s parameter for subdirectories (just like XCOPY) works just as well, and it automatically verifies the copy.

The two new programs to be concerned with are LWGCON.NLM and LWPCON.EXE. The LAN WorkGroup manual includes good advice concerning the initial setup: configure one or two workstations only until you fully understand the process. No sense retyping dozens of configuration files after you finally figure out the proper setup.

Unlike many manual configuration sheets, the one in LAN WorkGroup is worth filling out. It asks for strange things not normally required, such as the boot drive of each user's PC. Information about the shell and driver used before LAN WorkGroup is installed is necessary as well.

There are two sheets at the beginning, one for the Workstation Type and the other for Subnetwork Profile. Subnets to the UNIX world are the same as network segments to the NetWare world. If your NetWare server has more than one interface card, your network is "subnetted" (another example of verbing a noun in the computer business), whether you realize it or not.

The Subnetwork Profile screen, shown in Figure D.1, requires fairly simple entries, and the manual clearly spells out what to put for the Subnet Mask. If your network is using a name service, ask the UNIX administrators for the name and address of that server.

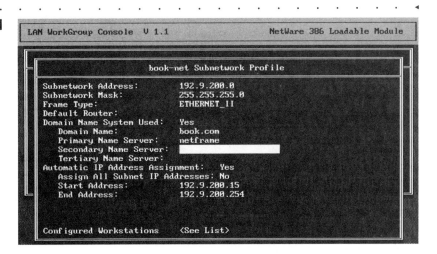

FIGURE D.1

The LAN WorkGroup Subnetwork Profile screen showing a simple network configuration

```
LAN WorkGroup Console   V 1.1                    NetWare 386 Loadable Module


                         book-net Subnetwork Profile

           Subnetwork Address:        192.9.200.0
           Subnetwork Mask:           255.255.255.0
           Frame Type:                ETHERNET_II
           Default Router:
           Domain Name System Used:   Yes
             Domain Name:             book.com
             Primary Name Server:     netframe
             Secondary Name Server:
             Tertiary Name Server:
           Automatic IP Address Assignment:   Yes
             Assign All Subnet IP Addresses: No
             Start Address:           192.9.200.15
             End Address:             192.9.200.254


           Configured Workstations    <See List>
```

The Default Router address is much like the name service information; the UNIX side of the house will know it. The four fields under Domain Names System Used won't appear if your response to the question is No. The same holds true for the Automatic IP Address Assignment screen. If you choose No for this, the next three lines stay hidden.

In the example in Figure D.1, the system was asked to assign IP addresses as clients logged in, but not to assign the range of IP addresses. When asked to supply the range, the system started at 192.9.200.1 and went up sequentially. Since there are conflicts in that address range, the problem was side-stepped by providing the starting and ending addresses.

This subnet information is not important when only one UNIX system is involved. In larger installations, the IP addresses of the name servers and routers are necessary for setup. Ask the UNIX administrators for these addresses. Better yet, get a copy of the UNIX hosts' /etc/hosts file; most of the information you need will be there.

SETTING UP THE BOOTPTAB FILE

Named for its UNIX counterpart, the BOOTPTAB file is the TABle for the BOOTP server software, and it's where configuration details for BOOTP are set. BOOTPTAB is an ASCII text file that the server reads when booting up. All those strange things you've been collecting, such as the boot disk location, are used here.

Luckily, you never touch the BOOTPTAB file. The information entered in the Workstation Type screen fills the file out for you.

SETTING UP THE WORKSTATION TYPE FILE

The intent of LAN WorkGroup is to keep the administrator from needing to manage each client station individually. Even with that goal being fairly well met, you must still configure the clients to receive the IPXODI drivers and up-to-date shells in place of the older IPX.COM program. The manual intimates that this process can be done automatically during any normal login process, but don't trust this to work until 50 or so have been done correctly.

There can be as many entries as needed in the Workstation Type table, shown in Figure D.2.

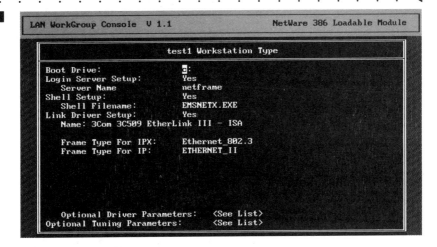

Novell has been politely trying to move users into the world of IPXODI for the last several years. It's a multiprotocol world, but IPX.COM is a single-protocol interface between the computer and the interface card. Don't get angry at the upgrade chores; get busy updating your shells. NetWare 4.0 upgrades the client drivers even more, but the IPXODI driver is still the heart of the client connection programs.

Configuration

The information required for the Workstation Type screen is much less than is ordinarily needed for BOOTPTAB files. When you press the Enter key on the Link Driver Setup field, more than 100 ODI driver files pop up. These include the adapters you might expect, such as the NE2000 and 3c503 from 3Com, but also include some unusual drivers. Most interesting in this group is the IBM FDDI MCA driver, for those of you interested in putting a workstation on Fiber Distributed Data Interface for 100 Mb/s transmissions.

If your particular driver is not in the list, you're somewhat out of luck. You need to leave this field blank and configure the details by hand in the NET.CFG file.

SETTING UP THE LANWORKGROUP USER GROUP

Each user planning to take advantage of the LAN WorkGroup product must be a member of the LANWORKGROUP user group on the BOOTP file server. Use NetWare's SYSCON (SYStem CONfiguration) utility to make these additions.

Each member of LANWORKGROUP must have the SYS:\NET\BIN directory in his or her search path. Novell recommends adding this line to the system login script:

```
include sys:public/syslogin.lwg
```

This processes the text file script pointed to in the file location. The alternative is to add the SYSLOGIN.LWG file to the login script directly. The SYS-LOGIN.LWG file consists of the following:

```
if member of "LANWORKGROUP" then begin
map f:=SYS:
map ins s1=SYS:net/bin
end
```

This inserts (with the ins command) a search drive (s1 stands for the first search drive) into the PATH statement of the PC. Since this search drive is inserted, when the PC is logged out, the original DOS search path will be restored properly.

The LANWORKGROUP user group is created automatically, but the "include" line must be inserted manually. If preferred, the SYSLOGIN.LWG file can be written (manually) into the system login script. Writing it in the system login script keeps all login instructions in the same place, and keeps the SYSLOGIN.LWG file itself out of harm's way. When installed, the file is flagged read-write in the public directory, where every user has access. If having the separate file appeals to you, put it in the SYS:SYSTEM directory; few users have access there.

WORKSTATION SETUP WITH WGSETUP

Once the Workstation Type options have been configured, one for every likely workstation setup, each client must be configured. This program must be run from the workstation by the regular user, or at least by someone using the user-name associated with that PC. The format of the command for setup is

WGSETUP *workstation-type*

The *workstation-type* must match one of the types configured earlier in the Workstation Type screen.

This command will churn for a bit, list on screen all the files it is copying, then congratulate you on all your hard work. That's not necessarily the end of configuration, though, since the NET.CFG, AUTOEXEC.BAT, and CONFIG.SYS files may or may not be in the form you need at the end of the file copying.

Generally, the installation works fairly well. The problems will come if the workstation type chosen when running WGSETUP is not right.

The other work is to find the entries placed into your AUTOEXEC.BAT file and load all those drivers high once again. All the drivers with LAN WorkGroup can be loaded high, but this must be done manually.

THE LANWG.BAT PROGRAM

The LANWG.BAT program is loaded onto the boot drive of the client PC (that's why the installation worksheets request this information) by the WGSETUP.EXE program, based on the details put into the WPGSETUP.CFG file. The LSL.COM and IPXODI.COM files are loaded, along with the proper NET program (NETX.COM, EMSNETX.COM, or XMSNETX.COM). The .COM file for the particular network interface card in use must be supplied by the manufacturer.

The result of this configuration exercise should be a LANWG.BAT program similar to this:

```
C:\yesno "Do you want to load the networking software? [y/n]:"
if errorlevel 1 goto noload
C:\LSL.COM
C:\NE2000.COM
C:\IPXODI.COM
C:\NETX.COM
F:LOGIN SERVER2/BDAVIS
WGTCPIP.EXE -C=F:\NET\NET.CFG
```

> SET NAME=BDAVIS
> BREAK ON
> :noload

The WGTCPIP.EXE program is the TCPIP.EXE program from LAN Work-Place, modified to use common configuration files. It now points to a network-based NET.CFG file that can be shared among all the PCs. It can point to the local NET.CFG file on the PC as well by listing

> C:\NET\NET.CFG

on the eighth line. If the IPXODI set of network drivers is already loaded, this file can be modified to match the circumstances by excluding the driver files. Most administrators prefer to keep the driver files in a separate \NET directory rather than in the root directory as shown here.

OTHER MODIFIED DOS FILES

The LAN WorkGroup setup sequence will modify several other files on the target PC. All the modified files are copied and renamed in the same directory where they were found for easy recovery. If a problem occurs, the UNINSTAL.BAT program in the SYS:\NET\INSTALL directory will delete the new files and rename the old ones to their original names.

The AUTOEXEC.BAT file gets the most changes of any DOS file. All the existing shell information is commented out, even if the IPXODI drivers are in use. The LANWG.BAT file will load all these from now on. After all else is done, the line

> CALL C:\LANWG.BAT

is added at the end of the AUTOEXEC.BAT file.

Usually, the modified file will work smoothly, but some things confound the process. Statements by various memory managers loading the network drivers in upper or expanded memory will be bypassed. If you've worked to get these drivers loaded conserving as much RAM as possible, don't let it get changed without a fight.

The setup sequence also checks CONFIG.SYS for ANSI.SYS. If ANSI.SYS is not found, it will be added. The TNVT220 terminal emulation program needs this file to handle color properly.

CHECKING THE INSTALLATION

There is a program named BOOTPCHK.EXE that will, believe it or not, check to see if there is an active BOOTP server on the network. The format is real tough: type **BOOTPCHK** on the command line. The result should look something like Figure D.3.

FIGURE D.3

The results of a successful BOOTPCHK test

```
F:\NET\BIN>bootpchk
IP Address = 192.9.200.15          IP Net Mask = 255.255.255.0
Bootp Server = 192.9.200.7
Hostname = JAMES
---------------------------------------------------------------------------
IP Address = 192.9.200.15          IP Net Mask = 255.255.255.0
Bootp Server = 192.9.200.7
Hostname = JAMES
---------------------------------------------------------------------------
2 BOOTP packets have been examined.
The following BOOTP server is currently running:

     192.9.200.7

===> No conflicting BOOTP packets have been found.


F:\NET\BIN>
```

The IP address listed, 192.9.200.7, is the NetFRAME file server running the LAN WorkGroup software. The Hostname=James is shown on the Workstation IP Address Assignment screen, as in Figure D.4. The name filled in comes from the SET NAME=JAMES line in the LANWG.BAT file.

The physical address, although needed by BOOTPTAB, is filled in by the system automatically. The program finds that value and fills in this blank. The IP address is the first of the pool of addresses you set up earlier.

USING THE LWPCON PROGRAM

Once the centralized portion is complete, there is another program that gives details concerning the host connection options in place. The LWPCON (LAN Work-Place CONfiguration) program has been inherited from the earlier, stand-alone LAN WorkPlace for DOS. This program is run from DOS rather than from the console.

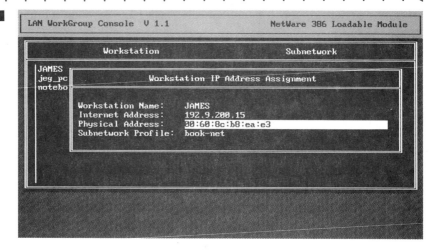

Checking the LAN
WorkGroup local
workstation information

The function of LWPCON is to allow testing and configuration checking for the local PC and remote host. Figure D.5 shows an echo test, which is essentially a PING of the remote host. You would run LWPCON when a user complains that he can't reach the host.

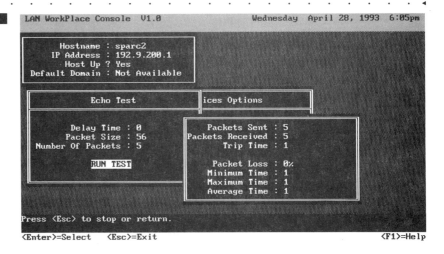

Echo testing (pinging) a
Sun SPARCstation2

SETTING UP LAN WORKGROUP FOR WINDOWS

The installation is smart enough to look for and find Windows on any local disk (Windows is too big to hide) and make the necessary changes automatically.

Although LAN WorkGroup is based on LAN WorkPlace for DOS, there are some fancy files in the Windows area. To take advantage of this, three Windows files are modified and one is created during setup:

- ▶ LWP.INI, the new file, provides lots of information (it starts out 200 lines long before any changes are made). Most of the information concerns file transfer, but details concerning terminal emulation and remote shell are handled here as well.

- ▶ SYSTEM.INI is changed to add networking. NetWare drivers and some configuration details must be included for every Windows installation, and WGSETUP adds or modifies those files. Little is added to existing NetWare clients, since the modifications needed for LAN WorkGroup are the same as those for any NetWare client.

- ▶ PROGMAN.INI gets LWG.GRP installed, which is the group for LAN WorkGroup. The LAN WorkGroup Windows programs are true Windows programs, but all the DOS utilities are included with their own icons.

- ▶ WIN.INI gets the extensions for the LAN WorkGroup programs added under the *[Extensions]* heading. The NWPOPUP program is added here as well. This allows normal NetWare status line messages to appear inside Windows.

Once these files are edited by the installation program, Windows should start with all the proper details in place. There are a few utility programs Windows needs and some DLL programs used, but the installation process does a good job of putting those in the right places. If something doesn't work, refer to the manual, which lists all the various files and their various hiding places.

Firefox's Novix Installation

The early version of Novix available here in the U.S. required a Configuration Pack as a copy-protection device. Often called a *software key* or *dongle* (derogatory slang), this device plugs into a parallel printer port. The companies in the U.S. lead the world in the fight against software piracy, and in recognition of this, the scheme has been dropped in version 2.0 of the product in the U.S.

In the current version, two sets of diskettes come with the product. The first is a Software Issue Diskette, which includes all the Novix software set. The second diskette (it may be more than one, depending on the product) is the Configuration Diskette, which provides the license protection now instead of the dongle. It creates a license file on the server. This is a "stacking license," meaning more functions or a larger user count can be added to existing licenses by use of another Configuration Diskette. These can only be used once, but the program doing the upgrading is not disabled until the upgraded license file is complete and checked.

This is a true NetWare application. A user must be logged in to a file server to run this product. You can't load it to a local hard disk and run it from there, as you can with LAN WorkGroup. The server running the gateway need not be the user's home server, but each user must be attached and be a member of an appropriate security group. Part of the advantage of Novix is the integration with Novell security, adding an extra layer of protection between the PC users and the UNIX hosts.

NOVIX SERVER INSTALLATION

Novix is installed to the NetWare 3.*x* and 4.*x* server from a PC workstation. The installer must be logged in as SUPERVISOR, not a user with SUPERVISOR equivalence. This is to bestow proper authorities on all user and system files installed during the installation.

Before starting the installation, you need the IP address of the NetWare server and some details concerning the UNIX hosts. Much of this information is the same as that required for LAN WorkGroup, and it's the kind of information needed for all NetWare to UNIX products.

The installation is run from the floppy disk drive containing the Server Configuration diskette (A: or B:). The target drive should be on the server acting as the gateway, and the drive should be pointing to the root of volume SYS. There is some flexibility in program file placement, but the server license file must be placed in the \TCPGWAY directory off the root of volume SYS.

Choosing the Install a New Novix System option from the opening menu gets things going. You can cancel the installation procedure at any time without jeopardizing the Configuration Diskette. Entering the name of your company is necessary to continue the installation.

The choices available for using the Configuration Diskette are update, finish the update, or abandon the installation. Each time additional features or user licenses are purchased, you must repeat this procedure. There is also an option to place a copy of the license file onto a blank diskette for safekeeping, which is recommended. If you're not paranoid about losing important files at the worst possible time, you haven't been managing a network long enough.

The license information is used to create the new NetWare Bindery (user profile and security files) entries for the rest of the installation. Several groups are created, and the proper trustee rights and permissions will be granted based on the provided information.

The software installation menu is simple; it offers to install the software to the NetWare server or stop. If the installation is stopped here, the license file will be placed into the \TCPGWAY directory created on the server during the previous step. There will be no other useful software there, however.

The software copied during this step depends on the license file and Configuration Diskette information. The user count particularly will be set by the license file. The program allows the placement of the Novix client software in any directory, but following the defaults on this type of program is always easier. Firefox has carefully not used any directory or group names that will conflict with existing names.

The next step is configuring either the VAP or NLM to run on your server, bridge, or router. Major installations in mixed environments tend to run NetWare 386, so we'll concentrate on NLMs. The Install program is fairly automatic, and there is little required that will make a NetWare administrator feel uncomfortable.

The local IP address requested is for the NetWare server acting as the gateway. The UNIX side of the house will have the number needed; if there is no UNIX side of the house, pick a number carefully. If your UNIX host has an address of 192.9.200.1, give your NetWare server an address in the range of 192.9.200.*x*. Each IP address must be unique or weird things happen. Don't try to use IP addresses that differ anywhere except in the fourth group of numbers unless the subnet masks are configured properly.

Once this step is finished, the software files are listed on the screen as they are copied to the server. A complete installation log is kept, so any miscues have a good chance of being solved without too much hair pulling and teeth gnashing.

THE NOVIX NVCONFIG PROGRAM

The next step in installation is using NVCONFIG, the configuration program for all of Novix. During installation, this program will be called at the appropriate time. If the program is called out of sequence, it will not work. The NetWare Bindery must have the Novix groups configured before NVCONFIG will start.

NVCONFIG is entirely menu-driven and written in much the style of NetWare. For UNIX administrators, this may not be good news; remember the F1 key for help and the Insert key to show pick lists.

Programs and Files to Modify

Two program files are created the first time NVCONFIG is exited. TCPGSVCE holds the details of the hosts and services set up with NVCONFIG and the connection details that go with them. TCLGUNIT holds the IP address mappings created. These files are read every time Novix starts; after changing configurations, the program must be forced to reread these files. This can be done by stopping and restarting, or by using the Host Connect Management commands on the NetWare console.

Each time the NVCONFIG program is used to modify settings, new copies of these files will be written. The existing files will be saved with a .BAK extension. If a change proves disastrous, you can return the settings to their prior condition by renaming TCPGSVCE.BAK to TCPGSVCE and TCPGUNIT.BAK to TCPGUNIT.

Saving these files under another name entirely may be a good idea. In a system so complicated as TCP/IP gateways with dozens of users, it's probable that some changes will have repercussions not felt for days or weeks. Keeping these older files in chronological order will act as breadcrumbs dropped behind a traveler going into a dangerous, unknown place (in other words, into a new configuration).

Printing the Installation Details

Novix includes a utility named PRNTCONF.EXE for listing all the installation details on paper or in a disk file. Although 90 percent of administrators won't keep current information anywhere, you should try to run this utility at least once. When the installation is working and settled, print this report to both paper and disk. Put the resulting report into the folder labeled TCP/IP Gateway. Feel good about your new organizational skills. Promptly lose the folder and never run PRINTCONF.EXE again. In other words, be a normal overworked network administrator.

NOVIX DOMAIN NAME SERVICE CONFIGURATION

To quote from the SCO Administration manuals concerning name services: "A name server is a network service that enables clients to name resources or objects and share this information with other objects in the network. The Berkeley Internet Name Domain (BIND) Server implements the DARPA Internet name server for the UNIX operating system. In effect, this is a distributed database system for objects in a computer network."

The name services available in UNIX have long been a goal of the PC LAN companies of the world. B+anyan took the early lead with their StreeTalk, the first wide-area name service for PC LANs. Even Microsoft's LAN Manager had a domain name service before Novell, although LAN Manager lagged behind Banyan. Only when Novell released NetWare 4.0 did the Big Red Horde take the lead in name services. Look for Novell to start integrating the NDS into standard UNIX domain name services. Until then, however, only special programs, such as Novix and Novell's NFS Gateway, allow a NetWare program to use UNIX name services.

Novix uses a domain name server to identify host systems once they've been identified during configuration. Novix uses its own Domain Name Resolver to contact the domain name servers in order to obtain the IP address of the requested host. Then the requested connection will be made, using IP and ARP (Address Resolution Protocol). This is exactly what any other UNIX host would do, and Novix makes the process easy and painless in the NetWare to UNIX arena.

Most UNIX networks have two name servers, the Primary and the Secondary. Up to eight name servers can be configured within Novix. These are listed, in order of importance, in the Configure Domain Name Servers submenu (reached from the main Novix menu). The most important point is to list the Primary name server first, the Secondary next, and so on. Servers will be queried in the order listed in this submenu.

You can insert a group name into the Accessible via Novell User Group field. Only members of that group will be able to use the name resolution service. The default is EVERYONE, and it should probably stay that way in most cases. Only the most security-conscious installations will need to hide the domain name servers from users.

NOVIX GATEWAY CONFIGURATION

Gateways in the UNIX world started back with the Internet itself. Unlike PC LANs, most UNIX machines can act as a gateway between two network segments. This is done by using two different network interface cards (usually both Ethernet, although Token Ring is starting to infiltrate the UNIX world), or between the local network and a remote network reached through a modem.

The gateway machine will have two different network IP addresses, one for each network segment attached. This is different than NetWare users are used to, but it makes sense once given some thought. The IP address names network nodes, not machines. Since there are two networks attached to the gateway, two network nodes are created, and two addresses are needed.

Information contained within the IP Gateway Definition screen includes the fields IP Address of Gateway, Gateway Network Address, Network/Subnet, and Accessible via Novell User Group.

Each gateway configured within Novix is given a name, but that name is used only within Novix. The local IP address must be entered into the IP Address of Gateway field. This IP address is the one all local connections will use in attaching to this host. The Gateway Network Address field is the physical address of the gateway's network interface card. This will be supplied by Novix using ARP.

Another excellent security and control device offered by Novix is the ability to exclude groups and users from accessing gateways. If you've enabled Novix Host Connect Security in the Host Connect Management program on the NetWare console, the Host Connect Security option will appear. By changing the default of EVERYONE in the Accessible via Novell User Group field, all users except members of the defined group will be excluded from gateway access.

NOVIX WORKSTATION CONFIGURATION

In Novix, you don't need to configure the workstation for the TCP/IP protocol stack support, as is necessary for LAN WorkGroup. The gateway program on the server handles those details. The client choices are simply whether to activate one host session or four, and how to remap the keyboard.

The DOS programs VT220-1.EXE and VT220-4.EXE are the single and multiple session executable programs for the clients. The user should run these programs from the directory where they reside, which defaults to \NOVIX\ FFDOSWS (FireFox DOS WorkStation), so that they can pick up any session configuration or keyboard mapping settings.

If only one host is defined in Novix, the opening screens will be skipped and the user will immediately see the UNIX host login prompt. When more hosts are defined, the VT220 Services Available on this Network screen appears. If the user isn't a member of a group allowed to connect to a particular host, that host description won't appear on this screen.

Configuration files are created by starting a session and selecting the Edit a VT Configuration option. You can set features such as the cursor mode, autowrap mode, character set, tab setting, print mode, insert mode, and so on, for a total of 17 available settings, some with multiple options. After you set up the terminal emulation exactly as you want it, choose the Save Configuration option from the menu and give that configuration a unique name. To use that configuration again, type **VT220-1** */cCONF1* (where *CONF1* is the actual name). Even when the client is connected to multiple hosts, each session can have its own configuration file. In this case, the command would be **VT220-4** */cCONF1 /cCONF2* and so on. All command line options can be set inside batch files. Other command line options include hot keys, color selection, auto logon sequences, and custom menu calling.

The procedure for auto login sequences uses an ASCII file to feed responses to the host, eliminating the need to interactively type them each time. Here is a sample logon sequence:

```
{Logon}fred[CR]
{Password}bloggs[CR]
{#}set term vt220[CR]
{cd/etc/network/[CR]
```

This will log in Fred with a password of bloggs (not a legal password to some UNIX systems, by the way). The terminal type is set for a vt220, and the directory is changed to */etc/network*.

You can modify the Help screens, both for terminal emulation and file-transfer options. Instructions for PC keyboard combinations to correspond to vt220 keystrokes are included.

You can also set up any number of dialogue files for any number of users. This does not violate the spirit of security in the program. Before this point, the user will pass through NetWare security, then the user and group filters of Novix. The UNIX host password is the least solid of all the security procedures involved, so skipping it does no great harm.

NOVIX GROUP SECURITY

Working down through the menus of NVCONFIG to the Host Service Definition screen, the Accessible via Novell User Group field can be amended for security purposes. Press the Enter key when this field is highlighted, and a pick list of all defined Novell groups appears. This is not magic; this is solid integration into the Novell Bindery system.

Press Enter on the desired group to change the group allowed access to the particular host session defined in the Host Service Definition screen. Each defined host may support a different group than every other defined host. Going further, each service to each host (Telnet or FTP) may support different groups.

NOVIX USER SECURITY

Security for individual users and even workstation addresses is controlled in much the same manner. You can define up to 200 descriptions of users, workstations, or groups. Planning is helpful here, since trying to spontaneously fabricate large numbers of user and group relationships is prone to mistakes.

As a rule of thumb for NetWare administration, try to avoid micro-managing down to the user level. Groups are handy and easy to set up and administer in NetWare, and users are numerous and change often. While it's nice to have the ability to control security down to the user in Novix, don't.

NOVIX EXCLUSIONARY SECURITY

If you need to exclude some users completely from accessing the Novix gateway, you can do so without creating some giant TCP group for everyone else on the network. Create a NetWare group named Barred and list as members those users that shouldn't have access to the TCP/IP gateway. In the Accessible via Novell User Group field in the Host Definition screen, list the group Barred. Novix will then prevent all of those group members from using the gateway.

Since the NetWare Bindery is queried by Novix during use, security profiles set inside NetWare will hold within Novix. The level of integration with Novix and NetWare security is greater than any other product seen to date.

Ipswitch's Catipult Installation

Running on a separate PC eliminates any direct involvement between the Catipult gateway and the NetWare server. This product is weighted heavily toward the TCP/IP user, so a NetWare-only administrator will need help from the local UNIX administrator.

An installation form is included, with instructions on faxing the completed form to Ipswitch. Try the organized approach and send in the form so you can get support and updates.

CATIPULT SERVER INSTALLATION

The installation must be run from the OS/2 machine slated to be the gateway. This ensures that the OS/2 client to NetWare server connection is working, although most of the application can be stored on the gateway machine if desired. Placing it on the NetWare server makes for easier management, however.

There are options for either one or two network interface cards in the gateway PC. This allows converting from Token Ring to Ethernet, or anything to Ethernet for that matter. It will also act somewhat as a bridge between two Ethernet segments. If both TCP/IP and IPX/SPX are running on the same physical network segment, one card in the gateway PC will suffice.

After rebooting the gateway PC, all the connections to the NetWare server need to be retested. Creation of the NetWare groups and permissions for those using the gateway are explained in some detail, and there's actually not much to it. Caveats concerning OS/2 version 1.3 (the one required for the gateway machine), which deal with mapping and search drive weirdness, are taken care of during installation or by easy changes in the login scripts.

For large installations with existing UNIX systems, IP name resolver files are included, along with spaces for a standard *hosts* file. If there is none of this available, Catipult provides sample files.

CATIPULT WORKSTATION INSTALLATION

Once the gateway is installed, set up the batch file named CATSTART.BAT for a basic user profile. More involved and more personal profiles are recommended, but casual users can certainly get to work using the defaults provided. The basic CATSTART.BAT file is as follows:

```
break on
set catipult=sys:\catipult\etc\catipult.cfg
netbios
catipult
```

These commands shouldn't be put into the login script; NetBIOS doesn't unload if loaded in the login script and will eat about 100K of lower memory. Call the Catipult user batch file at the end of the login script and avoid this bug. Then edit the CATSTART.BAT file and rename it for the user involved. Change the line

set catipult=sys:\catipult\etc\catipult.cfg

to read

set catipult=sys:*username*\catipult.cfg

Since the combinations of variables inside CONFIG.SYS, PROTOCOL.INI, NET.CFG, and STARTUP.CMD files stretch into the millions, sample files are included.

NetWare TCP/IP Gateway 386 Installation

Like Catipult, TCP/IP Gateway 386 looks much more like UNIX than NetWare, so a tag-team installation may be necessary. The license number is based on the Ethernet address of the NP600 network card and must be supplied by NCM. If you plan to install after regular work hours, call and get the license number first so people in your office won't laugh at you for working late two nights in a row to configure one gateway.

TCP/IP GATEWAY 386 SERVER INSTALLATION

NetWare TCP/IP Gateway 386 requires an OS/2 machine with two network interface cards installed. One connects the gateway to the existing NetWare network (Ethernet, Token Ring, or other), and the other is the intelligent TCP/IP processor.

Mail programs are supplied, and mail-relay information can be entered during installation. The hardware must be configured after the software is installed.

Changes made to CONFIG.SYS and NET.CFG are listed in the manual, and an installation log provides the changes for those preferring to modify these files manually.

Quite a bit of site-specific information is needed to configure this gateway. A sample TCPGATE.INI file is included in the manual, and it stretches for three pages. This is a good candidate for management by the UNIX side of the network.

TCP/IP GATEWAY 386 WORKSTATION INSTALLATION

Each NetWare client to use TCP/IP Gateway 386 must be configured with the HOMEDIR.EXE utility. You run this utility from the \PUBLIC\TCP-OPT directory where it was installed.

Since gateways are available to everyone, it makes sense to run everyone through the HOMEDIR.EXE utility, whether they plan to use the gateway or not. If a TCPUSER.PRO file isn't found in the user's home directory, one is created. Details are less necessary than the fact that the file exists; a standard file copied to each home directory will start things off smoothly.

To make a third-party terminal emulator the default choice for any user, edit the TCPUSER.PRO file and the name of the new software. However, each TCPUSER.PRO in each home directory may need to be modified if there are a variety of choices in use. This choice can also be made on the command line.

MCS UniLink Installation

The MCS UniLink manual is full of code examples and programming flavor. If the automatic installation script works properly, a NetWare administrator may be able to install the product. If the script doesn't work, usually because some of the necessary library files have been moved, only a UNIX administrator will have the courage to install the product. Manually editing files like */usr/sys/sun/conf.c* and */usr/sys/sun/str_conf.c*, linking a new kernel, renaming the current kernel, and rebooting the system are in UNIX power user territory.

MCS says that the Sun platforms are the ones most likely to be rearranged. The vast majority of installation problems happen on Suns, which is why they included so much detail in the manual for Sun systems. SCO systems use *custom*, and SVR4 systems use *installpkg*, the software installation utilities included with those operating systems. Support calls for these installations are negligible.

The UniLink manual comes with instructions for installing the NetBIOS/ix program as well, so check carefully before making changes. NetBIOS/ix allows connection between a PC client and a UNIX host over NetBIOS, including Novell's NetBIOS. Some network programs need NetBIOS even with Novell, and many networks (the LAN Manager family especially) use NetBIOS as the primary network programming interface.

UNILINK HOST INSTALLATION

The installation procedures load the software onto the target UNIX host. Once there, several files must be configured to accept terminal emulation clients. Of the four dozen small UniLink Basic host files, the following are the ones used after installation:

UNIX FILENAME	DESCRIPTION	LOCATION
loginxd	Login/ix daemon	/usr/hin/loginxd
ipxd	IPX daemon	/usr/hin/loginxd
ipxtab	IPX/SPX configuration file	/etc/ipxtab

If the proper device driver name for the network interface card and the proper network number (or 0) were entered during installation, little or no changes will be needed in the */etc/ipxtab* file. The important parameter to check is that *ethtype* (Ethernet type) is set to 802.3 for Novell-style packets. Details like the network interface name and the card driver were set up correctly in installation if no error messages were given.

Starting the host software is a three-step process: device drivers, IPX/SPX protocol, and the *loginixd* program. For the device drivers, enter **dlix** on the host command line (this should be done by *root* or *superuser*).

Next enter **ipxd** to start the daemon process on the host to support IPX/SPX protocol packets. Another small menu appears, with instructions to start, stop, or set up a new configuration file. The command **ipxd start** must be issued; no menu choices start the process.

The command **loginixd start** begins the host program that accepts login sessions from the PC clients. By using the MCS programming tools, a user can connect to a Login/ix process and run applications without going through the login procedure. For terminal emulation purposes, however, the login process is needed for security. This option should give you some ideas about the type of client-server programs that MCS programming tools support: automatically start a process on a UNIX system from an IPX/SPX client without the login hassle and interaction. Hmmmm...

UNILINK WORKSTATION INSTALLATION

The IPX/SPX protocol stack and shell programs must be resident. A NetWare server provides the client programs as part of the network operating system; MCS doesn't provide these drivers. The company assumes NetWare is on the network, or the customers wouldn't want terminal emulation over IPX/SPX.

Installation for the client software is fairly easy: run INSTALL from a floppy disk, and the program will create a directory named C:\LOGINPC (the default) and place six programs there. Finished.

To configure the software, type **LOGINPC** while in the default directory for the first time to bring up an empty Connect window. Press the A key to add a host name for connection purposes.

The required information is the host name, the interface type (IPX/SPX or NetBIOS), and the physical address of the Ethernet interface card for the card supporting IPX/SPX in the PC. Providing details like printer, mode (number of lines on screen), colors on screen (default is white letters on black), and a definition file name is optional.

Keyboard remapping is supported, but be prepared to enter hexadecimal codes. The definition file mentioned earlier controls the keyboard remapping, and multiple .DEF files can be kept and used with different hosts. Tie the hosts to the definition file name in the Quick Access Database screen, where the initial host connection information was entered.

Puzzle System's SoftNet Term Installation

As a testament to programming frugality, the entire product comes on one 3.5-inch high-density diskette. The beta version of their entire NetWare file server clone came on a single diskette as well. Both the server and workstation programs are on the one diskette: *tar* (tape archive) them to the host, then transfer the PC client files back for installation on the clients. Puzzle Systems assumes that you have some method of transferring files between UNIX and NetWare systems.

SOFTNET TERM HOST INSTALLATION

Instructions from Puzzle Systems suggest that the installer of the software have both NetWare and UNIX experience, but any minimal experience on both systems will suffice. The installation is as easy as any I've ever seen—in DOS, NetWare, or UNIX. The big requirement is to be running from whatever window manager comes with the UNIX system. The other requirement is to start this during working hours, so a call can be placed to Puzzle Systems for the serial number needed for security purposes. This would be more of an aggravation except that the installation puts little or no strain on the system, and the kernel doesn't need to be relinked and the system rebooted.

The default directory for the UNIX host files is */usr/softnet*, but any directory or file system may be used. This must be done manually, but typing **mkdir /usr/softnet** is not much work. Once the directory is created, a SOFTNET environment variable must be set. The environment variable works much the same in DOS and UNIX (I wonder where DOS got the idea?), and the command **setenv SOFTNET /usr/softnet** will be handled easily by any NetWare administrator that has done a login script.

Typing the **sninstall** command from the */usr/softnet* directory calls the installation programs. The programs run inside the windowing system, which gives SoftNet a classy, well-made feel. All the expected keystrokes and mouse movements are there and function as they should.

Nothing unusual is asked for in the installation sequence. Normal information, such as the network address number (important to the other NetWare servers involved), is all that's required.

SoftNet allows the product to take as much or as little of the host operating system priority as needed. With zero as the midpoint, the Process Priority field ranges from +20 (highest) to −20 (lowest) and anywhere in between. The default is set at zero, and this is a good place to start.

The Packet Frame Type field comes up with Ethernet_802.3 (the kind NetWare uses) as the default. Other details follow the same pattern: easy to understand, easy to configure, and with the proper choices set as defaults.

When everything is finished, start the host software by using the command **pvthost &**, and start communicating. The ampersand at the end of the file name places the program in the background. Within a few seconds of starting the program, PC clients are able to establish connection.

SOFTNET TERM WORKSTATION INSTALLATION

Four files are needed on the NetWare client for connection to the UNIX host: PVTLIST.EXE, PVTINST.EXE, PVT.EXE, and PVT52.EXE. The names make a play on NVT by using PVT (perhaps for Puzzle Virtual Terminal). These files must all be in the same directory. That's the end of PC client installation.

Configuration consists of running the PVTINST.EXE program with the same serial number as used during the host installation. This registers the client PVT.EXE program with the host and establishes that the two programs belong together. The process is rather painless as security procedures go. Installation and configuration are now finished.

Rational Data Systems' PopTerm/NVT Installation

The PopTerm/NVT automatic installation process offers a choice of placing the files directly on a client or on a NetWare server. The server version allows central management and file security, but it keeps individual configurations under separate file names. Even on a server with dozens of sessions defined, scrolling through the list of available hosts is simple.

RDS is adamant about not using the NVT.EXE program supplied by the Net-Ware for UNIX vendor. Go now to the \PUBLIC directory and rename the NVT.EXE file. If it stays, someone will run it and complain things don't work properly.

The installation program suggests default names for the directory, but any directory is acceptable. Remember the session files are in a subdirectory underneath the main PopTerm directory. If the PopTerm directory will be reached through a search path, remember to include the subdirectory as well, or the session files will not appear. Otherwise, users will call you on the phone and swear their computer is broken.

See anything concerning host installation? You won't. The NVT programs are loaded on the host server with all the other NetWare for UNIX utility files. The NVT daemon on the UNIX host is started by the other NetWare for UNIX programs. Once the client is ready to find the host, the host will be waiting.

Novell's FLeX/IP Installation

FLeX/IP ships on a single, high-density diskette, so installation is quick. The files are copied to the SYSTEM directory, since most of them are NLMs and configuration files. A few utility-type programs are copied to PUBLIC so that all Net-Ware users have access to them.

FLEX/IP SERVER INSTALLATION

In a typical NetWare installation procedure,, you use the INSTALL program at the server console to install FLeX/IP. An alternative is to use the XCOPY command to copy the disk contents to a directory on the server, and then install from there. You must use XCOPY to copy all the subdirectories. The command often used to be safe and get all subdirectories and "empty" (zero-length) files is

XCOPY A:*.* F: /S /E

If you copy the disk to the server before beginning installation, you must reference the location of the source files by NetWare volume, not drive. After the files have been copied to the server in a new directory named NEW.DSK, you will be prompted

Enter drive and/or path to new product source media

Respond **SYS:\NEW.DSK**.

The drive/path prompt appears immediately after INSTALL is started, and yes, UNIX fans, once again the Insert key must be pressed. No warning, no instruction, but if you want to add something anytime in NetWare, press Insert.

If TCP/IP was not configured on the server before, details such as the Internet address, host name, subnet mask, packet size, receive buffers, and the LAN driver must be given in the TCP/IP Configuration Parameters screen. Use the defaults when possible. The two most important items are the Internet address and host name. The host name is actually the server name in this case. You could use a different name here, but it's confusing and unnecessary. Keep the server name. NetWare administators can get unfamiliar information, such as the subnet mask, from the UNIX administrators. Hint: Try 255.255.255.0 for the subnet mask if the UNIX people are away from their phones.

FLEX/IP CONFIGURATION

The FLeX/IP disk actually contains three products, or at least the NetWare installation program counts them as three. Besides the FTP server program (FTPSRV), there are the two print gateways. Let's skip the printing now and go on to the FLEXCON (FLEX CONfiguration) program to get the FTP server going.

The first entry on the FLEXCON menu is Novice Configuration, which cycles through each of the product configurations in order. We don't care about that now, we just need to pick the Workstation IP Address choice.

This fills in the basic UNIX *hosts* file and puts it on the server just where it should be, in \ETC\HOSTS. If it helps, an existing *hosts* file can be copied there as well, since the format is the same. The entry screens are easy enough to use, but Novell thoughtfully provides a page in the manual describing the file format for those that enjoy using a manual editor.

Two configuration files are necessary for the FTPSERV program, and these are a mix of UNIX and NetWare parameters. The INETD.CFG (in UNIX, the *inetd* program is the Internet daemon, a superserver for the network programs specified in the */etc/inetd.conf* file) details the type of service and protocol used and calls the FTPSERV program. The default file, whose format is similar to that of the UNIX file, is

```
#svc   socktype protocol   program-name
ftp     stream   tcp        ftpserv
```

This file calls up the FTPSERV.NLM. The FTPSERV program reads the \ETC \FTPSERV.CFG program, which has the following information:

```
SESSION          9
NAMESPACE      DOS
USERDEF         /sys
GUESTDEF        /sys
```

The maximum number of concurrent sessions is 75. The default name space is DOS, but the NFS name space can be configured. This allows the FTP clients to see a more typical file listing, including the longer names allowed by UNIX. That puts the burden on the DOS users to make conversions, since DOS will be unable to display UNIX names properly. The least painful method may be to ask the UNIX FTP clients to use DOS-compatible names, since there are likely to be fewer FTP clients on the server than NetWare clients.

The NetWare SYS volume is referred to in UNIX style, since USERDEF refers to regular FTP clients with a name and password. The volume listed is the default directory for FTP clients upon attaching to the server. The GUESTDEF directory specifies where users attach (see Chapter 7 for information about anonymous FTP).

Novell's NFS Gateway Installation

NFS Gateway is a collection of 30 or so NLMs that run on NetWare 386 version 3.11 and above. It doesn't support NetWare 286 systems with VAPs. Since most large customers have migrated at least a portion of the NetWare servers to 386, the lack of VAP support shouldn't pose a problem.

The NFS Gateway user's manual does a good job of explaining NFS, how NetWare NFS Gateway works, and the information needed for a successful installation. But, hey, manuals are for weaklings, so you slapped the diskette into the file server floppy drive and went to work, right? Well, it may be time to back up and do it right.

PREPARING FOR NFS GATEWAY INSTALLATION

If you skipped all the neat worksheets Novell provided in the manual, go back. Take a few minutes to mentally organize who goes where on what system, then write it down. You can write it down either on the worksheet provided or a print out of your UNIX */etc/host* file, but write it down somewhere.

You may not need to write down everything on every worksheet. The most helpful information is the user and group listings for both systems.

You must know the remote system name, address, and mount point (where to attach to the UNIX file system). A lot of other information on the worksheets concerns the memory and disk space necessary to run NFS Gateway. Most important are the size of the shadow file to be created on the NetWare Gateway server and whether the server is configured properly for TCP/IP support.

Most of the other parameters on the worksheets for the NetWare server side can be ignored for now. Go with the defaults to get everything running. After things are working, go back over these lists and see if changes are necessary.

User and Group Listings

The more user and group setup done before installing NFS Gateway, the smoother the installation. Trust me, the NetWare User Setup option inside the Install program may not fully create the user. Better to have it done on each system before starting.

In the user and group listings, check both the *uid* and *gid* numbers. The *uid* number for UNIX is analogous to the User ID that's created automatically under NetWare. This number must be unique within systems; the number can be repeated under different operating systems without any problems. Your goal here is to map NetWare users to their UNIX names and *uid*. Better to plan it now rather than during installation.

You can allow groups of NetWare users access to the UNIX file system on a group, rather than individual, basis. Although this approach works, using individual usernames and *uid*'s raises the security level a bit. It also helps to engage file locking under NFS. If everyone comes into the UNIX system under the same name, file locking may not be engaged on that host. It takes only a few minutes to add individuals, and it will make the UNIX administrator happier.

Shadow File Location

The shadow file lists all the entries of the NFS file system that NFS Gateway users will access. This file organizes the UNIX permissions on the remote file system and the NetWare privileges for the NetWare user. The shadow file will grow as more file systems are added.

NetWare will place and track this file automatically. The only question for the administrator to answer is where to put the shadow file. Since this volume can grow and may not be included on any user warning list concerning file space, pick a volume with plenty of room. The default is in the SYS volume. You can use this volume, but remember that much of SYS may be taken up by spooled NetWare print jobs. If the SYS volume gets filled by spooled print files waiting on a printer, NetWare often shuts down or gives a variety of cryptic error messages. No sense having the NFS file system shadow file placed in danger if SYS overloads. Check VOLINFO or CHKVOL for space available before deciding where to put the shadow file.

TCP/IP Setup

Your NetWare server must be configured properly for TCP/IP before you can install NFS Gateway. Now is the time to recheck the IP address used on the server against the IP addresses of the UNIX systems. Since NetWare NFS Gateway is the new player in the network, it's more polite to change that address rather than the addresses of the UNIX systems. Go to the AUTOEXEC.NCF file and put the new TCP/IP address in now, while you're thinking of it. If you bring up NFS Gateway with a duplicate IP address, things will get weird quickly.

Something along these lines must be in the NetWare NFS Gateway AUTOEXEC.NCF file:

```
LOAD NE2000 PORT=320 INT=3 FRAME=ETHERNET_802.3
NAME=IPXLAN
LOAD NE2000 PORT=320 INT=3 FRAME=ETHERNET_II
NAME=TCPLAN
BIND IPX TO IPXLAN NET=12345
BIND IPX TO TCPLAN ADDR=192.9.200.1
```

Yes, the listing in all capitals looks garish to UNIX people, but that's the way Novell shows it in all their examples. Doing this listing in lowercase or mixed case is perfectly fine; DOS is case insensitive.

INSTALLING NFS GATEWAY

After you run the Install program on the console, choose Product Options, and press the Insert key, you may hit a roadblock. If TCP/IP isn't running, everything stops until it is. The reason is simple: NFS uses TCP/IP for a transport layer. If TCP/IP needs to be installed, do it now. The Install program will wait.

With TCP/IP running, you can continue the installation. Next, you supply the Local Host Name. This is the name for the NetWare file server that will be the NFS Gateway machine. Here's hoping you picked a server name that's reasonable, since you'll need to type it quite a few places around the network. Before you get far, the SUPERVISOR password will be required. Then you get to the fun stuff: the name services.

CONFIGURING NFS GATEWAY

The NFSCON program loads on the NetWare server console, just like MONITOR and TCPCON. This programs acts as a front-end to all the configuration files to be controlled for NFS Gateway. All the details concerning users, groups, and file systems become important here.

The NFS Gateway user's manual introduces you to NFSCON in Chapter 4, but the initial configuration of NFS Gateway is described in Chapter 6. Other important information is contained in the seven Appendices C through I. These list vital information about how to create users and groups on various UNIX operating systems. Included are AIX, NeXT, SCO, Solaris, SunOS, System V, and ULTRIX. Other operations detailed are discovering whether NIS or DNS is actually running on the UNIX system and how to add the NetWare Gateway server to the system's *hosts* list.

Even if you're familiar with these operations on your particular UNIX system, you should read what Novell has to say. The listings will show you what Novell engineers were thinking when they wrote the program and how they expect the UNIX system to be administered. If you're not familiar with these functions on a UNIX system, these pages give a clearer look at some basic administrative functions than most other references.

Configuring Name Services

In an existing NIS (Network Information Service) or DNS (Domain Name Service) network, NetWare NFS Gateway will happily use the existing UNIX name servers. You can use the documentation for both NetWare and UNIX for reference. The excellent appendices in the NFS Gateway manual explain how to discover which naming service is in use for all major UNIX systems. Importing that information to the NFS Gateway server is described in the appendix that covers installation.

If you don't already have a name service running, you may set up one on the NetWare server for NFS Gateway. Figure D.6 shows the Server Profile screen for a NetWare server handling the name service control. This may be the case when the network has a large NetWare group and a smaller UNIX group. There's no reason for name services if there are only a few UNIX machines in the network.

FIGURE D.6

The NFS Gateway Server Profile showing the NetWare server handling name service control

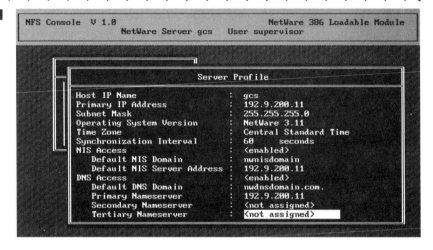

Many customers have only a single UNIX machine with multiple terminals (or PCs acting as terminals) attached, so there's even less reason for name services.

Getting the UNIX Host Files

With only one or two UNIX systems in the network you're setting up, it's easy to configure the various files by hand. If there are more systems, use the Perform File Operations menu choice in NFSCON to fetch all the files you need. In the FTP Server Login box, enter the name or address of the UNIX host where the files are located. If the default comes up with the Gateway server name instead, type over it. The name asked for on the second line must be a username on the UNIX host. A password is necessary; you can't log in to the remote host as an FTP client without a password. If necessary, go back to the UNIX system and add a password so the connection can be made. Figure D.7 shows file operations from NFS Gateway.

The FTP Operations box gives simple options for either getting or putting a file on the remote UNIX system. The directory listing option is quick and easy, and it tells you immediately if you have the right location. Unfortunately, there isn't a way to "tag" file names on the UNIX host and bring over a group at one time. The old-fashioned way of typing a file name, including the complete path

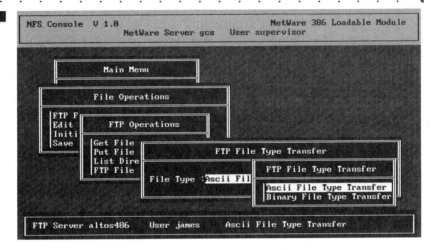

File operations from NFS Gateway

(*/etc/passwd*, for example), must be used. Choose ASCII or Binary files depending on the file type involved. ASCII is the default and will be needed for the name files you're interested in now.

The Perform File Operations option is handy for other file activities, even after NFS Gateway is up and running. Often, only one of several file systems on the UNIX host are attached with NFS Gateway. Using Perform File Operations allows you to retrieve files that don't reside on the attached file system.

User Setup

After the name service files are retrieved, choose the Initialize Nameservices option on the Perform File Operations menu to convert the UNIX system files into the format expected by NFS Gateway. Once the initialization is done, you can set up the users.

Here's where all the earlier work of setting up NetWare and UNIX users beforehand pays dividends. All the UNIX users imported within the UNIX system name files will be listed, along with an asterisk indicating that there is a matching NetWare user. Match them up per the manual's instructions, and your work is finished for the users.

Group Setup

For group setup, once again your preparation pays dividends. The NetWare and UNIX groups should match up, and you use the same procedure for converting them into the NFS Gateway format as you do to convert the users.

Several strange group names, such as *nfs_gateway_manager* and *nfs_host_manager*, appear. These are created by the NFS Gateway software, and you don't need to worry about them.

Host Setup

To set up the host, the NFS Gateway hostname and IP address must be in the */etc/hosts* file of the remote NFS server. To the UNIX NFS system, the NetWare NFS Gateway machine must look like any other NFS client. The UNIX system must be aware of NFS Gateway and know its address.

If your UNIX system doesn't have an */etc/hosts* file, see the relevant appendix of the NFS Gateway manual for help. System V UNIX will modify this file through the *sysadm* utility. SCO and SunOS will need to have the actual */etc/hosts* file modified with a text editor.

The other part of the host setup is telling the NFS Gateway server which hosts are in your network. To provide this information, choose Administer Services from the main menu, and then enter the host name and IP address in the Host Address Management box. There is also room to put the physical address, aliases, other IP addresses of that machine, machine type, and OS type. None of these are mandatory, although the Other IP Addresses field may be helpful. Figure D.8 shows the Host Information screen.

In UNIX networking, systems with multiple network connections must have multiple IP addresses. Addresses really signify a particular network node connection, not necessarily the machine itself. If there are two network connections, there will be two different IP addresses: one for each subnet. The alias names kept on a UNIX system are often the result of this situation; each network subnet has a particular name for a particular reason.

FIGURE D.8

NFS Gateway's Host

Information screen

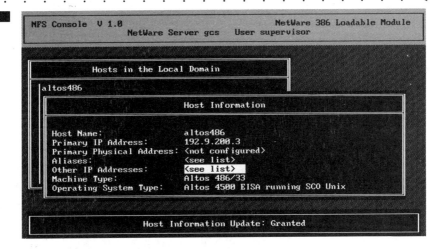

FIGURE D.8

NFS Gateway's Host

Information screen

```
NFS Console  V 1.0                         NetWare 386 Loadable Module
                    NetWare Server gcs   User supervisor


            ┌──────────── Hosts in the Local Domain ────────────┐
            │ altos486                                           │
            │        ┌───────────── Host Information ─────────────┐
            │        │                                            │
            │        │ Host Name:              altos486           │
            │        │ Primary IP Address:     192.9.200.3        │
            │        │ Primary Physical Address: <not configured> │
            │        │ Aliases:                <see list>         │
            │        │ Other IP Addresses:     <see list>         │
            │        │ Machine Type:           Altos 486/33       │
            │        │ Operating System Type:  Altos 4500 EISA running SCO Unix │
            │        └────────────────────────────────────────────┘

            ┌──────────── Host Information Update: Granted ──────────┐
            └────────────────────────────────────────────────────────┘
```

Setting Up the Gateway Volumes

The system used by NFS Gateway to present remote file systems to the Net-Ware client is clever and comfortable for the user. Each remote system is presented as a NetWare volume. Most NetWare servers have more than one volume (SYS must be first, then the common usage is VOL1, VOL2, and so on), so users are accustomed to mapping drives to multiple volumes. Some users may never know that one of the volumes they see is really a UNIX file system.

This conversion of a UNIX file system to a NetWare volume is complete. The NetWare utility VOLINFO shows each file system as a volume. The NetWare PERFORM utility, which measures performance and throughput by reading and/or writing to a NetWare volume, will function perfectly happily to one of these UNIX/NetWare volumes.

To match these NetWare volumes to the remote NFS file systems, choose Configure Volumes from the Administer Services menu in NFS Gateway's NFSCON. During setup, no volumes are listed, so remember the Novell trick here: when in doubt, press the Insert key. This summons the screen where you can configure new volumes.

This setup is in two parts. First, you must type in the NetWare volume name and the remote NFS path to match it to. The NetWare volume will be created from this information. It can be deleted from here, as well, but only if the volume

is not currently mounted. Once this volume name and remote mount point are provided, press Enter to move to the NFS Gateway Volume Information screen, shown in Figure D.9.

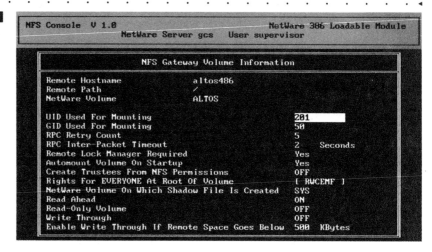

F I G U R E D.9

The NFS Gateway Volume

Information screen

The NFS Gateway Volume Information screen shows the name of the remote host, the path (mount point), and the corresponding NetWare volume. This information cannot be changed here, or anywhere else for that matter. If you find a mistake in the volume name or mount point, or the mount point needs to be changed for some reason, you're out of luck. You must delete the volume and then recreate it. This sounds drastic, but it's not. It only takes a few seconds to delete and recreate this volume information, so it was probably not worth the programming time to add an editing function.

The only two important blanks to fill in are the first and second, UID Used for Mounting and GID Used for Mounting. The defaults are 0 for both, identifying the UID as *root* and the GID as *wheel*. Both assume that the remote host has offered these file systems with most privileges available, root access, and a generic group. If the UNIX system has given specific mounting instructions during the *exports* command, those instructions will override your requests here.

The rest of the information in this screen is useful, but not yet. Get NFS Gateway up and running for a few weeks before making any changes here. The default values for RPC Retry Count, RPC Inter-Packet Timeout, and the rest will work. But do make sure that the default of Yes is set for the Remote Lock Manager Required field. This setting forces both NetWare and NFS on the remote host to be aware of potential file conflicts. The record of concurrent NFS and NetWare file locking with NFS Gateway is spotty, so force as much oversight as possible. It may not create all the locks that are needed, but you'll sleep better.

Novell's NFS Server Installation

NFS Server ships on a single, high-density diskette. Many people (including Your Humble Narrator) made suggestions that a product as expensive as NetWare NFS Server should contain more than a single diskette and a single, slim manual. So Novell dropped the price considerably, and now it even offers a "starter kit" that supports five NFS clients at a time at a lower price.

PREPARING FOR INSTALLATION

As with the other NetWare-to-UNIX products, taking some time to get things right before inserting that single diskette will help the installation go smoothly. In the NFS Server manual, you'll find details on the requirements for TCP/IP and NFS name space support. You'll also find worksheets, which you'll probably ignore to your later regret.

TCP Configuration

Before NFS Server can be installed, TCP/IP must be running and properly configured on the file server. The frame type of ETHERNET_II must be set, since that is the frame type used in the UNIX world.

Name Space Support

You'll also need to add the NFS name space support. NetWare's ability to translate UNIX file names depends on the NFS name space being initialized. Adding support for this new name space takes a certain amount of disk space and a certain amount of time to initialize, depending on the size of the volume adding the name space support. The support is added only for the volume specified, not for the entire server.

Worksheet Information

You will need to supply the host names and TCP/IP addresses, which are used to build the \ETC\HOSTS file. The product doesn't have an import mechanism for an existing UNIX /etc/hosts file (as does NFS Gateway). Look for Novell to standardize that type of function across all its NetWare to UNIX products in the next release or two.

Although the copy and update functions aren't implemented in NFS Server, copying an ASCII text file from a UNIX host and placing it in the \ETC directory will work. One note: aliases in the normal UNIX sense are not allowed. You can't list several UNIX host names on the same address line; each name must have its own address line. The IP addresses on multiple lines can be the same with different names for each. This adds a bit of typing, but isn't fatal.

Fill out the worksheets for the NFS *uid* and *gid* (user and group ID) carefully. There may be a bunch of them, because each NFS client username, not just the UNIX host name, must be identified. This is where an automatic update feature will be an improvement, since a new NetWare user and group must be created for each of the UNIX user and groups.

The next worksheet forces you to decide which directories to export and what the access levels will be for each of them. The Yes/No check boxes allow root access, read only or read/write access, and anonymous access. You also choose whether NFS clients can modify DOS file attributes and whether to change NetWare trustee rights when NFS permissions are added or changed. Novell recommends allowing modification of both, so the NetWare file system can track the actions the NFS users expect to be tracked. If you don't permit DOS attribute modifications, it's possible for the DOS and NetWare attributes to make the directory unusable by the NFS clients. The support phone will ring within seconds of that happening, so avoid headaches and allow the modifications.

The last worksheet concerns the printers and print queues. It includes spaces for the UNIX printer name, NetWare queue name, UNIX host name, UNIX IP address, and UNIX printer name. This information is used in configuring the NetWare to UNIX print gateway.

NFS SERVER CONFIGURATION

When you load the diskette from the NetWare INSTALL utility on the server console, it copies the files into their proper places. The rest of the installation is handled by the NFSADMIN program. This program is the point of contact for basically everything done inside NetWare NFS Server. The option labeled Novice Configuration doesn't give extra help for people new to NFS, but it progresses through the configuration menus in order.

Users and Groups

The *uid* comes first, so pull out the worksheet (didn't fill it out, did you?). Remember the magic NetWare trick of pressing the Insert key to add usernames and ID's. A little text window will ask for the *uid* and username in turn, and will keep on asking for more names until you press the Escape key.

If there is no NetWare name attached to the UNIX user, or that user has no access control rights to the file, the file's owner will be listed as *nobody*, or *uid -2*. If tracking the actual owner of files isn't important, much of this stuff can be skipped. However, the installation will work better and users will be happier if everything is configured normally for the users. That means the UNIX users expect to see proper ownership, especially when they are also users in the NetWare system.

A similar scheme works in listing the group ID. The files owned by groups not properly configured will show *gid -2*, or *nogroup*, as the owner.

You can manually edit the NetWare files NFSUSER and NFSGROUP. The NFSUSER file looks like this:

```
# "NFS uid" , "NetWare Username"
1493 bobd
1738 jimj
1584 keithb
```

1855 bobw
-2   nobody

Host Setup

You add the UNIX host names and addresses in another text window, found under the slightly misleading heading of Workstation IP Address in the Configuration submenu. The title should be HOSTS File Editing, but the meaning is decipherable. You add, delete, or edit the host names and addresses through this screen.

Server Setup

Next, configure the NetWare server directory to be exported. All the questions concerning DOS attributes and trustee rights are here. If you prefer to do this configuration manually, edit the NetWare file SYS:\ETC\EXPORTS. Figure D.10 shows the screen layout and the recommended attributes and trustee settings.

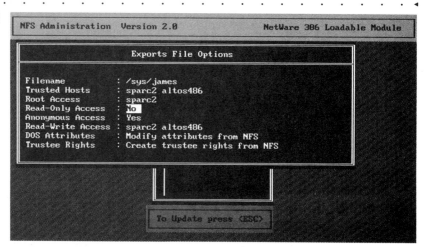

FIGURE D.10

Configuring the NetWare server NETFRAME to export a directory for UNIX clients SPARC2 and ALTOS486

The Trusted Hosts field names the systems authorized to access the server. If the field is left blank, any system can mount the server. Root Access, the next field, is more specialized. The systems named in this field have NetWare Supervisory rights to the file system. This is a bit dangerous. Systems not named in this field have the same rights as the NetWare user NOBODY. That user can be configured with strong access to certain directories, however, allowing more control over the privileges of the guest NFS systems without too many glaring holes in security.

The file attributes can be changed to give every NFS client full access, regardless of username and profile. By changing the files to All Rights for All Users and All Groups (setting the permissions to 777), all files are available. Let your security comfort level be the arbiter of this. If your system is on the Internet, and accessible from thousands of other systems, more caution may be advised. If this is the only UNIX and NetWare system being connected, security can be more relaxed.

INSTALLING NFS SERVER PRINTER SUPPORT

Printer setup, although done for a NetWare to UNIX gateway product, is very much a NetWare utility. All the screens look like those in other NetWare utilities, and all the same keystrokes are used. Remember to press the Insert key to call up your pick lists, and things will go easier.

There is an attempt to make these configuration programs the only utility needed for installation. You can add users and printers into the NetWare Bindery without leaving the configuration programs.

The NetWare to UNIX Printer System

Don't get confused, but there are two printer gateways that come with the NFS Server. One goes from NetWare to UNIX, and the other goes from UNIX to NetWare. The first one to be configured is the NetWare-to-UNIX Print Service.

The Print Server name must be shorter than 47 characters (that's an easy direction to follow), and it's written into the file SYS:\ETC\LPR$PSRV.NAM. This file can be written manually, but using the text box is easier. The field for listing UNIX printers is next, which is actually the name for the printer that NetWare clients will use. To the NetWare users, this is the UNIX printer name, since they don't need to address the UNIX printer system at all.

The UNIX host name must be listed in the SYS:\ETC\HOSTS file on the server. A pop-up pick list is available, and if your hosts are numerous, the list can be scrolled. When adding the UNIX printer name, be careful. This is the first entry that's case sensitive. Don't enter *Lp0* or *LP0*, because this name is passed exactly as is to the UNIX system, and UNIX expects *lp0*.

You must assign a NetWare print queue to service this printer connection. This is done through the window shown in Figure D.11. If a queue doesn't exist, it can be created from the UNIX Printer Setup Options window. Created means just that: a real NetWare print queue can be initialized from these screens. More than one NetWare queue can feed the UNIX printer system.

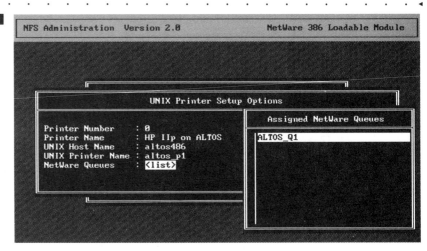

```
NFS Administration   Version 2.0                NetWare 386 Loadable Module




                          UNIX Printer Setup Options
                                              Assigned NetWare Queues
        Printer Number    : 0
        Printer Name      : HP IIp on ALTOS     ALTOS_Q1
        UNIX Host Name    : altos486
        UNIX Printer Name : altos_p1
        NetWare Queues    : <list>
```

The UNIX to NetWare Printer System

The UNIX to NetWare print gateway is not loaded with NFSADMIN, but with PLPDCFG (it's never explained, but the name comes from something like Printing Line Printer Daemon ConFiGuration). This NLM sits on the NetWare NFS Server awaiting input from a UNIX print queue. Its function is like the UNIX *lpd* (Line Printer Daemon).

Much of the installation is similar to the NetWare to UNIX print setup. One or more of the NetWare print queues must be exported so that the NFS clients can direct jobs to them. Queues can be created here as well. A pick list of available NetWare queues can be summoned, and one or more of those can be listed as available to NFS clients.

Printers must use the standard NetWare printer definitions, with one extra. The Print Filter option in the Print Filter and Device Configuration window, shown in Figure D.12, is something new. Two types of filters are available: Line Printer and PostScript. The PostScript filter can handle both ASCII and Post-Script input. The Line Printer filter normally gets only the basic vanilla jobs.

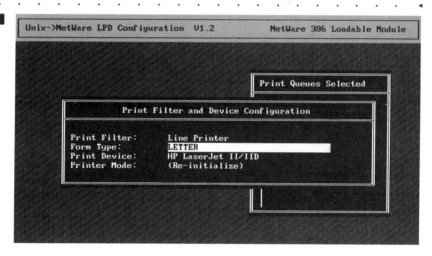

The Forms setting reads the PRINTDEF (PRINT DEFinition) utility database on the NetWare server. Pick any of the predefined forms, or skip this setting.

The Print Device field is a fancy name for printer, so pick an existing one and go on.

The Trusted Hosts screen comes back, so the UNIX systems listed in the SYS:\ETC\HOSTS file are once again presented for your approval. As few or as many hosts as you wish can be given access.

NetWare puts the username in the print banner for every print job, and there are several ways to gather that name from the UNIX host. Since the *uid* for users is known as they mount the system, the names can be translated in several ways.

The Single Account Mode is the simplest to administer. Every UNIX print job is listed as coming from one username, such as the NetWare user GUEST. You can choose other, more descriptive names. If no names are chosen here, any names not specifically listed in another access control table are refused. The warning in the manual is that there is no security for this setting. Any user on an authorized UNIX client system could then submit print jobs.

This seems like a minimal security threat, actually. If you really get hacked off if people use your printer, just wait and ambush them when they come to retrieve the printout. Or crumple all the pages and run.

The Table Based Mode lists each authorized user and maps the UNIX name to a NetWare username. Names can be mapped to different NetWare usernames than the UNIX names. For instance, several UNIX users can be mapped to the NetWare GUEST username.

Going one step further is the Client User Name Mode. If you chose this mode, each UNIX user wanting print support must have the same username on the Net-Ware system. Case sensitivity being the way it is, UNIX users *ray* and *jan* would be mapped to NetWare users RAY and JAN. Figure D.13 shows the name mapping choices.

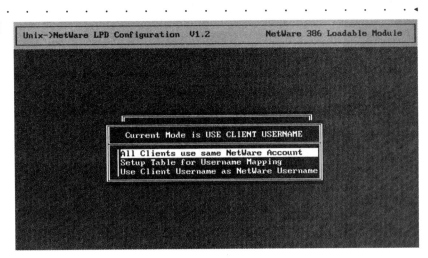

F I G U R E D.13

NFS Server name mapping choices

The NetWare to UNIX print modules are loaded by the LPR_PSRV.NLM and LPR_GWY.NLM programs. The UNIX to NetWare modules are loaded by PLPD.NLM, which calls the FILTER and FLTRLIB files. All the print modules are loaded automatically by the NFSSTART.NCF script file set up during installation.

Terminology: Translations and Definitions

This appendix consists of four main sections:

▶ Translating NetWare/DOS Terms to UNIX, which lists common Net-Ware/DOS functions, in alphabetical order, and the corresponding UNIX functions.

▶ Translating UNIX Terms to NetWare/DOS, which lists common UNIX functions, in alphabetical order, and the corresponding Net-Ware/DOS functions.

▶ Definition of Terms, which includes definitions for the terms used in this book, as well as other common networking terms.

▶ Acronyms and Abbreviations, which includes the acronyms and abbreviations used in this book, as well as other common networking acronyms and abbreviations.

Translating NetWare/DOS Terms to UNIX

The NetWare, DOS, and UNIX terms listed here often have flags or switches that modify the results. For example, the DIR and *ls -al* commands have a variety of switches to list directories in columns or one page at a time.

NETWARE/DOS TERM	UNIX TERM	DESCRIPTION
ATTACH	rlogin	Make connections and log in on another server/system
Backspace key	Delete key	Move the cursor to the left and delete any characters there
CD	cd	Change directory
CHKDSK	df	Show remaining disk space

NETWARE/DOS TERM	UNIX TERM	DESCRIPTION
COPY	cp	Copy files
DEL *.*	rm *	Delete all files in current directory
DEL	rm	Delete or remove file
DIR	ls -al	List files in current directory
DOWN (on server console)	shutdown, haltsys	Stop the system operating system
F3 key	!! (on some systems)	Repeat last command
FLAG	chmod	Change access privileges for files
HELP	man	Show help documentation for given term or command
LOGIN	login	Gain access to the system with username and password
LOGIN SCRIPT	.login	Script of user's rights executed upon login
LOGOUT	exit	Stop using the system
MD	mkdir	Make directory
MOUNT (on server console)	mount	Attach and use local disks
NDIR	ls -al	List files in current directory

NETWARE/DOS TERM	UNIX TERM	DESCRIPTION
NPRINT	lp	Print named file
PATH	path	Display the current path; set the search path
PCONSOLE	lpadmin	Set up and control printer
PRINT	lp	Print named file
PSTAT	lpstat	Check status of system printers
RD	rmdir	Remove directory
REN	mv	Rename files
SEND	wall	Send short message to every active user
SET	setenv	Set environment variables
SETPASS	passwd	Change current password
SYSCON	sysadmsh, sysadm	System administration program
TYPE	cat	Send file contents to the screen
USERLIST	finger	List current system users
VOLINFO	dfspace	Show volume listing with space available

Translating UNIX Terms to NetWare/DOS

The UNIX, NetWare, and DOS terms listed here often have flags or switches that modify the results. For example, the *ls -al* and DIR commands have a variety of switches to list directories in columns or one page at a time.

UNIX TERM	NETWARE/DOS TERM	DESCRIPTION
.login	LOGIN SCRIPT	Script of user's rights executed upon login
!! (on some systems)	F3 key	Repeats last command
cat	TYPE	Send file contents to the screen
cd	CD	Change directory
chmod	FLAG	Change access privileges for files
cp	COPY	Copy files
Delete key	Backspace key	Move the cursor to the left and delete any characters there
df	CHKDSK	Show remaining disk space
dfspace	VOLINFO	Show volume listing with space available
exit	LOGOUT	Stop using the system
finger	USERLIST	List current system users

UNIX TERM	NETWARE/DOS TERM	DESCRIPTION
login	LOGIN	Gain access to the system with username and password
lp	PRINT or NPRINT	Print named file
lpadmin	PCONSOLE	Set up and control printer
lpstat	PSTAT	Check status of system printers
ls -al	NDIR or DIR	List files in current directory
man	HELP	Show help documentation for given term or command
mkdir	MD	Make directory
mount	MOUNT (on server console)	Attach and use local disks
mv	REN	Rename files
passwd	SETPASS	Change current password
path	PATH	Display the current path; set the search path
rlogin	ATTACH	Make connections and log in on another server/system
rm	DEL	Delete or remove a file

UNIX TERM	NETWARE/DOS TERM	DESCRIPTION
rm *	DEL *.*	Delete all files in current directory
rmdir	RD	Remove directory
setenv	SET	Set environment variables
shutdown, haltsys	DOWN (on server console)	Stop the system operating system
sysadmsh, sysadm	SYSCON	System administration program
wall	SEND	Send short message to every active user

Definition of Terms

adapter: Hardware installed in a computer to connect the computer to other hardware.

AFP: See **Appletalk Filing Protocol**.

American National Standards Institute (ANSI): The association responsible for the establishment of many standards, including a number of data communications and terminal standards. ANSI is the recognized U.S. representative within CCITT (Consultative Committee on International Telegraph and Telephone) and ISO (International Standards Organization). See also **Consultative Committee on International Telegraph and Telephone and International Standards Organization.**

American Standard Code for Information Interchange (ASCII): A 7-bit code, intended as a U.S. standard for the interchange of information among communications devices.

ANSI: See **American National Standards Institute.**

API: See **Application Programming Interface.**

AppleShare: Apple Computer's networking solution. It requires a dedicated Macintosh as a network server and includes both server and workstation software. It uses **AppleTalk:** A set of communications protocols (such as SPX/IPX and NCP) used to define networking on an AppleShare network. Based on the OSI (Open Systems Interconnection) model, AppleTalk is comparable to NetWare communications protocols; both specify communications that range from application interfaces to media access.

AppleTalk Filing Protocol (AFP): A protocol that allows distributed file sharing across an AppleTalk network.

application: A software program or program package that makes calls to the operating system and manipulates data files, thus allowing a user to perform a specific job (such as accounting or word processing).

application interface: A set of software routines and associated conventions that permits application programmers to use that interface as a part of any application. In general, an application interface is used to access system or networking services that would require significant development effort to create from scratch. For example, the Btrieve application interface lets a programmer use Btrieve file structures and services within an application. See also **Application Programming Interface.**

Application Programming Interface (API): A means by which an application gains access to system resources, usually for the purpose of communication (sending and receiving data), data retrieval, or other system services. In the specific area of terminal emulation, an API provides for the simulation of keystrokes and for writing into and reading from the presentation space (device buffer). It may also provide for sending and receiving structured fields.

Arcnet (Attached Resource Computing Network): A proprietary token-bus networking architecture developed by Datapoint Corporation in the mid-1970's. Currently, Arcnet is widely licensed by third-party vendors and is a popular networking architecture, especially in smaller installations. It is relatively fast (2.5 Mbit/s) and reliable, and it supports coaxial, twisted pair, and fiber optic cable-based implementations.

ASCII: See **American Standard Code for Information Interchange**.

asynchronous: A data-transmission method in which each character is sent one bit at a time. Each character has a start and stop bit to synchronize signals between the sending and receiving devices. This allows a character to be sent at random after the preceding character has been sent. See also **synchronous**.

attach: To access a network server; particularly to access additional servers after logging in to one server.

attributes: A technique for describing access to and properties of files and directories within a filing system. For NetWare files, attributes include Read, Write, Create, Delete, and Execute Only (prevents files from being deleted or copied). For NetWare directories, attributes include Read, Write, Create, Execute and Hidden (hides information about the directory from file listings, preventing unauthorized access, deletions, or copying).

basic input/output system (BIOS): A set of programs, usually in firmware, that enables each computer's central processing unit to communicate with printers, disks, keyboards, consoles, and other attached input and output devices.
baud rate: The rate at which data is transferred over a serial interface.

Big Blue: A nickname for IBM (International Business Machines).

BIOS: See **basic input/output system**.

bridge: See **router**.

CCITT: See **Consultative Committee on International Telegraph and Telephone**.

coaxial: A type of cable that uses two conductors: a central, solid-wire core, surrounded by insulation, which is then surrounded by a braided-wire conductor sheath. This cable is particularly well suited for networking because it can accommodate high bandwidths but is relatively resistant to interference.

console: The monitor and keyboard from which you actually view and control server or host activity.

Consultative Committee on International Telegraph and Telephone (CCITT): A committee that recommends standards for communications equipment interfaces, communications protocols, modem modulation methods, and so on.

cron: Clock daemon on UNIX systems that executes *batch* and *at* commands along with other time-specific utilities.

daemon: A background UNIX process that is not under the control of any user. Examples are *cron* and the networking protocol controls such as FTP (File Transfer Protocol) and NFS (Network File Services).

DECnet: A set of networking protocols developed by Digital Equipment Corporation used in its VAX family of computers to exchange messages and other data. Although DECnet is currently a proprietary protocol, DEC is merging its protocols with OSI (Open System Interconnection) protocols .

dedicated line: A leased or private line communications line. Also called a leased line.

device driver: Software or firmware that translates operating system requests (such as input/output requests) into a format that is recognizable by specific hardware, such as adapters.

dial-up line: A communications line accessible via dial-up facilities, typically the public telephone network. See also **dedicated line**.

directory caching: A NetWare feature that copies the file allocation table and the directory entry table and writes them into the network server's memory. A file's location can then be read from memory, which is faster than reading it from a disk.

directory hashing: A NetWare feature that is a method of indexing file locations on disk, which speeds up file retrieval.

directory rights: Restrictions specific to a particular directory.

directory structure duplication: A NetWare feature that maintains duplicate copies of the directory table and the file allocation table on separate areas of the hard disk. If the primary copy is lost or destroyed, NetWare uses the secondary copy.

directory verification: A NetWare feature that performs a consistency check on duplicate sets of directory and file allocation tables to verify that the two copies are identical every time the server is turned on.

disk duplexing: Duplicating all the data on one hard disk on a second hard disk on a separate channel. Disk writes made to the original disk are also made to the second disk. If the original disk or channel fails, the duplicate disk takes over automatically. See also **disk mirroring**.

disk mirroring: Duplicating all the data on one hard disk on a second hard disk on the same channel. Disk writes to the original hard disk are also written to the second hard disk. If the original disk fails, the duplicate disk takes over automatically. See also **disk duplexing**.

distributed processing: A technique to enable multiple computers to cooperate in the completion of tasks, typically in a network environment. Each computer contributes to the completion of the total task by completing one or more individual subtasks independently of its peers, reporting the results from its subtasks as they are completed.

domain: A description of a machine, department, or site for naming purposes. Top-level domains must be registered to exchange mail outside the controlling organization. Local domains have meaning only within their organizations. Top-level domains must be registered by the DDN Network Information Center of SRI International (Phone: 800-235-3155).

domain name server: The particular machine that controls naming within its domain.

dongle: The slang name for a hardware security device that attaches to a computer's parallel printer port. The software sends signals to the device and must receive the proper response codes before it will continue program execution.

electronic mail: See **e-mail**.

elevator seeking: A NetWare feature that allows the disk read-write head to pick up files in the direction the head is traveling across the disk rather than in the order they were requested.

e-mail (electronic mail): A method of transferring files and sending messages among workstations.

Ethernet: A network cable and access protocol scheme originally developed by DEC (Digital Equipment Corporation), Intel, and Xerox (hence the DIX name for the 15-pin AUI connector for thick Ethernet cable devices).

Ethernet 802.3: A description of network packet contents, first developed by DEC (Digital Equipment Corporation), Intel, and Xerox. Ethernet 802.3 uses the Type field (the fourth field, bytes 21 and 22), unlike Ethernet II packets, which use the Length field. Novell packets are frame type Ethernet 802.3.

Ethernet II: A description of network packet contents. Ethernet II uses the Length field, unlike Ethernet 802.3 packets, which use the Type field.

FAT: See **file allocation table**.

FCONSOLE: A NetWare utility used to access information from the network server and fine-tune its performance. FCONSOLE is a virtual console utility, which allows the operator to control a server from any workstation on the network.

file allocation table (FAT): A record of file locations in a particular volume. NetWare divides each volume into blocks, and some files are stored in multiple blocks, which may not be adjacent. The FAT keeps track of the block numbers where different parts of the file are located. To retrieve a file, the software searches through the FAT until it finds the entries and corresponding block numbers for the requested file.

file sharing: An important feature of networking that allows more than one user to access the same file at the same time.

file system: In NetWare, the operating system controls the file system, and the user cannot configure the file system. In UNIX, there are several file systems. The most important is *root*, and most systems include a */u* or */usr* file system as well. UNIX file systems must be mounted upon booting, and they behave much like NetWare volumes in many respects.

FLeX/IP: Novell's NLM-based software that adds FTP server capability to an existing NetWare 3.11 or 4.*x* file server. Bidirectional printing support is also included, allowing UNIX print jobs to print on NetWare printers and vice versa.

gateway: A hareware/software package that runs on the OSI application layer and allows incompatible protocols to communicate (includes X.25 gateways). A gateway usually connects PCs to a host machine, such as an IBM mainframe.

GB: See **gigabyte**.

gid: In UNIX, the Group ID designation.

gigabyte (GB): A unit of measure for memory or disk storage capacity: ten to the ninth power (one billion) bytes.

HFS: See **Hierarchical File System**.

Hierarchical File System (HFS): A file system attached to AFP (AppleTalk Filing Protocol) in the Macintosh operating system. HFS manages files and directories.

host: A computer, attached to a network, that provides services to another computer beyond simply storing and forwarding information. It usually refers to mainframe and minicomputers.

Hot Fix: A NetWare feature that protects data from being written to a defective block on the disk. It sets aside a small portion of the hard disk's storage space as a redirection area. If read-after-write verification determines that there is a bad data block on the disk, Hot Fix redirects data that was to be stored in the bad block to the Hot Fix redirection area. It then marks the defective block as bad, and the server will not attempt to store data there again.

hybrid user: The UNIX user in NetWare for UNIX systems who has a corresponding NetWare username. The UNIX user has access to all the files of the

NetWare user of the same name. Hybrid users are created through the *hybrid* utility or in *sconsole*.

IEEE: See **Institute of Electrical and Electronic Engineers.**

Institute of Electrical and Electronic Engineers (IEEE): An association that creates standards for cabling, electrical topology, physical topology, and access schemes.

INT14: Interrupt 14, the PC BIOS interrupt used to reroute messages from the serial port to the network interface card.

International Standards Organization (ISO): An organization that develops standards for international and national data communications. It is based in Paris.

Internet address: A 32-bit (4-byte) numeric value that specifies a particular network and a node on that network. The standard format is "dotted decimal," as in 192.9.200.7. The three classes of Internet addresses are A, B, and C. Class C can support 254 hosts, while Class A can support up to 6 million. Class A values (the first group of the address) range from 0 to 127; Class B from 128 to 191, and Class C from 192 to 223.

Internet Protocol (IP): The protocol that defines the unreliable, connectionless delivery mechanism. IP defines the basic unit of data transfer and the format of all data using the protocol, with rules specifying packet processing and exception handling.

internetwork: Two or more networks connected by an internal or external router.

Internetwork Packet Exchange (IPX): A protocol that allows the exchange of message packets on an internetwork.

IP: See **Internet Protocol.**

IPX: See **Internetwork Packet Exchange.**

ISO: See **International Standards Organization.**

KB: See **kilobyte.**

kbit/s: See **kilobits per second.**

kbyte/s: See **kilobytes per second.**

kernel: The main UNIX system program that interfaces to all hardware, memory, and peripheral devices. It is similar to the NetWare SERVER.EXE program.

kilobits per second (kbit/s): A unit of measure commonly used for transfer rates to and from peripheral devices.

kilobyte (KB): A unit of measure for memory or disk storage capacity; two to the tenth power (1,024) bytes.

kilobytes per second (kbyte/s): A unit of measure commonly used for transfer rates to and from peripheral devices; 1024 bytes per second.

LAN: See **local area network.**

LAN WorkGroup: Novell's TCP/IP client software that is located and managed centrally at the NetWare server.

LAN WorkPlace: Novell's TCP/IP client software (for Macintosh and DOS systems) that resides on the client system.

leased line: See **dedicated line.**

local area network (LAN): A system that links computers together to form a network, usually with a wiring-based cabling scheme. LANs connect PCs and electronic office equipment, enabling users to communicate, share resources (such as data storage and printers), and access remote hosts or other networks.

LocalTalk: Shielded, twisted-pair cable introduced by Apple.

login script: A set of instructions that directs a workstation to perform specific actions when the user logs in to the network. It usually specifies individual drive mappings. The network supervisor can create a systemwide login script (which is the same for all users on the network) that instructs all workstations to perform the same actions upon login. The systemwide login script executes before any individual login scripts.

MB: See **megabyte.**

Megabyte (MB): A unit of measure for memory or disk storage capacity: two to the twentieth power (1,048,576) bytes.

Name space support: The NetWare system module that provides each non-DOS client file information in the format of the client system.

NetBIOS (Network Basic Input/Output System): A programmable entry into the network that allows systems to communicate over network hardware using a generic networking API (Application Programming Interface) that can run over multiple transports or media.

NetWare Bindery: The system database in NetWare 2.*x* and 3.*x* that keeps track of the access and security rights of users, groups, and all other server-based objects.

NetWare Loadable Module (NLM): A software module that can be added to the NetWare 3.*x* operating system to give a network server more functions. NLMs can be dynamically loaded on or unloaded from the NetWare server without the server being down.

NetWare NFS: Novell's software-only NLM product that adds NFS server capability to an existing NetWare 3.11 or 4.*x* file server. UNIX NFS clients will see the NetWare server as another NFS server.

NetWare NFS Gateway: A software-only NLM product from Novell that allows a NetWare server to mount and present UNIX file systems as NetWare volumes to NetWare clients. Full NetWare security is maintained, restricting access to the UNIX systems based on the NetWare client's privileges.

NetWare operating system: The operating system developed by Novell, Inc. The NetWare operating system is loaded on the server when the server is booted. It controls all system resources and the way information is processed on the entire network or internetwork.

NetWare Runtime operating system: A single-user version of NetWare provided to support NLMs and other server-based applications.

NetWare shell: The NetWare program loaded into the memory of each workstation. It builds itself around DOS and intercepts the workstation's network requests, rerouting them to a NetWare server.

network: A system that sends and receives data and messages, typically over a cable. A network enables a group of computers to communicate with each other, share peripheral devices (such as hard disks and printers), and access remote hosts or other networks.

network adapter: See **network interface card**.

Network File System (NFS): A distributed file system network protocol developed by Sun Microsystems.

Network Information Services (NIS): The new name for yellow pages, the security and file access databases on UNIX systems. The most important UNIX files in the naming system are */etc/passwd*, */etc/group*, and */etc/hosts*.

network interface board: See **network interface card**.

network interface card (NIC): The hardware installed in workstations and servers that enables them to communicate on a network.

NFS: See **Network File System**.

NIS: See **Network Information Services**.

NLM: See **NetWare Loadable Module**.

open systems: The somewhat vague and generic term describing computer systems, hardware, and software that follow available standards in order to interoperate with systems from different vendors. It has become a marketing term rather than an accurate description of particular hardware or software.

OSI (Open Systems Interconnection) reference model: A model for network communications consisting of seven layers that describe what happens when computers communicate with one another.

packet: The unit of information by which the network communicates. Each packet contains the identities of the sending and receiving stations, error-control information, a request for services, information on how to handle the request, and any data that must be transferred.

passwords: A system security feature for both NetWare and UNIX. Supervisors of both systems can require users to use a password when they log in to the network. If passwords are required, all users must have unique passwords. Passwords in NetWare are encrypted; that is, they are stored on the server in a format only the server can decode. Passwords in UNIX systems are stored in the */etc/passwd* file, but they cannot be edited in that form.

PCONSOLE: The NetWare utility program to set up, monitor, and manage the print queues and printers on a NetWare file server.

permissions: The elaborate UNIX system of file descriptors that detail which users on a system have read, write, and execute privileges on each file.

preemptive scheduling: An operating system type that allows certain system functions to interrupt other, less critical functions. UNIX is preemptive; NetWare is non-preemptive.

PRINTCON: The NetWare utility that defines the way that the printer handles print jobs, including the form type, the banner, the server and queue used, and the printer mode.

PRINTDEF: The NetWare utility that defines the database of printer parameters that control network printers.

Protocol: A formal description of message formats and the rules two or more machines must follow to exchange those messages.

protocol suite: A collection of networking protocols that provides the communications and services necessary for computers to exchange messages and other information. The protocols typically manage physical connections, communications services, and application support.

pseudo terminals: Terminal connections to a UNIX host that come through the Ethernet controller rather than through the async serial connection controller.

read-after-write verification: A NetWare feature that reads back the data NetWare writes to a block on the hard disk and compares it to the original data still in memory. If the data from the disk matches the data in memory, the data in memory is released. If the data does not match, Hot Fix marks that block on the disk as bad and redirects the data to another location on the hard disk. See also **Hot Fix.**

record locking: A feature of the network operating system that prevents two users from writing to the same record simultaneously.

Red Horde: A nickname for Novell, Inc.

.rhosts (Remote HOSTS): The file in the individual user account's home directory (or in the root directory for the user root) that works with the */etc/passwd* file to determine permissions and security controls of users logging in from remote systems.

rights: A NetWare security feature that controls which directories and files a user can access and what the user is allowed to do with those directories and files. Rights are assigned to directories and files by the network supervisor.

router: A software and hardware connection between two or more networks, usually of similar design, that permits traffic to be routed from one network. A NetWare router (formerly known as an internal or external bridge) can connect networks that use different network adapters or transmission media as long as both sides of the connection use the same protocols. If a router is located in a server, it is called an *internal router*; a router in a workstation is an *external router*.

RPRINTER: An executable program that runs on a Novell client workstation to allow an attached printer to be accessible to all users.

Sequenced Packet Exchange (SPX): A protocol by which two workstations or applications communicate across the network. SPX uses NetWare IPX to deliver the messages, but SPX guarantees delivery of the messages and maintains the order of messages on the packet stream.

SFT: See **System Fault Tolerance**.

shell: See **NetWare shell**.

SPX: See **Sequenced Packet Exchange**.

subnet mask: The filter that separates subnetted addresses into network and local portions. Local systems will have a subnet mask in order to restrict broadcasts to the local network only.

subnetting: The process allowing a complex network to be seen as a single address from outside the network.

superuser: The privileged UNIX account with unrestricted access to all files and commands.

supervisor: The person responsible for the administration and maintenance of a network or database. A supervisor has all access rights to all volumes, directories, and files.

SYSCON: The NetWare utility used to add, delete, and modify all details of the user accounts on the system.

System Fault Tolerance (SFT): A method of duplicating data on multiple storage devices so that if one storage device fails, the data is available from another device. There are several levels of hardware and software SFT. Each level of redundancy (duplication) decreases the possibility of data loss.

systemwide login script: See **login script.**

TCP: See **Transmission Control Protocol.**

TCP/IP (Transmission Control Protocol/Internet Protocol): A protocol suite and related applications developed for the U.S. Department of Defense in the 1970's and 1980's specifically to permit different types of computers to communicate and exchange information. TCP/IP is currently mandated as an official Department of Defense protocol and is also widely used in UNIX systems.

TelAPI: A feature in LAN WorkGroup that supports third-party programs by providing TCP/IP transport services.

Telnet: The Internet protocol for remote terminal connection service.

terminal: A device, usually equipped with a keyboard and display, capable of sending and receiving data over a communications link.

topology: The physical layout of network components (cable, stations, gateways, hubs, and so on). There are three basic interconnection topologies: star, ring, and bus networks.

Transaction Tracking System (TTS): A NetWare feature that protects the integrity of databases by backing out of incomplete transactions that result from a failure in a network component.

Transmission Control Protocol (TCP): The communication protocol that provides reliable stream service on the Internet. The protocol specification is fairly complex, yet so standard now that all TCP software implementations will work with all others.

trustee rights: A NetWare security feature that controls a specific user's rights to use a particular directory.

TTS: See **Transaction Tracking System**.

UID: User ID, the unique number assigned to each UNIX user.

uninterruptible power supply (UPS): A backup power unit that provides continuous power even when the normal power supply is interrupted.

UNIX: An operating system developed by AT&T Bell Laboratories. It allows a computer to handle multiple users and programs simultaneously.

UPS: See **uninterruptible power supply**.

UPS monitoring: A NetWare feature that monitors the status of the UPS (uninterruptible power supply) attached to the server.

user: Any person who attaches to a server or host.

user account: An account that determines what name the user uses to log in to the network, the groups the user belongs to, and the user's trustee assignments. Each user on a NetWare network has a user account. User accounts are maintained by the network supervisor.

username: The unique name each NetWare client uses to log in to a system.

value-added process (VAP): An application that runs on top of NetWare 2.*x* operating systems. VAPs tie in with the network operating system so that print servers, archive servers, and database servers can provide services without interfering with the network's normal operation.

VAP: See **value-added process**.

volume: The highest level in the NetWare directory structure. It is the same level as a DOS root directory. A volume represents a physical amount of hard-disk storage space.

vt52, vt100, vt220: Specific terminal types used to connect to UNIX systems, based on the old video terminal developed by DEC (Digital Equipment Corporation) to replace vacuum tube terminals.

WAN: See **wide area network**.

wide area network (WAN): Two or more LANs in separate geographic locations connected by a remote link.

workstation: Any individual personal computer that is connected to a network.

wyse50, wyse 60: Specific terminal types popularized by the Wyse company. The keyboards match the standard PC keyboard better than most other UNIX terminal types.

yellow pages (ypages): The former name for UNIX services to maintain name, user, group, and security control. See **Network Information Services.**

yellow pages server (ypserver): The name server for a network with yellow pages service installed.

ypages: See **yellow pages.**

ypserver: See **yellow pages server.**

Acronyms and Abbreviations

ACL	Access Control List
ANSI	American National Standards Institute
API	Application Programming Interface
ARP	Address Resolution Protocol
ASCII	American Standard Code for Information Interchange
BIND	Berkeley Internet Name Domain
BIOS	basic input/output system
BOOTP	Boot Protocol
BOOTPD	Boot Protocol Daemon
BSD	Berkeley Software Distribution

BSL	Berkeley Socket Library
CAD/CAM	computer-aided design/computer-aided manufacturing
CBT	computer-based training
CCITT	Consultative Committee on International Telegraph and Telephone
CD-ROM	compact disc read-only memory
CGA	color graphic adapter
CLIB	C-Library
CNE	Certified NetWare Engineer
CNI	Certified NetWare Instructor
CORBA	Common ORB Architecture
CPI-C	Common Programming Interface-Communications
CP/M	Control Program for Microprocessors
CPU	central processing unit
CSMA/CA	carrier sense multiple access with collision avoidance
CSMA/CD	carrier sense multiple access with collision detection
CUT	control-unit terminal
DAL	Data Access Language
DBMS	database management system
DDE	Dynamic Data Exchange (Windows)
DDS	Direct Digital Service

DEC	Digital Equipment Corporation
DFS	Direct File System
DG	Data General
DLL	Dynamic Link Library
DMA	direct memory access
DNS	Domain Name Service
DOMS	Distributed Object Management System
DPA	Demand Protocol Architecture
EAB	Extended Attributes
EDI	electronic data interchange
EGA	enhanced graphic adapter
EISA	Extended Industry Standard Architecture
ELS	Entry Level Solution
ESDI	Enhanced Small Disk Interface
FAT	file allocation table
FSP	file service process
FTAM	File Telecommunications Access Method
FTP	File Transfer Protocol
FTPD	File Transfer Protocol Daemon
GB	gigabyte
GE	General Electric
GID	Group ID
GOSIP	Government OSI Protocols

GUI	graphical user interface
HMI	Hub Management Interface
HP	Hewlett Packard
HSL	Hub Support Layer
I/O	input/output
ICMP	Internet Control Message Protocol
IEEE	Institute of Electrical and Electronic Engineers
IETF	Internet Engineering Task Force
IMSP	Independent Manufacturer Support Program
INT14	Interrupt 14
IPC	interprocess communications
IPX	Internetwork Packet Exchange
IRQ	interrupt request line
ISA	Industry Standard Architecture
ISO	International Standards Organization
KB	kilobyte
LAN	local area network
LAT	Local Area Transport
LLC	Logical Link Control
LPD	Line Printer Daemon
LPDGWY	Line Printer Gateway
MAC	Media Access Control
MB	megabyte

MCGA	multicolor graphics array
MCS	Micro Computer Systems, Inc.
MHS	Message Handling Service
MSAU, MAU	Multistation Access Unit
MULTICS	Multiplexed Information and Computing System
MVS	Multiple Virtual Storage
NACS	NetWare Asynchronous Communication Services
NAEC	Novell Authorized Education Center
NAS	Network Application Support
NAUN	Nearest Active Upstream Neighbor
NCB	Network Control Block
NCP	NetWare Core Protocol
NDIS	Network Device Interface Specification
NDS	NetWare Directory Service
NEST	Novell Enhanced Support Training
NFS	Network File System
NGM	NetWare Global Messaging
NICA	Novell Integrated Computing Architecture
NIS	Network Information Services
NLM	NetWare Loadable Module
NMA	NetWare Management Agent
NNS	NetWare Name Service

NOS	Network Operating System
NOSA	Network Open Services Architecture
NSE	Network Support Encyclopedia
NSM	NetWare Services Manager
NTS	Novell Technical Support
NUI	NetWare Users International
NVT	NetWare Virtual Terminal
ODI	Open Data-Link Interface
OEM	original equipment manufacturer
OLTP	online transaction processor
OMG	Object Management Group
OOPS	Object Oriented Programming System
OPT	Open Protocol Technology
ORB	Object Request Broker
OS	operating system
OSF	Open Software Foundation
OSI	Open Systems Interconnection
PDN	public data network
PDP	Professional Developers' Program
PROM	program read-only memory
QBE	query by example
RAM	random-access memory
RARP	Reverse Address Resolution Protocol

RCS	Resource Construction Set
RDS	Rational Data Systems
RFC	Request For Comment
RIP	Routing Information Protocol
RISC	reduced instruction set computing
RMF	Remote Management Facility
ROM	read-only memory
RPC	remote procedure call
RSH	Remote Shell
RSHD	Remote Shell Daemon
SAP	Service Advertising Protocol
SBK	System Builder's Kit
SCO	Santa Cruz Operation
SCSI	Small Computer System Interface
SDK	Software Developer's Kit
SDLC	Synchronous Data Link Control
SES	Strategic Engineering Support
SFT	System Fault Tolerance
SMGP	Simple Gateway Management Protocol
SMB	Server Message Block
SMF	Standard Message Format
SMIT	Systems Maintenance Interface Tool
SMTP	Simple Mail Transport Protocol

SNMP	Simple Network Management Protocol
SPG	Service Protocol Gateway
SPX	Sequenced Packet Exchange
SQL	Structured Query Language
STP	Software Testing Program
TB	tetrabyte
TCP/IP	Transmission Control Protocol/Internet Protocol
TES	Terminal Emulation Service
TFTP	Trivial File Transfer Protocol
TIDB	Technical Information Database
TLI	Transport Level Interface
TSA	Technical Support Alliance
TSR	terminate-and-stay-resident
TTS	Transaction Tracking System
UDP	User Datagram Protocol
UID	User ID
UPS	uninterruptible power supply
USL	UNIX Software Laboratories
VADD	value-added disk driver
VAN	Value-Added Network
VAP	value-added process
VAR	Value-Added Reseller
VGA	video graphics array

VM/CMS	Virtual Machine/Conversational Monitor System (IBM)
VMS	Virtual Memory System
WAN	wide area network
WNIM	Wide Area Network Interface Module
WORM	write once, read many
WOSA	Windows Open Services Architecture
XDR	External Data Representation

Index

This index differentiates between *mentions* of items and *explanations* of items. Explanations are listed as **bold** page numbers and mentions as roman page numbers. Figures are listed as *italic* page numbers.

V

VMS (Virtual Management System), 52
VMUNIX (UNIX), 13
VOLINFO command, 134, 135, 287
volumes, 320. *See also* NFS volumes
vt52 emulation, 68, 91, 320
vt100 emulation, 68, 90, 320
VT200-1.EXE program, 267
VT220-4.EXE program, 267
vt220 keyboard, 68–69, *69*
vt220 emulation, 68, 90, 320
 by Novix, 82

W

WAITFOR.COM, 109
WAITSECS.EXE, 109
Walker Richer & Quinn, Reflection 1, 91
WANs (wide-area networks), 26, 320
Wellfleet, 50
WGSETUP, to set up LAN WorkGroup
 workstation, 256–257
wide-area networks (WANs), 26, 320
Windows clients, FTP server on, 124
Windows (Microsoft), 38
 applications for, 209
 databases for, 201
 as NetWare client, 135
 network protocols with, 46
 printer in, 187
 running LAN WorkGroup under, 74–78
 running Novix under, **84**
 running PopTerm/NVT under, **96**
 running UniLink under, 90
 TNVT220 difference under, 76–77
Windows NT, network protocols with, 46
Windows Open Services Architecture (WOSA), 211
Windows programs, (LAN WorkGroup), **103–107**
WIN.INI file, for LAN WorkGroup for Windows, 261

WinTerm for Windows, 231
wiring, unshielded-twisted-pair (UTP), 24
WordPerfect, 27, 59, **197–199**, 233
WordPerfect Office, **197–199**
WordPerfect for Windows, 210
worksheets, for NFS Gateway, 280
Workstation Type table, setting up, 254–255
workstations, 320
 installing for Catipult, **270–271**
 installing for NetWare TCP/IP Gateway 386, **272**
 installing for SoftNet Term (Puzzle System), **276**
 installing for UniLink, **274–275**
 Novix for NetWare configuration, 267–268
 setup in LAN WorkGroup, 256–257
worldwide directory services, 196
WOSA (Windows Open Services Architecture), 211
Wyse50 terminal emulation, 68, 321
Wyse60 terminal emulation, 68, 90, 321

X

X Windows, **28**, 38, 151
 client-server applications, **202–203**
X.400 e-mail addresses, 196
X.500 e-mail addresses, 196
XCONSOLE program, 28, 151, 202
XDR (external Data Representation) routines, 128
XENIX, 6
Xerox Network Services (XNS) protocol, 46, 219
XMSNETX.COM program, 257
XNS (Xerox Network Services) protocol, 46, 219

Y

Yellow pages, 145, 321. *See also* NIS (Network
 Information Service)

SYBEX

FREE BROCHURE!

Complete this form today, and we'll send you a full-color brochure of Sybex bestsellers.

Please supply the name of the Sybex book purchased.

_____

How would you rate it?

_____ Excellent   _____ Very Good   _____ Average   _____ Poor

Why did you select this particular book?

_____ Recommended to me by a friend

_____ Recommended to me by store personnel

_____ Saw an advertisement in _____

_____ Author's reputation

_____ Saw in Sybex catalog

_____ Required textbook

_____ Sybex reputation

_____ Read book review in _____

_____ In-store display

_____ Other _____

Where did you buy it?

_____ Bookstore

_____ Computer Store or Software Store

_____ Catalog (name: _____)

_____ Direct from Sybex

_____ Other: _____

Did you buy this book with your personal funds?

_____ Yes   _____ No

About how many computer books do you buy each year?

_____ 1-3   _____ 3-5   _____ 5-7   _____ 7-9   _____ 10+

About how many Sybex books do you own?

_____ 1-3   _____ 3-5   _____ 5-7   _____ 7-9   _____ 10+

Please indicate your level of experience with the software covered in this book:

_____ Beginner   _____ Intermediate   _____ Advanced

Which types of software packages do you use regularly?

_____ Accounting	_____ Databases	_____ Networks
_____ Amiga	_____ Desktop Publishing	_____ Operating Systems
_____ Apple/Mac	_____ File Utilities	_____ Spreadsheets
_____ CAD	_____ Money Management	_____ Word Processing
_____ Communications	_____ Languages	_____ Other _____

(please specify)

Which of the following best describes your job title?

_____ Administrative/Secretarial _____ President/CEO

_____ Director _____ Manager/Supervisor

_____ Engineer/Technician _____ Other _____
(please specify)

Comments on the weaknesses/strengths of this book: _____

_____

_____

_____

_____

Name _____

Street _____

City/State/Zip _____

Phone _____

PLEASE FOLD, SEAL, AND MAIL TO SYBEX

SYBEX, INC.
Department M
2021 CHALLENGER DR.
ALAMEDA, CALIFORNIA USA
94501

SYBEX

NetWare to UNIX Connection Goals and Quick Recommendations

CONNECTING NETWARE AND UNIX WITH NFS

QUICK RECOMMENDATION	PRODUCT OR PRODUCT SOURCE	PAGE
NetWare gateway to NFS	NetWare NFS Gateway	130
NetWare server as NFS server	NetWare NFS Server	148
NetWare server on UNIX host	NetWare for UNIX	159

PRINTING FROM A NETWARE CLIENT TO A UNIX HOST

QUICK RECOMMENDATION	PRODUCT OR PRODUCT SOURCE	PAGE
TCP/IP software on a NetWare client	LAN WorkGroup	176
TCP/IP gateways	Firefox	178
	Ipswitch	178
Printing through the server to the UNIX host	FLeX/IP	168
	NetWare NFS Server	168
	NetWare for UNIX	173